THE PILGRIM ROAD TO NIDAROS

St Olav's Way: Oslo to Trondheim

THE PILGRIM ROAD TO NIDAROS

St Olav's Way: Oslo to Trondheim

by

Alison Raju

2 POLICE SQUARE, MILNTHORPE, CUMBRIA, LA7 7PY
www.cicerone.co.uk

© **Alison Raju** 2001
© **Photographs**: Alison Raju and Eivind Luthen
ISBN 1 85284 314 4
A catalogue record for this book is available from the British Library.

Maps drawn by Harveys Maps

About the Author

Alison Raju is a former teacher of French, German and Spanish to adults and the author of two other guides published by Cicerone Press: *The Way of St James: Le Puy to Santiago – A Walker's Guide* and *Via de la Plata: Seville to Santiago*.

for Jim

I would like to thank Andreas and
Leva Kiil Eivind Luthen and the
Pilegrimsfellesskapet St. Jakob
Norge for their assistance.

Front cover: Nidaros cathedral (photo: Eivind Luthen)

CONTENTS

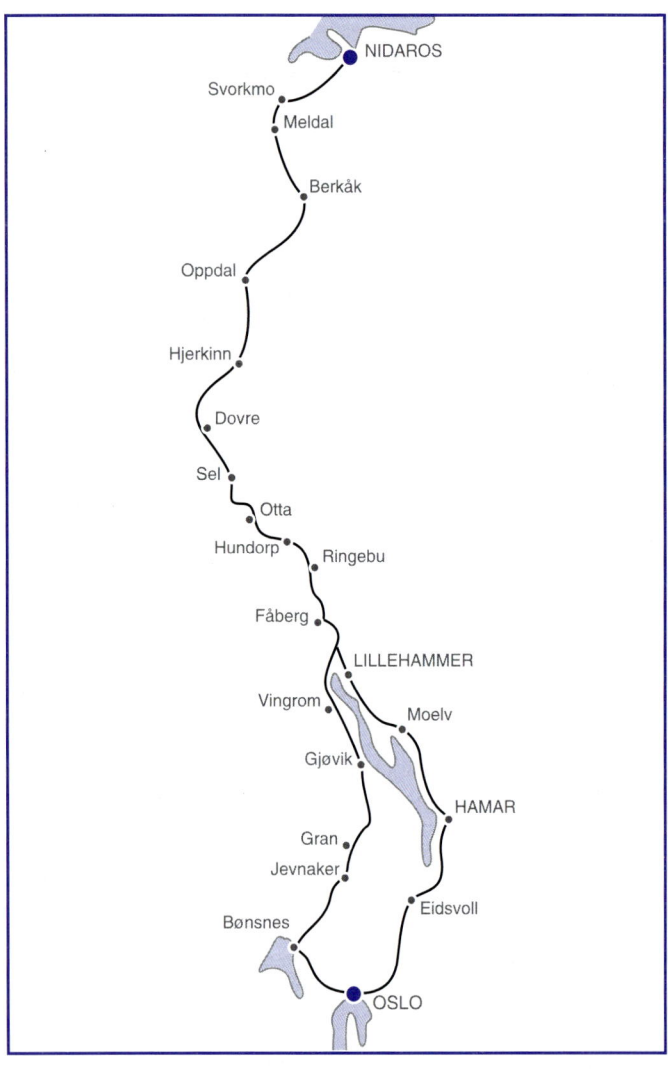

INTRODUCTION

The Pilgrim Road to Nidaros as described in this book is a long-distance footpath with a difference. People walked the 643km medieval pilgrim road (*pilegrimsleden* in Norwegian) from Oslo to Nidaros (the old name for Trondheim) cathedral for over 500 years to visit the place where St. Olav, king, and responsible for much of the conversion of Norway to Christianity, was buried. His shrine was the focus not only of many miracles but also of the fourth most important pilgrim route in Europe (after Rome, Jerusalem and Santiago de Compostela), and from the 10th century until the Reformation it attracted pilgrims in their thousands, not only from Norway and the rest of Scandinavia, Iceland and Greenland, but from Russia, the Baltic countries, Germany and Britain as well. After 1537 the route fell into disuse, with the arrival of the Reformation in Norway and the prohibition of pilgrimages; most of the 'hospitals' and other accommodation set up by religious orders along the way to minister to the needs of pilgrims have long since disappeared, as have the many holy wells and 'Olav fields' or resting places for pilgrims and their horses.

The route has recently been 'rediscovered', however, and is being very actively promoted as a walking pilgrim path with places of historical and cultural interest along the way, as well as just its landscapes and scenery. The old tracks were cleared and reopened between 1994 and 1996, and the western (cultural) route via Gjøvik was waymarked in its entirety for the first time in 1997 to celebrate the millennium of the saint's death and the founding of Nidaros cathedral. The eastern (historic) route was also waymarked from Hamar onwards, the two branches joining up some 20km north of Lillehammer to continue as one path thereafter. The remaining section of the historic route, from Oslo to Hamar, was waymarked in 2000. Both options are described in this book. A walker's guidebook to the Pilgrim Road to Nidaros is available in Norwegian but this does not really address the practical needs of walkers or modern pilgrims, even those with a knowledge of the language, and the present volume, the only guide to the route in English, has been written to fill this gap.

Originally there were several ways to Nidaros. One of these, from just over the Swedish border and passing through Stiklestad (where St. Olav was slain), is also waymarked and is outlined in Appendix A.

Other appendices contain a list of suggestions for further reading, a glossary of geographical and other useful terms and an index of the principal place names along the way. Sketch maps are at the scale indicated on the map.

Anyone who is fairly fit and who also likes to visit places of interest along the way should be able to complete the journey in a month. Even in July and August there may be occasional snow in some of the higher sections but the route is normally practicable, for those suitably clad, from mid-May to mid-September. It can be undertaken in sections, too, by those who lack the time to do it all in one go, and indications are given in the text as to how to reach (or leave) the larger places along the way, though it is obviously preferable to complete it as a single experience, especially if you are doing it as a pilgrimage. Some sections of the route are suitable for mountain bikes but many are definitely not, and prospective pilgrims are advised to walk rather than attempt to ride it. Anyone who is contemplating undertaking any part of the Pilgrim Road to Nidaros should also consider contacting (in English) the very helpful Pilegrimskontoret (pilgrim office) in Oslo for the latest information on accommodation (see Appendix B for address).

HISTORY

Saint Olav

Saint Olav, as he is known today, was born Olav Haraldsson in 995 and grew up in Ringerike in south-eastern Norway. When he was still only quite young he set out as a Viking and served as an officer for noblemen in different places in England and northern France. Somewhere on these travels he was converted to Christianity, probably through contact with the Benedictine movement, and was baptized while he was in Rouen. On his return to Norway in 1015, to claim the royal throne there, he took a number of English bishops and other clerics back with him, indicating that he must already have seen something of the instrumental role he was to play in completing the conversion of Norway to Christianity.

On his return Olav Haraldsson (i.e. Olav II, to distinguish him from Olav I, Olav Tryggvason) became the first national king to rule over the entire country. What is now known as Norway had hitherto been a collection of regions, each with their own petty king or local chieftain, as up until the 9th century these areas did not form a united whole. The unifying process lasted a long while, but by the time Olav II came to the throne he was able to wield his power over the entire country, gradually setting up an administrative network and legal system that enabled him to hold the country together. He went on a large number of missionary forays to those parts of Norway that were not yet fully Christianised, such as the inland areas and the north, and built churches and ordained priests so as to set up an ecclesiastical structure on a national level.

At first he apparently pursued his crusading activities unhindered, but he was not without opposition, and his methods were at times harsh and open to question. However, King (later Saint) Olav was not the sole force in the conversion of Norway to Christianity (though very definitely a major one), as this had already been introduced into the country over a period of time, probably some 200 years, and came from at least three different sources. Celtic Christianity reached Norway through contacts with Scotland and Ireland, as is evident, for example, by the setting up of St. Sunniva's convent on the island of Selja (on the west coast). Missionary activity from countries east and south of the Baltic introduced Orthodox Christianity to Norway, while the Catholic version came from areas that are now Germany and France, influencing the many Norwegians (i.e. Vikings) visiting these places, just as other versions had had an impact on those visiting what are now the British Isles and Russia. Olav II thus played a very important role in spreading Christianity throughout his kingdom, a Norway that was by now politically unified, and in establishing a permanent base for a Norwegian church, but he was by no means bringing a completely new religion into virgin territory. He was thus responsible not for the introduction of Christianity as such to Norway but for completion of an already ongoing process.

As a result of opposition to King Olav's rule his power gradually eroded and he was forced to flee the country. He spent the last year of his life on earth in Kiev with his brother-in-law Grand Duke Jaroslav, in a city which had become one of the most powerful spiritual centres in eastern Europe and where theology, monasteries and religious art flourished. Olav decided to return to Norway, though, influenced by one of several powerful dreams that occured at decisive moments in his career, and in 1030 set off back home to try to regain power. He was slain at the Battle of Stiklestad on July 29th and his body smuggled away to be buried on the spot where Nidaros cathedral now stands.

Immediately after his death, however, reports of miraculous cures began to occur, with innumerable accounts of the king's healing powers. One such concerns one of the men who had slain the king, whose wounded hand is said to have been healed instantaneously after a drop of King Olav's blood fell on it and who subsequently set off on a pilgrimage of atonement to Jerusalem. The body of the king was exhumed a year later and, as often occurs in accounts of the same process with other saints, it was found to be intact. He was canonised on August 3rd 1031, an apostle for having completed the Christianisation of Norway and a martyr for having died for his faith under the sign of the cross. The Battle of Stiklestad may have ended his earthly life but through his death as a martyr Olav's two main objectives, the unification and Christianising of Norway, were accomplished. Much of what is known about the life and work of St. Olav was recorded by Archbishop Øystein (of Nidaros) in his *Passio Olavi*, in the writings of the historian Adam von Bremen and in Snorri Sturluson's detailed account in the Icelandic Sagas.

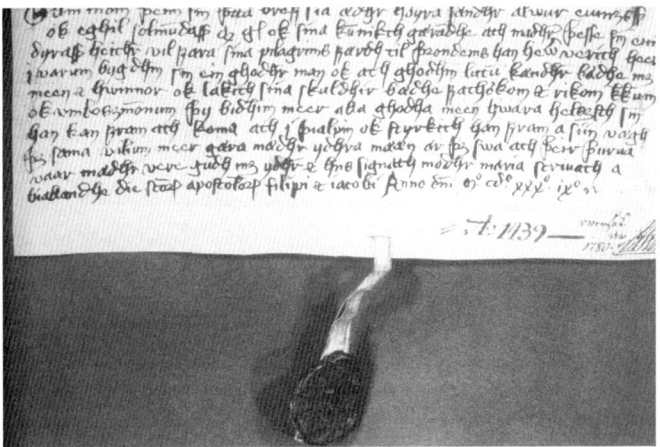

Pilgrim passport, dating from 1439 (Eivind Luthen)

The pilgrimage and the routes to Nidaros

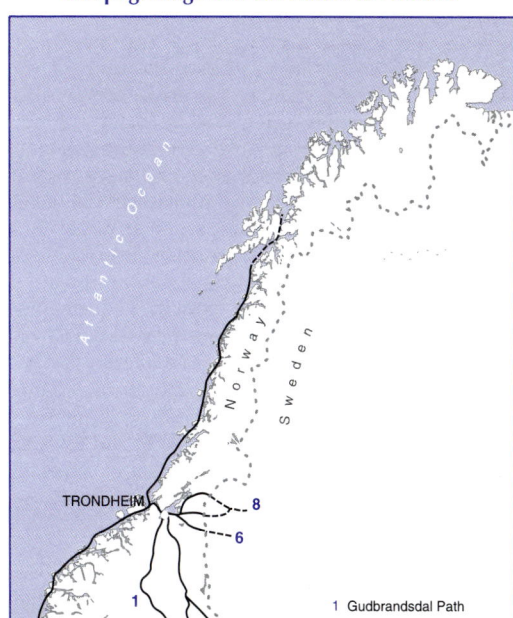

1 Gudbrandsdal Path
2 Tønsberg
3 Stavanger
4 Värmland - Østerdal
  Värmland - Trysil
6 Härjedal - Tydal
7 Jämtland - Stjørdal
8 Jämtland - Verdal
9 Coastal Route

After Olav's death and canonisation miracles continued to be reported and an increasing number of people began to make the pilgrimage to the shrine of St. Olav in the different churches that were built over the place where his grave is believed to have been. The exact whereabouts of the saint's remains are uncertain; the last Catholic bishop of Nidaros is understood to have taken them from the grave to ensure that they were not removed by the Protestants and then hidden them somewhere, perhaps under the cathedral. As explained above, though, there was not just one route to Nidaros, since pilgrims set off from their own homes in very different parts of Norway, Sweden and other countries either on foot or, if they were wealthier, on horseback (possibly with a considerable retinue), using the existing road network. With time and use, however, these itineraries fell into a pattern of several principal routes (see map p11), with subsidiary paths joining them at points along the way. One of these, the route described in this book, was the Gudbrandsdal path, leading from medieval Oslo up the valley to the Dovrefjell, over Hjerkinnhø and through Oppdal and Meldal to approach Trondheim from the south. There were also routes from Stavanger in south-western Norway, Tønsberg in the south and at least four routes from Sweden. Two of these came from the south-west of that country to link up and reach Nidaros from the south whilst others came directly west, joining up to reach it from the north-east, one of which, the northern-most Skalstugan route, is now waymarked. The other means of journeying to Nidaros was, of course, by sea, and there were routes approaching it from both the north and the south, south-west and west of Norway, as well as from England, Scotland, Ireland, the Isle of Man, Iceland, Greenland and the Faroe Islands.

It is often forgotten that Norway was a Catholic country for over 500 years, a longer period, in fact, than it has been Lutheran, and it is known that Norwegian pilgrims travelled to Rome, Jerusalem and even Santiago de Compostela during this time. Pilgrimages to Nidaros continued throughout the early and late Middle Ages (1031–1537), when the Reformation, introduced by royal decree (Norway was then under Danish rule), brought these journeys to a halt and put an abrupt end to the offical veneration of Saint Olav.

Pilgrims would normally complete the journey from Oslo to Nidaros in 25 days, arriving there for the saint's day on July 29th and the Olsok (Olav's Wake) celebrations. Each day was divided into four 'rosts', or stages of 8–10km, at the end of which was an 'Olav field', or resting and grazing place for horses. On the last day they only did one rost (i.e. roughly from Lian on the outskirts of modern Trondheim), presumably so as to arrive at the cathedral early in the day. The Gudbrandsdal pilgrim in the Middle Ages had his first good view of the town and the cathedral, the goal of his journey, from a point on a hill above it, the Feginsbrekken (literally 'glad hill') or Mountjoy. Then, of course, once they had attained their goal, they had to start back on the return trip by the same means and retrace their steps. Nowadays, however, the pilgrimage is a 'one-way street', all the more so since it is waymarked in only one direction, for unlike his historical counterpart the modern pilgrim no longer returns home on foot.

Olavkilde near Brøttum (author)

As well as Olav fields along the way there were also holy wells (Olavbrunnen) and springs reputed to have healing properties (Olavskilde), and on the modern route a number of these still exist along the way. There was also a network of hospices or hospitals (*spitaler* or *spedaler*), which provided places to sleep and feed pilgrims, and *saelehuser*, overnight shelters where pilgrims and wayfarers had to fend for themselves. These have long since disappeared, though it is known where a number of them were located, and these places are indicated in the text. However, although there are accounts of general travellers' itineraries through Norway in previous centuries which provide information about the roads in use and their condition, unlike the pilgrimages to Jerusalem, Rome and Santiago de Compostela, where there are many extant accounts of pilgrim journeys and descriptions of places passed through en route, there are no surviving written records of the Nidaros pilgrimage to give an idea of how many pilgrims were walking the route prior to the Reformation, where they came from or details about their experiences. What are available, however, are pilgrim badges and a collection of holy water jars which throw light on some of these matters.

Pilgrims were a source of revenue for the (Catholic) church in the Middle Ages as they came bearing gifts and offerings, and badges were sold to them to serve as souvenirs of their arrival at their destination. These badges were not peculiar to the Nidaros pilgrimage, however, but were common to other shrines too. Made of a lead alloy, usually some 5–10cm high, they bore the relief image of the saint in question and his or her attributes, though not always an inscription. They were intended to be attached to clothing (frequently hats) or luggage and are often found with loops for this purpose. The oldest pilgrim badges in Europe date from the 12th century, but those depicting St. Olav, seated on a throne or standing, with an axe in one hand and a crowned orb in the other, date from the 14th and 15th. Those extant are not very numerous, but the places where they were found suggest that pilgrims to Nidaros came mainly from Nordic countries, though some have been found in Britain and elsewhere in Europe. The most extensive collection of pilgrim badges in Britain (325 examples, from various sources) is in the Salisbury Museum.

One of the attractions of the Nidaros pilgrimage was the holy water from the spring in the cathedral which was sought as a remedy, and a number of small jars for taking this home have been found in the pilgrims' home settings. There are about 150 of these still extant and they, too, tell us something about the origins of those who journeyed to the shrine of St. Olav.

Apart from seeking cures people also made the pilgrimage to Nidaros as a form of penance, to atone for their sins, and the more arduous the journey to the pilgrim destination the greater was the merit earned thereby. Pilgrims in the past – unlike many of their modern counterparts – normally travelled light, with just a hat, staff, bag for food and a cape. They frequently carried a letter of recommendation from their parish priest, identifying the bearer as a bona fide pilgrim; there are 10 of these still extant, such as the one issued on May 1st 1439 to one Eivind Dyrasson. 'Credencials' or 'pilgrim passports' continue to be issued to those walking the ways of Saint James to Santiago de Compostela, but this practice has not yet been revived on the Pilgrim Road to Nidaros.

Churches

Many churches dedicated to St. Olav were built all over Norway prior to 1537, and 17 of the original 52 still survive today, three of them along the *pilegrimsleden*: Skedsmo, Ringsaker and Bønsnes. Skaun church is also believed to have been dedicated to St. Olav, and the original Ullensaker church was dedicated jointly to both St. Olav and John the Baptist. Nidaros cathedral is not, however, and as is often supposed, dedicated to the saint-king buried under its high altar but is a Christchurch instead. There were also 45 Olav (Olaf or Olave) churches in the British Isles (of which 17 survive today), 75 in Sweden, 20 in Denmark, 13 in Finland and an astonishing 75 in Iceland. It should be remembered, however, that only churches built in Norway **before** the Reformation were dedicated to a saint; those erected afterwards bear only the name of their locality, as do most non-conformist churches and chapels in Britain. There are recent St. Olav churches in Oslo (19th century) and Trondheim (20th) but these are both Roman Catholic; the original Olav church in the latter city is now buried under the present public library building, while that in the former has become the city's Catholic cathedral church.

Ruins of Mariakirke, Old Oslo (author)

There are many churches of medieval origin along the *pilegrimsleden*, on both the eastern and western routes, though only some of those, built in stone, survive intact. The earliest churches were built of wood (*trekirker*), with walls of upright planks and posts, but as these were embedded in the ground they eventually rotted and these buildings were replaced, from the 12th century onwards, by a new type of design, the stave church (*stavkirke*). Here the staves (plank walls) were set in a horizontal base or sill, thus raising them above ground level, a method that proved so effective that some of these still exist today. Of the 29 left only one, at Ringebu, is on the pilgrim route, but it is still in regular use as a parish church. Other medieval churches were built in stone and obviously survived better; there are several along the route, such as the Gamle Aker in Oslo, Bønsnes church and the 'Sister churches' in Granavollen. However, much of the furniture, fittings, doors, panel paintings and such like from many medieval and later churches are no longer *in situ*, but have been removed for safe keeping to museums in Oslo and Trondheim; pilgrims interested in church artefacts will find it interesting to visit them at the end of their journey when they have seen the original settings. For complete churches the Trøndelag museum at Sverresborg (which you pass on entering Trondheim) and the Norsk Folk Museum in Oslo each contain one that has been dismantled and re-erected there.

Eystein church, Hjerkinn (author)

In 1723, an important landmark in the history of Norwegian church building, the king of Denmark (who at that time ruled over Norway too), in straightened financial circumstances after fighting several wars, decided to sell off all the churches in Norway either to a wealthy individual or to the local community. As the sale of the church also included land, farms and part-farms this was obviously an interesting proposition, though the terms of the transaction stipulated that the churches be maintained in good condition and that they be large enough to accommodate all the parishoners. As many stave churches were both too small and by then in a very bad state of repair they were demolished and replaced by cruciform timber churches (*tømmerkirke*). Hence you will see many 18th-century churches along the way, and all those passed in the Gudbrandsdal valley – Lillehammer (replaced twice), Fåberg, Øyer, Tretten, Vinstra, Sel and Dovre – are examples of this phenomenon. In these, too, you will also see fine examples of the famous Gudbrandsdal woodcarving tradition on pulpits, altarpieces and communion tables. This was brought to Norway by woodcarvers from the Netherlands at the time the new cathedral in Oslo was built (1699), and from there the characteristic acanthus style of decoration spread to other parts of the country where it still lives on today. Contemporary churches, on the other hand, are only three in number along the route: Veldre church, between Brumunddal and Moelv, of stave church design and under construction in 1999, replaces one destroyed by fire a few years ago; Søre Ål (1964) as you enter Lillehammer; and the Eystein church at Hjerkinn (1969), designed by the architect Magnus Poulsson.

Saint Olav is sometimes represented in art (on altar panel paintings, for example) as having one of his dreams, whilst at other times he is depicted in much the same way as on the pilgrim badges, sometimes seated on a throne wearing a crown, sometimes standing as a warrior with a sword, sometimes with red hair and beard, sometimes black, with the axe and crowned orb as his attributes. The head (or complete body in miniature) that he is frequently seen treading underfoot with one leg is said to be his former heathen self that he now rejects. Representations of St. Olav have been found in several different countries, including one as far away as Bethlehem. Norway's other two indigenous national saints are Sunniva (female) and Hallvard (patron saint of Oslo); Øystein (archbishop of Nidaros and church builder), Ansgar and Torfín, bishop of Hamar, are local saints, as originally only episcopal (and not papal) blessing was needed to declare a person a saint. (There are stained-glass windows of each one of these in Oslo's Catholic cathedral.) The major European religious orders were also present in Norway in the Middle Ages: Dominicans, Benedictines, Franciscans and Cistercians, not only in medieval Oslo but at other points along the way as well.

The pilgrim route today

Today the *pilegrimsleden* (also referred to in the text as PL) has begun, slowly but surely, to undergo something of a revival, and a small trickle of pilgrims has begun to walk the route. As explained, the waymarked route from Oslo follows the line of the old 'Gudbrandsdal path' but, as a glance at the map (page 6) will reveal, it is in two parts to begin with, passing to either side of Lake Mjøsa before joining up to form a single route. Historically, when pilgrims set out from medieval Oslo they left the city along the traces of what is now the Strømveien in a north-easterly direction, to continue up the Grorud valley and via Skedsmo, Frogner, Ullensaker and Eidsvoll to Hamar, the only medieval city in Norway that was not on the coast. However, when the Gudbrandsdal path was 'revived', cleared and prepared in the mid-1990s and waymarked in 1997, it was apparently considered that today's pilgrim would not want to walk out of the city of Oslo through a largely industrial area, and a western option (referred to in this book as the 'cultural' one) was designed instead; this leaves Oslo to the west, following the traces of medieval roads where possible but not the main historic pilgrim route north out of the city.

River swollen after the snow has melted (author)

The preparation of the *pilegrimsleden* (the word *leden* refers, in fact, to the course of a sea rather than a land journey) was the responsibility of the Riksantikvaren (the State Department of Antiquities) who, surprisingly for such an undertaking, appear to have consulted neither walking organisations nor pilgrims associations while the work was being carried out. Walking is Norway's most popular and most practised sport, but the country does not have a tradition of long-distance walking from place to place, as exists in Britain and France, for example, with long-distance walks with a historical, geographical or other theme, such as the Pennine Way, the Coast to Coast path or the many long walks in the extensive French network of *grandes randonnées*. In Norway people walk from hut to hut in the mountains, often for several days at a time, or walk local waymarked footpaths of varying lengths on a Saturday or Sunday, for example, but the idea of setting off for two or more weeks at a time along a specified route is seemingly unknown, and the author of this guide frequently encountered people surprised at the undertaking. Norway, as a Protestant country, does not have a (recent) tradition of pilgrimage either, so on both these counts it was apparently inconceivable that anyone would actually walk the entire route at one go, once it was waymarked. It was expected instead that people would walk the stretches in their own local area, which accounts for the often exhausting climbs and immediately following descents the pilgrim will encounter, designed for people without a rucksack (or certainly not a heavy one). This accounts, too, for the lack of provision for bad weather alternatives in the waymarking, since people out for a Sunday afternoon walk in their own area can simply postpone their outing in unsuitable or inclement weather.

When the *pilegrimsleden* was to be officially opened it was apparently envisaged that on one designated day local groups all along the route would walk their own patch, but what happened in practice was that a group left Oslo on June 21st 1998 (and another departed from Skalstugan on July 18th) in order to arrive at Nidaros cathedral in time for the Olsok celebrations. A core of some 20 people walked all the way from Oslo, few of them experienced walkers, accompanied for stretches of varying lengths by many hundreds of others. Since then a trickle of individual pilgrims has completed the entire route at one go and an increasing number of organised groups have undertaken certain stretches, the most popular being from Dovre onwards. Because of the way the route, and especially the western option, was conceived, pilgrims in the early 21st century may often feel that they are being led along a route to see where those in the past would have walked, rather than being shown how to be a pilgrim themselves. This is changing gradually, though, with time, and this book hopes to redress the balance as far as possible.

As explained already, the whole of the western (cultural) route was waymarked as well as the eastern toute from Hamar onwards, but not, initially, the historic route out of Oslo. However, permission was subsequently obtained from the Department of the Environment to waymark this section, and this has now been completed. The historic route is described in this guide, though if users prefer they can walk as far as Gjøvik along the western route and then cross over to Hamar, either by bus (frequent service) or, as the group did in June 1997 and as pilgrims coming from that part of Norway would have done anyway in the past, go by boat: the *Skibladner*, the world's oldest working paddle steamer, operates a daily service between Gjøvik and Hamar in the summer months.

Those who have already walked the pilgrims roads through France and Spain, for example, will not encounter the same organised pilgrim infrastructure along the road to Nidaros. There is no comprehensive network of specifically pilgrim accommodation yet, for example, though several places which offer accommodation to the general public taking an outdoor holiday are beginning to add facilities for pilgrims. As regards to pilgrims' spiritual, as opposed to purely physical, needs, there are also the beginnings of an organisation on this level too, and the dioceses of Hamar (in Dovre) and Nidaros have each appointed a priest with attention to the needs of pilgrims as a specific part of their duties.

Traditionally many pilgrims arrived at the cathedral in Nidaros for the Olsokmesse or 'Olav wake'. This begins during the evening of July

28th and continues throughout the night, and its celebration is becoming more widespread again, with an increasing number of churches observing the festival today. In Trondheim there is now a week-long festival of music and other cultural events to mark the occasion, too, as well as the religious activities.

Stone relic jar, used for collecting holy water (Eivind Luthen)

TOPOGRAPHY AND LANGUAGE
Roads, paths and regions

The *pilegrimsleden* itself is fairly strenuous, due to terrain, to the need to avoid the (usually flat) main roads below you and because the waymarked route often takes you on short detours to visit places of historical, scenic or local interest before returning you to the straight and narrow. The walking is not difficult, though, in the sense that it is a walk (and not a scramble), and pilgrims do not have to have a good head for heights. From time to time there are stretches on minor roads, but much of the walking is on either footpaths or old tracks, whether the latter were originally public roads (*allmuevegen*, literally 'common people's road') or the numerous historic *kongeveien*. To begin with these 'royal' or 'king's roads' were only narrow bridlepaths (often just sunken *hulvei* or 'hollow roads') until they were eventually widened out to take horse-drawn vehicular traffic; today they may survive as anything from very narrow indistinct paths to wide tracks resembling present-day drove roads.

Modern roads in Norway are classified according to who maintains them (*riksvei* if they are national roads, *fylkesvei* if the county of local area looks after them; abbreviated as Rv and Fv respectively in the text) and according to their type of construction or function: a *bygdevei* ('built road') usually has a shale or loosely tarmacked surface while a *grusvei* is a gravelled lane. A *gårdvei* is one leading to (or from) a farm, a *saeterveg* one to a summer farm; a *driftvei* is one of fairly temporary construction, such as forest or works roads, while a *bomvei* is a gated road or one with a barrier across its entrance, often requiring a toll (for vehicles) to use it. A *privatveg* as its name suggests is a private road, a *blindveg* (i.e. 'blind way') a cul-de-sac; a *ridevei* is a bridlepath while a *gågate* or *gangvei* in a town is for pedestrians only (i.e. a road on which you 'go' or walk). A *turvei* (track) or *tursti* (path) is a recreational (usually waymarked) walking route, whilst in marshy areas such as the Dovrefjell a hybrid *kalvbru* or bridge road is encountered, a causeway made of logs to keep the route clear of the water. You will see many of these terms on signs and notices along the way.

Norway is divided up, for administrative purposes, into *fylker* (counties) which are in turn sub-divided into *kommuner*. Oppland *fylke*, for example, contains 26 *kommuner*, of which the *pilegrimsleden* passes through Vang, Gran, Jevnaker, Vestre Toten, Østre Toten, Øyer, Ringebu, Sør-Fron, Sel, Nord-Fron and Dovre. Many *kommuner* along the way publish their own guides to the pilgrim road in their area – mainly in Norwegian, though some of them have summaries in English. These are useful for more detailed information on the history, culture, flora and fauna of the places concerned, though not many are much good for detailed way-finding. These guides are available from local tourist offices and some from Pilegrimskontoret. Dovre has a particularly good one – except that it is written in Nynorsk!

The route

After leaving Oslo and its outskirts to the east up the industrial Groruddal valley the historic route continues out into open countryside, largely undulating agricultural land and woods, with increasingly large farms as far as Hamar. It then becomes hillier as it continues up the eastern side of the Mjøsa towards Lillehammer. After that the long slog up the Gudbrandsdal valley begins, with the river Lågen continuing where the lake left off, the route climbing steadily, with many ups and downs and the valley becoming steeper and narrower as it progresses further north. After passing the Håkåberget with its splendid views it reaches the farm at Skåe i Øyer, where the cultural route joins it from the west.

Olav logo stencilled on cairn, Dovrefjell (author)

For those who decide to leave Oslo to the west the first day is an interesting urban walk along quiet streets taking in places of historical and cultural interest; this can be undertaken separately before setting out on the main walk proper. After that it continues west via the Lommerdal valley and the hilly woods of the Krokskogen up to the Kongensutsikt (a hill with spectacular views) before descending to Sundvoll between the Tyri and the Steinsfjorden. From here it continues, via Jevnaker and then Lillehammer, up above the Ragnafjord to the west and up the left-hand side of the Gudbrandsdal valley itself, passing through a mixture of increasingly hilly agricultural land and forests, at times coinciding with other (differently waymarked) footpaths.

Once the two options fuse at Skåe i Øyer the route continues steadily upwards through the increasingly narrow and steeper valley, with the river Lågen below all the time, either to one side or the other, through open woodland and an increasing amount of forest, descending briefly into the wide, bowl-like valley around Kvam before climbing once again until it reaches the wide expanses of the Dovre plateau at nearly 1000m, with spectacular views in clear weather. The number of ascents and descents increase both in quantity and strenuousness the farther north you go.

After Hjerkinnhø, the highest point of the route at 1200m, the way continues north over the hills along the Gamlekongveien (an old drove-type road) and then down along the side of the Drivedal valley to Oppdal. From there the route continues via more stretches of the Gamlekongveien near Berkåk and Svorkmo and via Buvika to cross the river Gaula and enter Trondheim over the hills from the west; the last 8km are a continuous descent with splendid views out over the approaching town, the Trondheimsfjord and all the surrounding countryside. The walking, then, in general is a mixture of different types of terrain, with mountains, lakes, a lot of rivers, both large and small (which become raging torrents in the spring time after the snow has melted), waterfalls, open woodland, agricultural land and an often seemingly endless succession of (chiefly conifer) forest paths and tracks. The three main types of economic activity the pilgrim will encounter along the way are agriculture, sheep farming and forestry.

Recurrent features

Certain recurrent features will attract the pilgrim's attention as he or she walks along. The main unit of population outside of towns of any size is not the village as we know it in Britain and other parts of Europe, with its classic combination of church, pub and a larger or smaller cluster of houses, but the *gård* or **farm**. Farms are comprised not of a farmhouse and a couple of barns or other outbuildings, as might be expected, but often of a very large collection of both dwelling houses and functional buildings, sometimes as many as 20 or more, all belonging to the same family. Norwegian law prevents the sale of farms or any of the farm buildings except in certain very specific, limited situations, and the *gård* is passed from one generation to the next via the oldest son or daughter and so remain static in size. Typically there is the main farmhouse, often extremely large with a great number of rooms (all of them contain a ballroom on the first floor for weddings, festivities, etc.), and these have several common plans, one of which is the central sitting-room model, detectable by the balcony built outside. There are usually other houses, too, for the retired farmer and his wife once the younger generation has taken over the running of the farm, for example, and others for brothers, sisters and other relatives. The pilgrim will probably notice too that these are nearly always painted white whilst the functional buildings are red; this is because, traditionally, white paint was much more expensive than red presumably because of its ingredients. The custom has continued, however, and though other colours are now used this is not a very common practice. The functional buildings, barns (one of them usually surmounted by a belltower to summon people to meals), granaries and other storehouses raised up on 'legs' or pillars (the *stabbur*) also form part of the complex (those for dairy produce, on the other hand, are usually half-sunk into the ground) and are frequently grouped, along with the dwelling houses, around a central yard or *gårdstun*. An interesting example of one surrounded by largely arable land is at Lie between Hoff and Kapp churches, while Budsjord, 4km after Dovre, is a good example of a mountain farm (this is open to visitors). The *saeter* (or high-level farm) to which farmers took their animals for grazing during the summer months is much smaller and of much simpler construction. The *prestegård* is the 'priest's farm', many of which were extremely substantial, though the term is also used nowadays to refer to his vicarage and office. Norway has many open-air and folk museums, including several along the *pilegrimsleden*, and pilgrims interested in vernacular architecture will find these a good source of examples.

Stabbur, Budsjord (author)

Churches, the pilgrim will no doubt notice, are often situated on hill-tops and on main roads, away from population centres. As a great many of them are painted white they are visible from afar and thus function as landmarks to orient the walker. They are usually surrounded by their (extremely well looked-after) church yard in which, especially in many of the larger ones on the southern part of the route, you will see a 'mini-church' or cemetery chapel, originally built for the funeral services of the lower-classes (the well-to-do having theirs in the main church itself). Several churches are used as place-names in the text, though it should be remembered that they may well be at some distance from the centre of population they serve; Oppdal kirke, for example, is 3km from Oppdal sentrum.

Another feature that pilgrims cannot help but notice as they make their journey, if only because, initially, the waymarks draw attention to them, are the numerous **burial mounds** along the way. Many of these date from the Iron Age. The dead person was laid on the ground, along with all his worldly possessions, a burial chamber built around him and earth piled on top of it all to form an (often enormous) mound. Raknehaugen, the largest one in Norway, 15m high and 95m in diameter at its base, is located on the eastern route, a little to the north of Hovin church, while a visit to the inside of the Olav mound at Hundorp will give you an idea of their interior construction.

Those walking the *pilegrimsleden* will also notice that the air is very clear and unpolluted (Norway has little heavy industry and is a very environmentally conscious country) and that the countryside is 99.9% litter-free. Spring comes later than in countries farther south, so that the trees remain bare until late May/early June and flowers that make their appearance at the end of March or the beginning of April in Britain, for example, do not come into bloom until some two months later. As for animals you will encounter along the way – apart from sheep, horses, and cows, etc. – you may also see deer and elk, if you are attentive, as they are well camouflaged. Places where musk oxen have been reintroduced (from Greenland in the 1950s) are indicated in the text, as they should be given a very wide berth. Dogs are not normally a problem as their owners are nearly always nearby and will call them in if they start to annoy you.

Language

Norwegian, like Danish, Swedish and Icelandic (but not Finnish), is an Indo-European language and a 'grandchild' of Old Norse, just as French, Spanish and Italian, for example, are 'grandchildren' of Classical Latin. Norwegian is therefore a 'second-cousin' of English, German and Dutch, and speakers of any of these languages will therefore find a lot of similarities with their own once they start to 'tune in'. Norwegian is in a somewhat different situation than many other European languages, however, in that it officially exists in two versions (something linguists refer to as a *diglossia* situation): Bokmål (literally 'book language') and Nynorsk ('new Norwegian'). Bokmål is based on written Danish and is used in cities, in newspapers, and the like, while Nysnorsk, based on regional forms, is used more in rural areas, though it has enjoyed something of a revival and is taught in all Norwegian schools. You will find, though, that for many people in Norway English is almost their second language, and employees in stations, hotels, banks, offices and so on will automatically be able to speak it (and well). Nevertheless, it is recommended that you take along a small pocket dictionary and a phrase book as this will help you in rural areas and to read/understand notices. (Note that the three letters in the Norwegian alphabet ae, ø and å are placed at the end in the dictionary for words starting with them and after the other vowels when they occur within other words.)

Norwegian is not, in fact, a very complicated language to learn to read, and anyone with an extensive (passive) vocabulary in English and who also speaks German will not find it hard to understand once they have spotted the differences in spelling in words of the same origin (hus/house, for example, myrin/mire, bog, fjell/fell, bekke/beck, nedre/nether, lower, and so on). Spoken Norwegian, however, with its very 'sing-song' intonation is quite another matter...

In the text some words which occur frequently, are cumbersome to translate or do not give precisely the same meaning in English are left in the original Norwegian and are set in italic (*stabbur*, *husmannsplass*, *prestegård*, for example). A glossary of geographical and other useful items is given in Appendix D.

PREPARATION

Before you go

- Try to read up as much as you can about the road to Nidaros, its history, background, art, architecture and geography; a bibliography is given in Appendix B.

- Pilgrims already used to fairly strenuous walking will not encounter any difficulty on the *pilegrimsleden*, but those not accustomed to walking at all (and many pilgrims, as opposed to walkers, are not), to walking in hilly terrain or to carrying a (possibly heavy) rucksack day in and day out are strongly urged to train before they set out and get in plenty of practice. If this applies to you, consider joining your local rambling club at least six months in advance and go out with them as often as you possibly can. Most clubs have walks of different lengths and speeds so you can start with a shorter, slower one if you need to and gradually build up your speed and stamina. The advantages of this are that you can walk with other people (usually friendly), walk in the countryside, have someone to lead who knows the way and suitable places to walk (which you may not) and you can also practise walking in hilly places (which you will definitely need). Then, start increasing the amount of weight and gear you take out with you until you can carry all you need. After that, go out walking on at least two days in a row on several occasions, in strenuous terrain, carrying all your proposed gear with you; it's a very different matter walking 20–25km on a 'one-off' basis from getting up again the following morning, probably stiff and possibly footsore, and starting out all over again. In this way you should have an enjoyable journey, with trouble-free back and feet.

• Decide what footwear you will be taking to walk in and break it in well before you go.

EQUIPMENT

In general, try to travel as light as you can (not just because of the weight but because of the constant climbs and descents in many parts of the route), and leave out anything not entirely necessary. Remember, though, that it can be cold (as well as hot) in Norway, and as sections of the route are high up you will need gloves, hat and scarf as well as other warm clothing, even in summer.

The items listed below are given as a general guide only.

1. **Rucksack** – at least 50 litres
2. **Footwear** – both to walk in and a spare pair (e.g. lightweight trainers)
3. **Anorak**
4. **Waterproofs**
5. **Pullover**
6. **First aid kit** (including a needle for draining blisters)

   The type of elastoplast sold by the metre is more useful than individual dressings; take elastic bandage and scissors as well

7. **Torch**
8. **Water bottle**
9. **Sleeping bag**
10. **Sleeping mat** if carrying a tent

11. **Stick** – useful for testing terrain, hilly terrain, snow, etc.

12. **Guide book**

13. **Maps**

14. **Small dictionary** – Berlitz does a pocket-sized one

15. **Compass**

16. **Hat, scarf** and **gloves**

17. **Mug, spoon** and **knife**

18. **Tent** if you intend to camp regularly

THERE AND BACK

How to get there

- **By air to Oslo:** several flights a day from Heathrow with SAS, Braathens and British Airways to Oslo's new Gardermoen airport, with frequent train and bus connections to centre city. It is usually cheaper, as well as quicker, to fly to Norway than travel there by any other means. The various airlines often have special offers so it is worth doing your 'homework' thoroughly before you make a decision.

- **By boat from Newcastle to Bergen or Stavanger** and train from there to Oslo. Color Line runs a regular service from Newcastle to Bergen/Stavanger two to three times a week, journey time 23–25 hours according to which Norwegian port it goes to first (this depends on the day of the week you travel). The prices vary greatly not only according to the type of accommodation you chose, from five-star cabins down to 'sleeperettes' (reclining seats), but there are also considerable variations according to the season and day you travel. If you live in the north of England this may seem like an interesting proposition (especially if you want to visit either Bergen and/or Stavanger and you are lucky with the weather – the ride along the coast is beautiful), but it works out relatively expensive as the train fares to and from Oslo are between £30 to £50 single, again according to the time you travel, and the food and drink on these journeys is extremely expensive. The train journey from either Bergen or Stavanger to Oslo is between seven and eight hours.

- **By coach from London:** Eurolines runs a service to Oslo, once to three times a week according to the time of year, which takes 36 hours and costs about £180 return. This is a long, tiring ride, however, with three ferry crossings and lengthy customs clearances in each direction as the bus goes via Amsterdam.

- **Other places along the way:** Gjøvik, Hamar, Lillehammer, Dovre, Oppdal, etc., are easy to reach (or leave) either by train or coach (Bussekpress) as most of the places along the *pilegrimsleden* are on their Oslo–Trondheim services.

Returning from Trondheim

- **By train to Oslo** – journey time seven to eight hours.
- **By bus to Oslo** – journey time nine to ten hours.

In either case it is suggested that you travel back during the daytime as both of these options take you through areas you will now be familiar with and you can thus 'rewalk' in your mind much of the route in reverse.

- **By boat to Bergen** if you are not in a hurry. There is a continuous regular boat service along the coast from Bergen up to Kirkenes (on the border of Russia in the north) known as the Hurtigrute (the 'fast route') which stops and starts in a very large number of places along the way (in both directions). You could therefore get on in Trondheim and travel back to Bergen by this method (pricey but nice in good weather).
- **Bergen by train** from Trondheim is via Oslo.
- **Bergen by coach** from Trondheim – the Bussekspress has a regular service, journey time nine to ten hours.

BEING THERE

Accommodation

There is accommodation of different types (farms offering B&B, youth hostels, campsites, hotel and guest houses) all along the way, but as Norway is an expensive country and as the cheaper type of accommodation is not uniformly available everywhere on the route the walker on a budget would be well advised to carry a tent. There is very little specifically pilgrim-oriented accommodation as yet on this route (as there is, for example, on the pilgrim Ways of St. James through France and Spain), but as the Pilgrim Road to Nidaros becomes better known and more regularly walked this is expected to follow.

Prices for accommodation in farms, guesthouses, hotels and youth hostels normally include (a very copious) breakfast. Most campsites also have hut accommodation, each suitable for about 4–6 people, so that if there are two or three people walking together this could be a good option (these huts also have simple cooking facilities). Those carrying a tent can either sleep on a campsite (charges vary according to size) or, in many cases, pitch it in the grounds in farm-type B&B accommodation (and have meals or not, as you prefer). Those wanting to camp elsewhere can do so anywhere outside city limits provided the tent is more than 150m from a house, a fence or boundary surrounding private property, and as long as campers do not light a fire, leave litter or stay more than two nights. (For this type of camping, ensure that you have adequate supplies of water.) Check first, however, if you are in an area classified as a national park or a nature reserve, as other restrictions may apply.

Unless you are camping on spec or have a very small tent you will need to reserve your accommodation ahead. It is suggested, however, that you only do this for three to four days at a time to allow for flexibility, tiredness, rest days, etc. Places where accommodation is available are indicated in the text as you go along, with phone numbers and information on how to walk there where necessary. 'E' after an entry means that you will normally be able to speak English face to face with at least one person on the premises; 'EE' indicates that you can speak English on the telephone when booking ahead, though it may not always be the person who initially answers the phone. 'CF' is the abbreviation for 'cooking facilities'. You may find it helpful to read through the text before you set out and mark possible stopping places with a highlighter pen.

Apart from the information given in Appendix B the Pilegrimskontoret in Oslo publishes a booklet entitled *Overnatt-ungsguiden*. This lists accommodation in route order, with addresses, telephone numbers and an indication of prices. It is in Norwegian but is not hard to decipher and has an English glossary at the end.

If the type of accommodation you require is not available at the daily distances that suit you, you can also, in many places, adopt the 'bus method'. That is, with some prior organisation you can often stay two nights in the same place and advance or return by public transport. In many areas bus services (normally frequent) between larger population centres (e.g. Hamar–Gjøvik, Lillehammer–Otta, Oslo–Eidsvoll) pass through and stop in or near the smaller places along the way. Area timetables for services in a whole region are available from tourist offices, bus and train stations and some hotels. This will make you journey a slightly less 'pilgrim' one, but it could help you avoid walking longer distances in some places than you would otherwise find comfortable.

Planning the day

Walkers elsewhere often calculate a speed of 4km per hour as average. In Norway, though, and on the *pilegrimsleden* in particular, with its constant (and exhausting) ups and downs, you should probably reckon on only 3km in some sections (i.e. a little under 2mph), especially if you have a heavy rucksack. You will, however, have the advantage of plenty of daylight between mid-May and the beginning of September.

If you intend to visit places of interest such as open-air museums allow 1–2 hours according to their size and interest. Church visiting times have been indicated in the text where known, but as churches are often open earlier on in the day rather than later they may not always coincide with your schedule. To visit larger places (Hamar, Lillehammer, Gjøvik, for example) you will need to allow half a day or may decide to include these in a rest day; how many of these you take – and how often – will depend on how tired you are or how much time you have. You may also have to plan your daily stages around the accommodation available, rather than the distances you would prefer to walk, though as more places to stay become available this should change. If you are extremely tired, though, and actually want to rest (rather than visit), two nights in the same place with no sight-seeing opportunities will not only help you recuperate your strength but also, if you have problems with them, work wonders with your feet.

Food and drink: there are some cafeterias and cafés along the way (indicated where known in the text), but in many places you will not enter, during the entire day, a centre of population big enough to offer these facilities (or a shop), so you will need to carry sufficient food with you all the time. As indicated above, a copious breakfast is normally included when you stay in farm, guesthouse, hotel or youth hostel accommodation. Water is normally safe to drink from streams in high-level places.

OTHER PRACTICAL INFORMATION

Opening and closing times

Shops: supermarkets – most are open 10.00–21.00 Monday to Friday and until 18.00 on Saturday. Alcohol is **very** expensive in Norway and only beer is available in supermarkets (until 20.00 weekdays, 18.00 Saturdays); all other alcoholic drink for home consumption must be purchased from one of the Vinmomopolet (state-run liquor) shops which have limited opening hours (and are closed on Sundays). N.B. the term 'supermarket' used in the text refers to a self-service shop – not necessarily a large one – selling food but often other things as well.

Post Offices (Postkontor): Mon–Fri 9.00–17.00, Sat 10.00–14.00.

Banks: Mon–Fri 08.15–15.30 (Thurs 17.00, closed Sat).

Changing money: this can be done in all banks and post offices, as well as in 'hole-in-the-wall' machines ('minibank' in Norwegian). In Oslo Central Station there is also a note-changing machine which gives a considerably better rate for sterling and dollar bills than, for example, changing them over the counter at the desk beside it.

Norwegian coins (*myntene*) are available in denominations of 10 øre, 50 øre, 1 krone, 5 kroner, 10 kroner and 20 kroner. Notes (*sedlene*) are in amounts of 50, 100 and 1000 kroner.

Telephones: Phone booths are few and far between apart from in large places (Hamar, Lillehammer, Gjøvik, etc.), though in a place with at least one shop there is often one nearby. Phone booths take 1, 5, 10 and 20 kroner coins (minimum 2 kroner), though many in central Oslo only take phone cards. These (*telekort* in Norwegian) are available (from Narvesen newsagents and post offices) in units of 150, 65 and 22; calls are cheaper per unit the more expensive the card is (i.e. the units are longer). It is cheaper to ring between 22.00 and 08.00, weekends included – there are only two price bands. The international prefix is 00, the country code for Norway is 47 and emergency numbers (free) are 110 (fire), 112 (police) and 113 (ambulance).

Note: Norway does not have internal dialling codes so the subscriber numbers are for the whole country.

Public Holidays: Nine in total: January 1st, Maundy Thursday, Good Friday, Easter Monday, May 1st, May 17th (Constitution Day), Whit Monday (the seventh Monday after Easter), December 25th and 26th.

Temperatures: at sea level are much the same as in Britain during June,

July and August. On higher ground, however, they will obviously be lower, particularly at night.

Church services: are normally on Sundays only, frequently at 11am. However, note that in many country places they are held only once a fortnight.

USING THIS GUIDE

Waymarking

Apart from the section of the eastern (historic) route between Oslo and Hamar (waymarked with yellow arrows) the *pilegrimsleden* described here is waymarked throughout with a logo that is a mixture of a Saint Olav cross and the symbol commonly found on maps and signs to indicate places of historical interest. These are placed at junctions and points on the route where there are changes of direction and, given the nature of the route, it is intended to be walked in one direction only (south to north). Only very minimal waymarkings are provided, however, and only one in each place; so if they are missing (for example, because a road has been repaired or, more frequently, trees have been cut down) you may have to go a long way till you see the next one. Which turning you take will therefore often be a question of trial and error, though this book does try to minimise this as far as possible (and for this reason the route descriptions may appear at times to contain more detail than is required). There are rarely any 'reassurance' waymarks along the way, either, to let you know, for example, after a long stretch on the straight, that you are, in fact, still on the right track. If you don't see any waymarks before too long, though, especially when you change direction, you are probably lost. Go back to the previous one and try again.

There are four types of waymarks: stone, wood, mini and enamel. The stone ones, like large tombstones, tell you how many kilometres are left to Nidaros and are usually placed outside prominent churches. Wooden ones, marker posts some 2ft high, with a metal relief pilgrim logo on one face, are of two kinds: directional (simply with an arrow) and topographical/historical, often existing side by side with the directional markers. If you see one, for instance, with 'gravhaugen' (burial mound) and an arrow, this is to indicate where the mounds are located, not that the route continues in that direction. Many of these wooden posts also have 'forminne' on one face, indicating a historical or archaeological reference. The mini waymarks are square-cut sticks with a PL (*pilegrimsleden*) logo stencilled on their tops or even just red paint in some places, whilst the enamel ones are found on the walls of buildings, in towns, for example. On Dovrefjell you will also see red waymarks in the form of the PL logo stencilled onto rocks and boulders.

There are also information boards (historical, cultural, flora and fauna, etc.) in several places along way, many of them bilingual or with English summaries.

Marble-type waymark, Hamar Domkirkeodde (author)

Maps

Although Ordinance Survey type maps are readily available in Norway the *pilegrimsleden* is not yet marked on them, so detailed sketch maps of the route are included in this book. The scale is indicated on each sketch map. Walker's and other maps of Norway can be obtained from the larger bookshops in Oslo such as Norlis Bokhandel or Tanum (see Appendix B for addresses) or by writing (if you know which ones you need) to the Statens Kartverk, Landdivisjonen, Kartverksveien 21, 3511 Hønefoss. In Britain you can obtain them from Stanfords book and map shop in Covent Garden and from the Map Shop, Upton upon Severn. The Statens Kartverk produces a series entitled 'Topografisk Hovedkartserie, Norge 1:50 000', but you will need between 20 and

```
┌─────────────────────────────────────────┐
│                                           │
│    Key to Sketch Maps                     │
│                                           │
│                                           │
│    Pilgrim route on a road ═══════        │
│   Pilgrim route on a track --------       │
│                   Road ═══════            │
│               Railway ┝┼┼┼┼┼              │
│                 Track --------            │
│      County boundary · · · · · ·          │
│                 Water  ∼∼∼∼∼              │
│                 River  ∽∽∽                │
│                Church    ⬩                 │
│            Settlement    •                 │
│                                           │
└─────────────────────────────────────────┘
```

30 maps to cover the entire route; the names and reference numbers of all of the relevant ones are given in Appendix C.

You will probably find it easier to follow the first part of the walk to the Oslo city boundary, whether you choose the eastern or the western option, if you have either Capelan's 'Stor-Oslo 60' (Greater Oslo) map or at least the A3-size tear-off street plan provided free by the Tourist Office and mark out the route beforehand with a highlighter pen; that way you will have less stoppings and startings and have a general idea in advance of where you are going.

Textual description

Each section begins with the distance walked from the previous one and, before giving directions for walking that part of the route, provides a description of the practical facilities available such as shops, cafés, banks, public transport and accommodation, a brief history, where applicable, and an indication of the places of interest to visit or look out for. (Pilgrims wishing to spend time in any of the larger towns should obtain information leaflets and a street plan from the Tourist Office there.) The text is not divided into daily stages but runs continuously, thus enabling the walker to cover the distance he or she prefers each day. The figures after each place name heading indicate the height in metres where known and, in parentheses, the distance in kilometres from both Oslo and Nidaros. Place names and other names that help in wayfinding, such as street names, the names of prominent buildings, rivers, etc., appear in the text in bold type. Norwegian words retained in the original are in italic.

Since the spellings of certain words – veien/vegen (way, road), for example, gate/gata (street) – can vary there are some seeming inconsistencies of presentation in the text. This is because the spellings have been copied from the street or place-name boards *in situ*. Also (see Glossary), as the word for 'the' in Norwegian (-en) is tacked onto the end of words you will see variations in the way a street name is presented on signs and notice-boards: Strømvei/Strømveien, for example, Fossumveg/Fossumvegen. In the text 'the' is omitted in English if the '-en' is attached to the end of the word but used if not: e.g. 'turn L up the Fossumvei' but 'turn L up 'Fossumvegen'.

'Turn L, turn R, turn L and then L again', etc., means you do these maneouvres in quick succession so no distances are given. 'More or less'/'roughly in a straight line' means that from A to B the general direction is straight, even though there may be some 'kinks' in the path between the two points. Streams are normally only named if of any size.

Waymark on bridge over the river Gisna to mark the border between Oppdal and Rennebu kommuner (author)

Abbreviations have been kept to a minimum.

L indicates that you should turn/fork left

R that you should turn/fork right

(L) and **(R)** mean that something you pass is to your left or right

KSO keep straight on

KSO(L) or **KSO(R)** means that you should keep straight on to L (or R)

FP footpath

FB footbridge

// parallel

km kilometre

KM kilometre in road numbers

NSB is the abbreviation for the Norwegian national railway network.

Fv *fylkesvei* (i.e. county-maintained road)

Rv *riksvei* (i.e. nationally-maintained or 'A' class road)

BV *bygdevei* road with shale or loosely tarmacked surface

m.o.h. *meter over havn* (i.e. metres above sea level)

PL pilegrimsleden

HT high tension (cables, etc.)

CF cooking facilities

PO post office

CD cash dispenser

Unlike pilgrimages to Lourdes, Fatima or other locations where miracles are sought, help for specific problems requested and where being in the pilgrim destination itself is the most important factor, on the Pilgrim Road to Nidaros today (like the Ways of St. James through France and Spain to Santiago de Compostela) it is the making of the journey that is the pilgrim's principal concern, the arrival in Nidaros being only a conclusion to the rest of the undertaking. If you bear this in mind it will help you not to feel, on your arrival in a town where modern pilgrims are still not very common, that reaching your destination has been something of a 'let down'.

THE ROUTE

Oslo

Population 500,000. All facilities. **Accommodation** in all prices brackets. Youth Hostels: a) Haraldsheim, Haraldsheimveien 4 (tel: 22.22.29.65/22.15.50.43), open all year; b) Holtekilen, Micheletsveien 55 (tel: 67.53.38.53), open mid-May/mid-August; c) LBM-Ekeberg, Kongveien 82 (tel: 22.74.50.90), open end May/August; d) Albertine hostel, Storgata 55 (tel: 22.99.72.00), open early June/mid- to end August. Campsite: Ekeberg Camping, Ekebergveien 65 (tel: 22.19.85.68), end May/end August (3km from city centre). **Tourist Office**: a) Vestbaneplassen 1 (near City Hall); b) Oslo Central Station (also has accommodation service).

If this is your first visit to Norway you may wish to visit some of the (non-pilgrim) 'sights' before you start the walk. You can get more information from the Tourist Office (including a series of very informative leaflets in English on different aspects of Norwegian life, art, music, history, buildings, etc.) but the 'musts', as well as the Domkirke (cathedral) are the Vigeland Sculpture park, the Viking ship, Fram and Kontiki museums, and for those who like paintings the Munch museum (the National Gallery – entrance free – also contains a number of his works). The Norwegian Folk Museum is also interesting – perhaps at the end of your journey if you are returning to Oslo – when you will have seen some examples of the vernacular architecture exhibited there and be able to situate it better in its context. An interesting city walk (on a nice day) is to follow the Akerselva (river) from the Maridalvannet (lake) on the northern edge of the city gently downhill to the Grønland district in central Oslo, some 7–8km along a footpath which changes from one side of the river to the other occasionally. (Take the bus or tram to Kjelsås and get off at the terminus by the Norsk Teknisk Museum.) You can also do a short detour from the middle section of this walk to visit the 12th-century Gamle Aker church (still in regular use) if you are walking the eastern route to Hamar (the western passes it anyway (see page 84). And if you are interested in medieval religious orders it is worth visiting (again in nice weather) the ruins of the 12th-century Cistercian abbey on Hovedøya (an island, a short boat journey from the pier at Vippetangen).

Travelling about in Oslo If you intend to make more than two journeys within 24 hours it is worth buying 'et dagkort' (a 'day-card'), obtainable from bus and tram drivers, metro stations, etc., which are valid for unlimited free travel within the city on buses, trams, metro, ferry services to the islands and local trains. If you intend to visit several museums or other 'sights' involving entrance fees within a short space of time an 'Oslo card' (valid for one, two or three days, including unlimited travel as desribed for the 'dagkort') is definitely worth considering. These are obtainable from the Tourist Office, Narvesen newsagents, hotels in Oslo and some post offices and are valid for the relevant period from the time you first use it.

Bookshops Tanum, one of the biggest general bookshops in Norway, with a large branch in the city centre at Karl Johansgata 37, and Norlis Bokhandel, Universitets gaten 20–24, both have extensive stocks of books in English, of all types, and also sell maps. St. Olav Bokhandel, Akersveien 14 (a small street at the side of the St. Olav church) is an up-market religious bookshop with a 'pilgrim department' (in various languages) on the first floor.

Setting off As the route on the first day, whichever option you chose, is basically an urban walk it is suggested you leave your rucksack in the place where you are staying and spend another night there, returning to your point of departure by public transport: by metro/T-bane from Stovner station on the eastern route, for example, or Haslum on the western; there is no point in walking all through the town and its outer suburbs lugging all your (probably heavy) belongings with you...

The *pilegrimsleden* starts in Old Oslo, a short distance to the southeast of the modern town on a tongue of land between the river Alna and the sea, in the general direction of the Ekeberg. *This is where the city of Oslo was located from its beginnings around the year 1000 until it was completely destroyed by fire in 1624, after which it was rebuilt further west near the Akershus fortress by Christian IV (and thereafter known as Christiania).*

To reach medieval Oslo from the modern town centre *(for example from Oslo Central Station)*, take tram no. 18 or 19 *(both in the direction of Lyabru, unless you want to walk)*, and get off at the stop marked 'Oslo Hospital'. Across the road you will see a cemetery (to the L) and opposite it, on the R, the old **Oslo Hospital**, *founded in 1538 on the site of the original Franciscan monastery. The hospital church was restored in 1934 and has the old hospital building itself (now an old people's home) adjoining it to the R.*

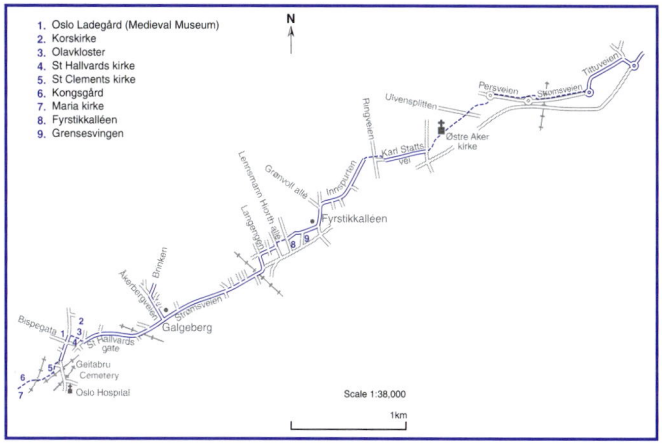

1. Oslo Ladegård (Medieval Museum)
2. Korskirke
3. Olavkloster
4. St Hallvards kirke
5. St Clements kirke
6. Kongsgård
7. Maria kirke
8. Fyrstikkalléen
9. Grensesvingen

Scale 1:38,000

1km

After getting off the tram turn back over the railway bridge you have just crossed *(on the site of the former Gjeitbru – 'goat bridge' – over the river Alna, which was used to take the animals to and from their pasture on the Ekeberg, the mountain behind)*. Turn L down **Saxegaardsgata** (first waymark on building on your R) and continue ahead to cross FB over railway line. The ruins in front of you are those of the *Mariakirke (the royal church) and the Kongsgård (royal court): see explanatory notice board for its history (with English summary). The church was very large, as its ruined outline shows, though the original building on the site, mid-11th century, was only a small wooden one. It was replaced by a stone church at the beginning of the 12th century and then expanded several times, with two tall brick towers. It caught fire in 1523 and after that fell into such bad condition that it was demolished later in the century. The Kongsgård (royal palace) complex dates from the early 12th century, the first buildings in wood* and earth being replaced by a stone castle early in the 13th century. This too fell into disrepair, and in the late Middle Ages the administration that was formerly carried out there was transferred west to the Akershus fortress.

Gamlebyen (Old Oslo) (0/643)

The route itself (either branch) starts from the ruins of the Mariakirke, so from here go back over the FB. *The building to your R is the* **Saxegård**, *a 14th-century city farm rebuilt in the 18th century, but with medieval stonework in its cellar. It is shortly to be restored as a museum for the Clemenskirke and as a community centre for this section of Oslo.*

On the L is the **Clemenskirke**, *a stone church from the 11th–12th centuries, dedicated to St. Clement and replacing two wooden buildings on the same site; this was Oslo's first parish (as opposed to royal or episcopal) church. As its outline shows, it was considerably smaller than either the Mariakirke or the St. Hallvardkirke nearby. It had a tower in the north-west corner but was unusual in design in having twin naves separated by a row of columns. (See information board for history, etc., with English summary. A plan was afoot in early 1999 for it to be enclosed by a protective glass dome, along the lines of the 'glass' cathedral in Hamar.) The Clemenskirke was in regular use until the Reformation reached Norway in 1537, after which it was demolished. An archaeological dig in 1970–71 unearthed 140 graves, the oldest dating from 930–1030 AD.*

Medieval Oslo had two centres, the 'King's Town' to the south, at the mouth of the river, with the Maria and Clemens churches and the royal palace, and the 'Bishop's Town' to the north near the Bispegata/Oslogata junction, with the Bishop's Palace, St. Olav monastery, St. Hallvard cathedral and the Korskirke (Church of the Holy Cross).

It is difficult to imagine, nowadays, with the southern site surrounded on three sides by railway sidings and the motorway, and the northern one with its industrial buildings, what it must all have looked like in medieval times, but it must have been construction on a grand scale for the period, judging by the extent of these and most of the other ruins in the area, as well as the buildings already referred to. Oslo around the year 1300, with an adult population of 3000, also had two other monasteries and a leper hospital.

Continue back along the **Saxegaardsgata** and along the **Oslogata** to its junction with the Bispegata and cross this. *On the LH side is the*

Ladegård/Bispeborget; the original building was used as a store for corn and hay, but it was later taken over in 1618 for use as the Town Hall. After a fire in 1721 it was rebuilt in 1725 using the original medieval foundations and is currently being restored as a medieval museum, with the land behind it being landscaped as a Baroque garden.

Opposite, on the R, are the ruins of the **St. Hallvardkirke**, Oslo's first cathedral. It was a vast structure, dedicated to St. Hallvard, the patron saint of the city of Oslo, and built of natural stone in Romanesque style. It was begun in the 12th century and had rounded arches, a central tower and transverse nave, but was rebuilt and altered several times, Gothic pointed arches being added in the 13th century. It was in regular use until 1660, when the present Domkirke in the modern city centre was built. After that the original cathedral fell into disrepair and much of the stonework was 'recycled' when the Akerhus fortress was built, further over to the west in the new town. Oslo's existing churches, in general, deteriorated after the arrival of the Reformation in 1537.

Next door to the St. Hallvardkirke are the ruins of the **Olavkloster**, adjoining the more modern part which is still standing (open on Sundays, times on door). It was established in 1239 and was one of the first Dominican monasteries in the north. Other religious orders in Oslo in the Middle Ages included Benedictine nuns (1161), Franciscans (1290) and Cistercians; the latter came from England and founded an abbey on the Hovedøya (island in the Oslofjord) in 1147.

To the L of the Olavskirke are the ruins of the **Korskirke** (Church of the Holy Cross), set in what is now a public garden. This is much smaller and was also a parish church, dating from the 12th century, for as well as having two centres, royal and ecclesiastical, medieval Oslo also had two parishes.

Leave the grounds of the St. Hallvard kirke by the gate opposite the one you entered from, into the **St. Hallvards gate**. The school on this street is built on the site of the former Oslo cathedral school, the town's first educational establishment. The modern industrial building a little further up on the L is on the site of the medieval Laurentius church and leper hospital.

Continue up the **St. Hallvard gate** to the junction with **Akerbergveien**; this is the area known as the

2.5km Galgeberg (2.5/640.5)

Literally 'gallows mountain', this is where hangings used to take place (the last was in 1864) and was the most important cross-

roads in the Middle Ages. This is also the point at which the eastern (historic) route through Groruddal to Hamar and the western (cultural) option via Baerum and up through Gjøvik part company.

For the first alternative KSO ahead here; for the second, turn L into **Akerbergveien** and then turn to page 83 to continue.

Eastern (Historic) Route

KSO into **Strømsveien** and then at roundabout cross over to LH side of road, turn R under the underpass and turn L and then R into **Langengen**. Turn L into **Lensmann Hiorths allé**, R onto cycle track veering R and L into **Svovelstikka** past the

1.5km Fyrstikktorget (4/639)

Formerly a match factory, until it was bought by a Swedish firm and the plant moved to Sweden, this is now a tastefully modernised shopping precinct. (Worth a look inside; if so, turn R at exit and emerge in the Grønvoll allé.)

Turn L into **Grensenveien** *(i.e. if you didn't come out on the Grønvoll allé – in which case cross Grensenveien)* and continue along **Innspurten** and then alongside the **Valle Hovin sportsground**. Continue on cycle track and cross **Ringveien** *(ring road)*, continue ahead on the **Karl Staatts vei** on other side and then KSO into the Østre Aker churchyard past the church.

1.5km Østre Aker kirke (5.5/637.5)

The oldest (1860) and biggest church in Groruddal (with seating for 900 people).

Go through churchyard, cross over **Ulvensplitten** and continue on cart track over waste ground, veering L down to **Persveien**. Cross over it and turn R into **Strømsveien** again. Go under road and railway line *(passing Hell's Angels HQ on L)*.

Continue to roundabout *(the A-møbler furniture store is now on your R, just after crossing the river Alna, navigable in the Middle Ages)* and turn L (watch out carefully for this) into gap between sections of high protective fencing *(to screen residential area from the railway)* marked 'Gangvei til Tittuveien'.

Continue along **Tittuveien** *(this part is the historical pilgrims' path)*

and at end turn R and immediately L into **Strømsveien** once again *(this was the old route out of Oslo to the north-east)*, along its cycle track until you get to just past the post office sorting office. Turn L here onto FP, veer R and pass either to L of farm ahead or go through farmyard to pick up path again on other side. This is **Alfaset gård** (Arveset), *a farm known to have been in existence as early as 1361 and a listed property. It belonged to the church in the 16th century, to the crown in the 17th and today is owned by Oslo kommune. There were previously many farms in this area, but in the 1950s, when the city of Oslo needed land for housing, the farm houses themselves were left standing (and you will spot several more as you walk through this area) but the land was subject to compulsory purchase order for residential development, which is why you will see old farm houses interspersed amongst modern flats and other buildings.*

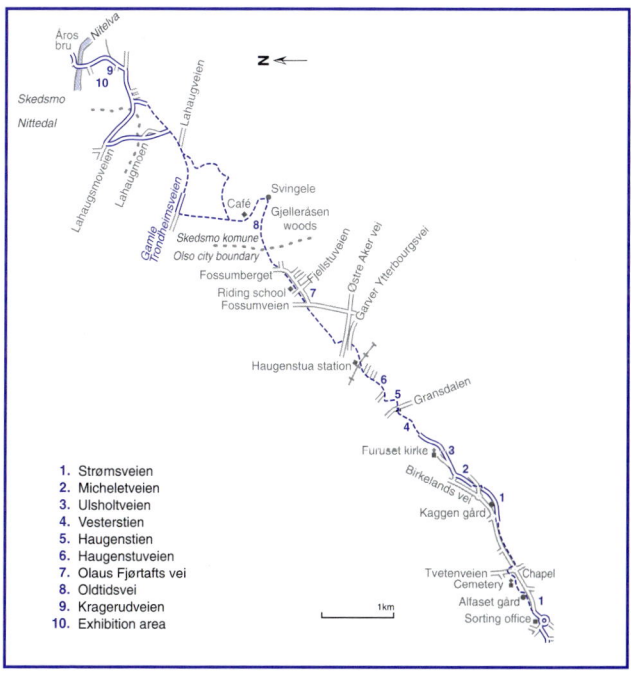

1. Strømsveien
2. Micheletveien
3. Ulsholtveien
4. Vesterstien
5. Haugenstien
6. Haugenstuveien
7. Olaus Fjørtafts vei
8. Oldtidsvei
9. Kragerudveien
10. Exhibition area

Continue along line of trees to R *with the graves of German soldiers from World War II in the cemetery on their other side (R), three to a grave. (The modern cemetery is over to your L.)* Veer R past chapel *(Muslim graveyard to RH side)* to return to **Strømsveien** once more, turn R to cross the **Nedre Kalbakkvei** via an underpass and then turn L under another (to cross **Tvetenveien**) and continue ahead up the cycle track on the RH side of **Strømsveien**.

Pass the Ikea store (R) and **Kaggen gård** on L, at no. 336, *the last farm in Groruddal to be used as such and lived in until very recently by a brother and a sister. It takes its name from the word for keg (*kagge*), a reference to those used for storing brandy and to the fact that the building was also a well-known drinking establishment, serving the needs of both carriers and other travellers from the 18th century onwards.*

Continue to the very end of **Strømsveien**, which finishes in an industrial estate. Veer L and then R and turn L over FB over the **Sam Eydes vei**. Continue ahead on the **Micheletvei**, turning R to continue on **Ulsholtveien** until *(note traditional farm on L)* you reach the top of the hill and

5km Furuset kirke (10.5/632.5)

The present church is only 20 years old but the former medieval one is believed to be buried somewhere next to it or nearby; its exact location is at present unknown but is the subject of ongoing archaelogical investigations by the Riksantikvaren, and excavations in 1998 unearthed two medieval keys, now on display in the modern church.

Continue along **Ulsholtveien** and then on **Vesterstien** down to cross the **Gransdalen** (supermarket opposite). Go up **Haugenstien** on the other side, veering L uphill. Continue on **Haugenstustien**, passing **Haugen skole** (L) and go under railway line by **Haugen stasjon**. KSO under another road (the **Ole Brummsvei**), veering L to go under the **Garve Ytterborgs vei** and the **Østre Aker vei**.

Veer R on other side past a kindergarten (L), pass to LH side of sports ground and turn R on cycle track coming from L, which leads you under the Fossumvei. Go up bank on other side, turn L into the Olaus Fjørtofts vei. Cross Fjellstuveien via underpass (or turn L here if you want to go to Stovner station and take the T-bane back into central Oslo) and pass riding school (on L), using bridlepath // to road. Cross three cycle tracks and continue under the Fossumberget (marked 'Privat vei') and along the Oldtidsvei (this is den Trondhjemske Kongevei, the old 'royal road' which starts here), crossing the Oslo city boundary into the kommune of Skedsmo.

3.5 km Fossumberget/Oldtidsveien (14/629)

Continue ahead into the woods and then turn L at T-junction with a seat *(this is **Svingele**). Today the Gjelleråsen woods are a recreational area with waymarked footpaths, but in the past the Oldtidsvei ('Olden times road'), the main route out of Oslo until the 1770s, passed through this area, rich in burial mounds from the stone and iron ages. Watch out carefully for the waymarks as there are few distinguishing features; from here to the military base at Lahaugsmoen the route is waymarked with red and blue flashes, sometimes with red ribbon markers.*

Fork L, pass behind the **Liastua** (a café) and veer R downhill to valley bottom. Continue ahead and then, when you reach a fork some 500m later, you can either a) fork R steeply uphill or b) KSO ahead.

a) After forking R uphill the track becomes a FP, waymarked with both red flashes (painted) and red ribbon markers. Turn L at signpost (to 'Lahaugsmoen') and L at next (indicating 'Lahaugsmoen 1km'). Pass house and veer L and R to a bigger junction. Turn R there and KSO downhill on old wide paved road *(Kongeveien again)*. After 1km reach a gate, the side entrance to the military base *(used by a medical regiment)* at Lahaugsmoen *(see next paragraph)*.

b) This option is slightly longer but not so hilly and the track is much wider. KSO, undulating, for 1km until you reach a road on the edge of a residential area: this is the **Gamle Trondheimsveien**. Turn R, KSO ahead up lane (to short-cut bend in road) by house no. 14 and at top turn R and then immediately L back onto **Gamle Trondheimsveien.** This continues as a forest road *(waymarked in red)*. After 1km you will reach the military base at

3km Lahaugsmoen 230m (17/626)

Go through gate, pass through the carpark *(probably full of army ambulances)* and turn L alongside lawned area with flagpole towards the main entrance. *(There is, in fact, another entrance/exit, more or less straight ahead of you, which would considerably shorten the route, but it is closed at present, though there are plans to waymark this eventually. When this is open you will then turn R along the Rv 22 here).* Go through the gates and KSO for 1km to the Rv 22. Turn R on cycle track, passing the boundary between Nittedal and (back into) Skedsmo *kommune* again, pass the turning (R) to Hellerud *(shop)* and a large exhibition area (the Hellerudsutstillingsområde) on L, which you turn down the side of 1km later; this is **Kragerudsveien** but it is not marked. Continue down to cross the

3km Åros bru 122m (20/623)

The bridge is closed to vehicles at present, though not to pedestrians.

Turn R on other side onto **Ramstadveien** and cross a small river.

[When the route is waymarked and a footbridge constructed it is intended to continue along the LH (i.e. northern) side of the **Nitelva** from here almost to the E6 then veer L up to join the **Gamle Trondheimsvei**, 1km after the Åros bru, and continue to Jogstad 400–500m later. From here the path will continue // to the E6, cross **Brånåsveiein** and (modern) **Trondheimsveien** and continue ahead along **Vestvollveien** under the E6 to Skedsmo kirke.] In the meantime continue along **Ramstadveien**, *high up, open and with good views, passing several farms and a large golf course. This is a very long road (little traffic) which you continue on until you reach the junction with Solbergveien* 5km later.

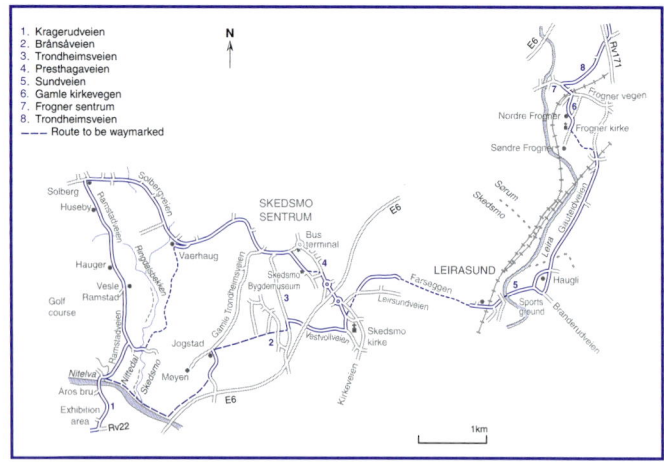

1. Kragerudveien
2. Brånsåveien
3. Trondheimsveien
4. Presthagaveien
5. Sundveien
6. Gamle kirkevegen
7. Frogner sentrum
8. Trondheimsveien
--- Route to be waymarked

[However, it is also possible, until the route is waymarked, to short-cut a substantial section of these roads by turning first R off the **Ramstadveien**. Continue past the turning to **Ramstad** *(a farm)*, cross the **Ringdalsbekken** *(a small river)* and then turn L up a FP which brings you out at Vaerhaug *(a farm)*, turn R to join **Solbergveien** and KSO for 1.5km to **Skedsmokorset**.]

5km Solbergveien/Rv 20 (25/618)

Turn R and KSO for 4km to

4km Skedsmokorset (29/614)

When you reach a junction (**Midtskogen**) KSO(L) and turn R after supermarket and other shops, signposted 'Skedsmotun bo-og behandlingssenter'. *N.B. If you KSO here you come to the Skedsmo bus terminal 200m later, with hourly buses to central Oslo (Bus Terminal), service No. 402.*

Pass the **Skedsmo Bygemuseum-Husaby** *(open mid-June to mid-August, Wed & Thurs 10.00-14.00, Sat & Sun 12.00–16.00, free admission).* Veer L *(Skedsmo church spire visible ahead)* round to road and 200m later turn R on cycle track (of Rv 120), crossing to LH side when it starts there.

Cross **Furuveien**. KSO(L) ahead (Rv 120), cross the E6 and 500m later turn R under the Rv 120. Continue ahead on the other side (**Gjoleidveien**) past playing field (R) and 300m later reach

1km Skedsmo kirke 180m (30/613)

Church dedicated to St. Olav, built in stone 1180 on site of a wooden church dating from 1022, rebuilt and enlarged in 1860. Visits mid-June to mid-August, Mon–Fri 12.00-18.00 (guided tours available).

Go back up **Gjoleidveien** (you came down it to visit the church) and after **Nordvollen** go through a cut-through to the Rv 120, cross it carefully and continue on other side on a *grusvei (this is Oldtidsveien again)* and then KSO on other side: this is **Farseggen**, a small road which becomes a track. 800m later pass **Søndre gård** *(farm)* on L, cross railway line, turn L and then R onto the cycle track of **Branderudveien** (Rv 120) and cross the bridge over the river **Leira** (you are now on **Sundveien**) in

2km Leirsund 122m (32/611)

Either: turn L up the Rv 171 (just after sportsground) or (short-cutting bend) turn L onto cart track opposite sportsground, veering R. Turn R at junction with another cart track and L at the top to road (Rv 171). Turn L (opposite house no. 54).

Cross border into Sorum *kommune and shortly afterwards you will see Frogner church ahead, on the skyline. (Road becomes Fv 259 after boundary.)* Cross railway line and when cycle track stops turn L off road and continue ahead alongside field, L ahead, veering L round border with another one, veering R, veering L and continue ahead across last field to

3.5km Frogner kirke 150m (35.5/607.5)

The original 12th-century church (its dedication is unknown) burned down on Midsummer's Eve 1918; the present building was completed in 1925. You can visit the church if any of its employees are working in the churchyard. Note gravestone with scallop shell (a pilgrim symbol).

Turn second R through farmyard and leave on *grusvei* on other side, leading down to road. Turn L under railway line and come to a junction 200m ahead in

0.5km Frogner sentrum (36/607)

Supermarket, PO, bank, other shops.

Turn R at petrol station *(***Frognerveien, Fv 260***)* and continue along its cycle track in the direction of Kløfta and Jessheim. After 1km cross Rv 171 and 350m later turn R into **Lindbergveien** and go under the railway line.

[When the route is fully cleared and prepared you will then take the third turn on the R (**Ulverudveien**) which continues as a track passing to the left (i.e. north) of **Kjerkefjellet** (216m) and **Vibergsfjellet** (220m): *this is St. Olavs gang, where it is thought that pilgrims passed on their way from Frogner to Ullensaker church, via those at Asak and Refsum (farm churches), which are no longer there today but which existed in the Middle Ages.* You will then continue ahead on **Vilbergveien** to **Øvre Vilberg** *(farm)* before taking a path left (i.e. north) to **Arteid vestre** *(another farm).* From there you will continue north and join **Ilevegen**, turn L along it and continue as described below (*).]

In the meantime, however, KSO along **Lindbergveien** after going under the railway line and 500m later, at a fork, KSO(R) along **Arteidvegen**. Turn L 500m later at a T-junction into **Isingrudveien** which retains its name, goes under the E6 shortly after passing from Sørum into Ullensaker *kommune* and runs into a bigger road joining you from back L. *You are now on the outskirts of **Kløfta**.* Turn L into **Ilevegen** (*) and at junction with **Kongsvingervegen** turn R. *(If you want to go into Kløfta – all facilities, including a regular train service to central Oslo –*

turn L here and then retrace your steps to continue.)
   Recross the E6, KSO, take second L turn and reach

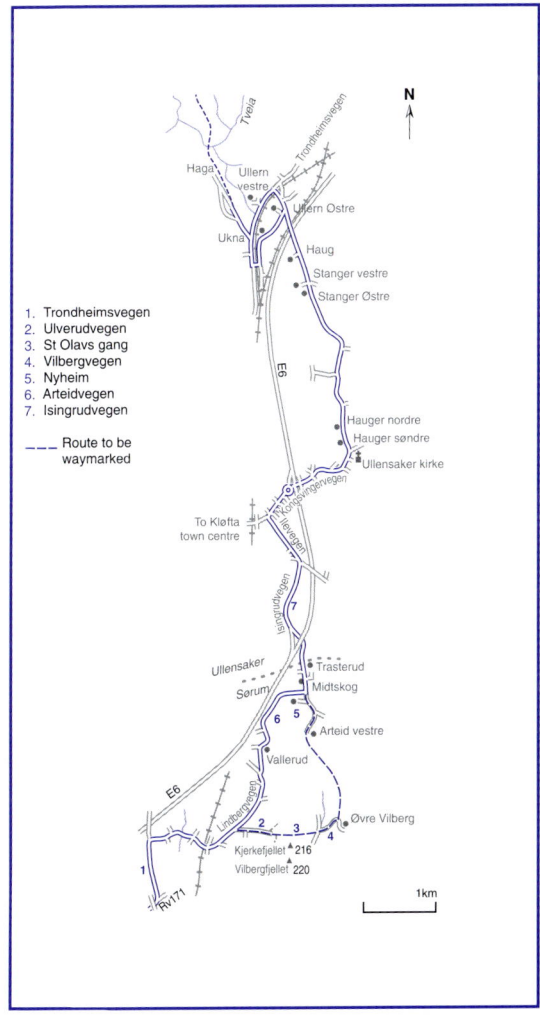

1. Trondheimsvegen
2. Ulverudvegen
3. St Olavs gang
4. Vilbergvegen
5. Nyheim
6. Arteidvegen
7. Isingrudvegen

— — — Route to be
        waymarked

N

Haga
Ullern vestre
Ullern Østre
Ukna
Haug
Stanger vestre
Stanger Østre

Hauger nordre
Hauger søndre
Ullensaker kirke

To Kløfta
town centre

Ullensaker
Sørum
Trasterud
Midtskog
Arteid vestre

Vallerud

Øvre Vilberg

Kjerkefjellet 216
Vilbergfjellet 220

E6

Rv171

1km

8km Ullensaker kirke (44/599)

The present building, from 1958, replaces several much older churches; there have been at least four on this site, the first one dating from 1430 and dedicated jointly to St. Olav and John the Baptist. Open 1st July to mid-August, Tues-Fri 10.00-15.00 (guided tours). From here continue on road (that you turned L onto to reach church), passing farm (R) at **Hauger** after 500m and **Haug** 3km later (500m before reaching the E6 once again). Here it is, in fact, possible to return to the Fv 454 by a FP by turning hard L at **Ullern østre**, but if you miss it you can continue past **Ullern vestre** and then backtrack to it (L). *Note that there are two farms called Ullern, one on the eastern side of the railway line (**Ullern østre**) and the E6, the other (**Ullern vestre**) on the west (i.e. LH) side, where simple accommodation may be available if you phone ahead. [Ullern gård vestre. 2040 Kløfta, tel: 63.97.77.77, EE, CF, sleeping bag needed.]*

[In very misty weather you may prefer to continue along the Fv 454 to Jessheim, then walk west on the Rv 174 (Gardermovegen) till you reach the entrance to Raknehaugen (down the Haug allé, an elm-lined road to your L, shortly after crossing the E6. In this case KSO to pick up the PL again when it turns 5th R into Vilbergvegen.)]

Otherwise – after crossing the E6 and the railway line turn L along Fv 454 (i.e. towards Kløfta) for 500m then turn R up farm road leading to **Haga**. At top of ridge turn R towards woods, passing to L of them. *(There are elk in woods though you probably won't see them as they are afraid of people, but you may well see their large, round cloven footprints in mud or snow.)*

Continue along the edge of the woods for 1km, past the white farm at a bend in the minor road over to your L, then veer R sharply downhill, and 10m after the bend to the L by two prominent trees make your way downhill to the river **Tveia** 20m below you *(you can see/hear it)*, veering slightly R.

Originally there was a water mill here, until the beginning of the 20th century, when electricity took over from water as a source of power, and there was also a wooden bridge for carts here too. A new, solid but simple FB was constructed here in late 1999, so it is now possible to cross without difficulty.

On the other side of the river *(waymark on tree)* veer slightly L and make your way uphill (there are some small FPs) – about 100m in all, veering a little L at the top to emerge on what was obviously formerly an old road downhill. Turn right here, up towards a clearing on a ridge and follow it round to the L to a very large field. Turn L along its LH edge then cross over to the RH side and continue along the edge of the woods until you pick up a tractor track *(Bjørke – a farm – is visible ahead.)* When the tractor track veers sharp L KSO ahead towards farm **(Bjørke S)**. *Hovin church – all white – is now visible ahead.* After passing farm (and until the route is waymarked) either:

a) turn R on track towards white house amongst trees and continue behind it on FP alongside/between edge of fields, veering L to pick up track which goes L to a farm road shortly before the church, or:

b) continue on the farm road after **Bjørke** until 200–300m before you reach the Rv 178 and then turn R next to a double garage between a garden and a field, veering R and then L downhill between two fields towards woods in a dip ahead, passing to L of them. Veer L towards farm, join farm road and turn R up to

7.5km Hovin kirke 175m (51.5/591.5)

The present church dates from 1675. Hovin was originally the N/S–E/W road crossing point until it was later moved east to Jessheim.

Continue to road, turn R onto Rv 178 and then turn R (signposted 'Raknehaugen') and fork L down a lane **(Ljøgodtveien)**. *This leads you past a lake (L) and the largest ancient mound in Norway (R), from 400–600 BC, 15m high and 95m in diameter around its base.*

Continue to **Haug gård** and turn L down the **Haug allé**, *lined with elm trees.* Reach **Gardermoveien** *(Rv 174, shop opposite; Oslo's Gardermoen international airport is only a couple of kilometres away to your L by now)* and then R and then turn second R along **Vilbergveien**. KSO for 3.5km and turn L at the junction at

4.5km Vilberg 212m (56/587)

700m later cross a minor (disused) railway line and then turn R alongside of woods on lane marked 'Privat vei', downhill. KSO for 2km to a junction with the Fv 462 at

3km Elstad 190m (59/584)

Turn L and KSO. *There is a large lake, the Hersjøen, in the valley to your R, but you can't see it because of the trees.*

Continue on this road, passing various farms *(good views as you are level but high up, with valleys/dips below you to either side)* until you reach the old (restored) bridge over the river *Risa.*

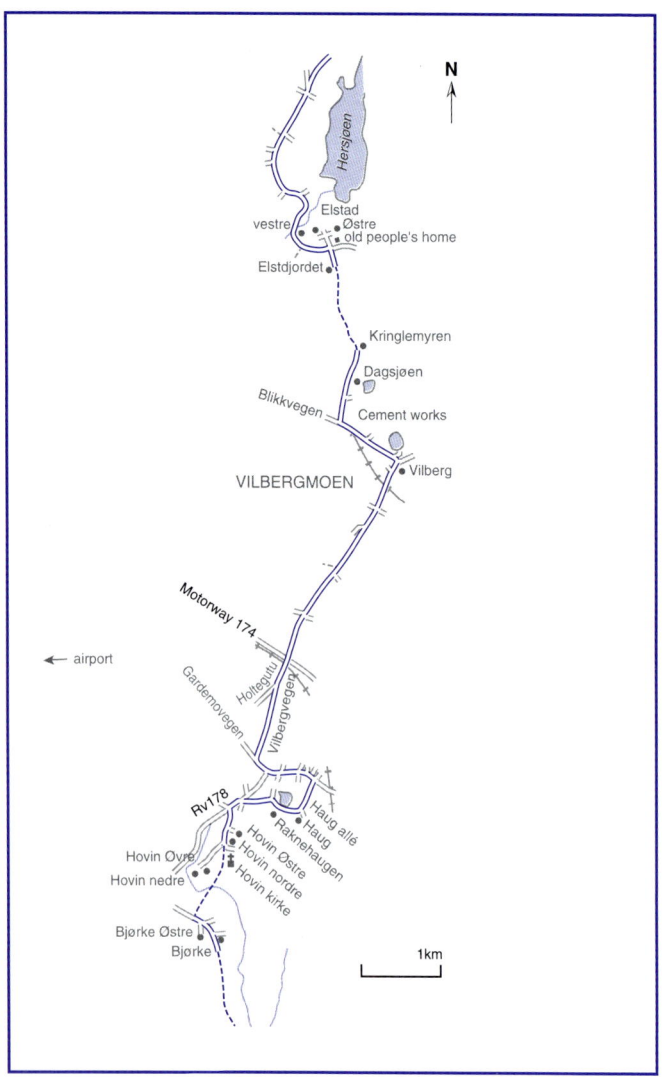

6km Risebru 190m (65/578)

Bridge over the Risa, giving rise to the place name. Oldtidsveien ('Road from the old times', a road dating from the Stone Age) and Trondheimsveien, from the 1770s, both used to cross the Risa here. The first bridge was wooden (originally it was just a fording place). Stone bridge built 1827, restored 1994. Seats.

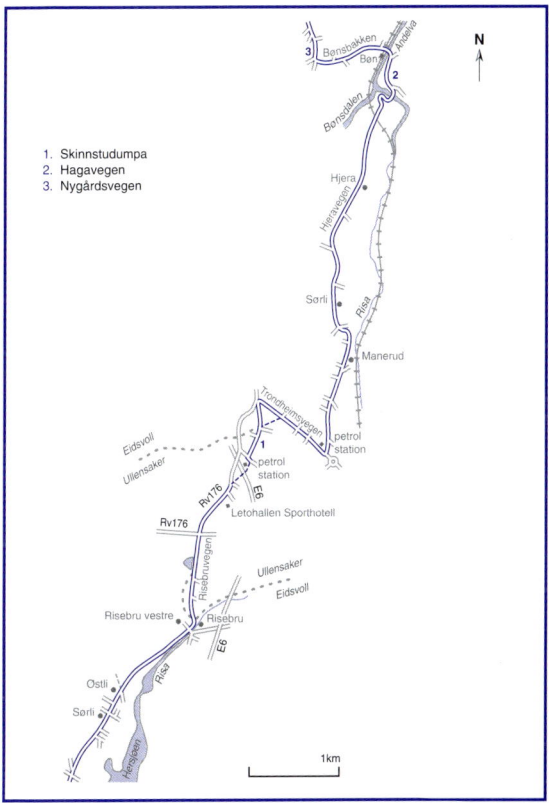

1. Skinnstudumpa
2. Hagavegen
3. Nygårdsvegen

To continue turn L up a lane between houses **(Risebruvegen)** before you get to the bridge, uphill to the top. Continue to the Rv 176, cross it, passing **Sportshotellet Letohallen** on R. [*Accommodation: tel: 63.95.50.00, E (EE?); address 2072 Dal.*] Pass the boundary between

Ullensaker and Eidsvoll *kommuner*, continue on cycle track and cross the E6. Turn L by petrol station and then turn R on the Fv 501, signposted 'Dal'. 500m later turn R (also signposted 'Dal') and 700m after that turn L down **Hjeravegen** *(Fv 504)* by a petrol station on L *(snack bar)*.

3km Dal (68/575.5)

After 2km pass a junction with **Kjerkevegen** *(Bøn stasjon is 3km ahead on Hjeravegen)*. Cross bridge over the river **Risa** after 4km and over the **Andelva** by

5km Bøn stasjon (73/570)

Railway station on Oslo-Eidsvoll line.

KSO on other side of railway line *(Fv 505)* and after 1km reach junction at

1km Nygård (74/569)

Supermarket.

Turn R along **Nygårdvegen** (signposted 'Eidsvoll Verk 3km') and KSO, crossing railway line 1km later. KSO (road becomes **Dønnumskia**) ignoring turns, and 4km later reach junction with Rv 181. Turn R for 500m then KSO ahead (marked 'Eidsvollbakken 2') to visit

4.5km Eidsvoll kirke (78.5/564.5)

Church containing an Olav altar, with walls and choir from 12th century, dedicated to Saints Peter and Paul; restored 1885. Statue of Camilla Collett (1813–1895) outside, sister of Henrik Wergeland, both of them 19th-century Norwegian writers (Eidsvoll Prestegård, their childhood home, is over to the R beyond church).

Continue past church, downhill, to main road (Rv 181) again, go under it and turn R on cycle track to cross railway line. Continue ahead and then take second L turn to cross first the railway line and then the **Sundbrua** over the river **Vorma** in

1.5km Eidsvoll (80/563)

Shops, banks, cafés, PO, railway station (trains to Oslo).

Turn L on other side of the bridge onto **Sundgata**. *[Turn L to sleep in Solli Pensjonat at Torvet 5, 2080 Eidsvoll, tel: 63.96.45.09, EE. This is only 50m off route, facing the Eidsvoll railway staion on the other side of the river.]* Turn L again by **Vilberg Skole** *(opposite petrol station)* up

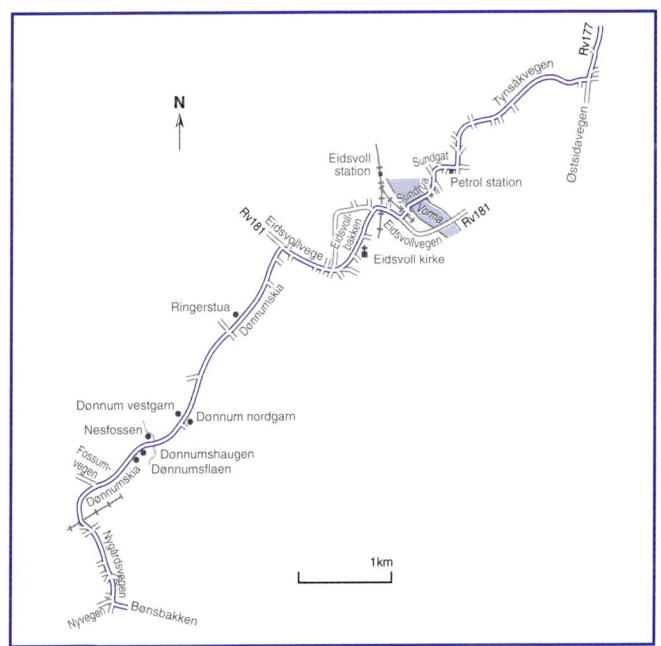

Tynsåkvegen. Follow this round, veering R, and KSO for 1.5km until you reach a junction *(shop to L)* at **Elstad**.

Turn L here (this is **Østsidavegen**, *the Rv 177 to Minnesund)* and KSO; more or less level *(quite a lot of seats by side of road)*.

KSO, passing farms at **Hemli**, **Habberstad** and **Brostad**. Then, between road KM 7 and KM 7.5 fork R at junction marked 'Hamar 53' (where the Rv 177 does a sharp bend to the L). Continue ahead (this is Fv 511) and after 1.5km pass **Sollihøgda Trevarafabrikk** *(on R, a factory)*. Here:

a) you can, in fact, turn R and 300m later turn R again onto a *tursti* (marked in yellow) which leads you to another *tursti* (marked in red) where you can turn R and go straight to **Fløyta**, quite a bit shorter (some 2.5km) and more direct than going to **Langset** and picking up the same red *tursti* via a 2.5km blue one. Otherwise:

b) continue for 500m more (i.e. beyond the factory) and turn second
    L (after the **Hans Aansurds veg**) down an unmarked lane to

12km Langset kirke (92/551)

Built 1859.

You do not, in fact, need to go as far as the church, but turn R instead opposite the start of the lane (on your L) leading to the church, up a tursti waymarked in blue (handy map on information board at start). The track (a FP) is well waymarked with blue wooden tags hanging from the trees and goes uphill at first, then undulates, describing a sort of arc-like quarter-circle to R (east). Cross gravelled road and continue ahead (without going over cattle-grid on L).

After 2.5km reach a T-junction with a much wider track and a signpost *(the direct route from the Trevare-fabrikk joins you here)*. Turn L to 'Fløyta N' (waymarked in red now) and at junction 100m later KSO(L) ahead.

This sti *(track) is well waymarked (with red wooden tags) but watch out carefully, especially in the section where it becomes a FP for a while, as there are no distinguishing features to orient you apart from a HT pylon (at your feet) and a wooden observation platform (to your L) until you reach the junction of paths at Kvernhus Vika and you can see the Fløyta (a lake) in front of you.*

Turn L here (signposted 'Fløyta N') and follow path round top of lake, veering R inside the woods for 1km until you reach the *badeplassen* (swimming area) at the north end of the

5.5km Fløyta-sjøen (97.5/545.5)

Nice place for a swim (weather permitting), picnic area.

Continue on wide *grusvei*. 1km later turn R at T-junction. KSO(L) at next junction and 1km later pass isolated house at **Dorrsvangen**.

KSO ahead here, on centre track (i.e. to L of house – **not** on LH track, though it looks more prominent and crosses the river), and at end of track, 500m later, continue ahead R on FP with pilgrim logo on tree and old sign saying 'Lysjøen'. This is waymarked with white tags; follow it, alongside the **Lysåa** *(a stream)* for much of the time, until you reach a clearing where the waymarked route continues ahead and you turn L over a 'bridge' *(logs)*.

On the other side there is, in fact, a wide, clear forest track parallel to the river and 50–100m away from it, but at present you can't see it. Make your way straight ahead as best you can through the scrubby trees and turn R when you reach the forest track. (If you can't find it easily continue R after crossing river along its bank until you see two buildings ahead L and make your way to them – they are on the track.)

KSO for 500m until you reach the

4.5km Lysjøen 353m (102/541)

Another (considerably bigger) lake. There were many saeter (summer farms) in this area, and pilgrims would have originally taken the roads leading from one to another, where food, lodging and medicine would have been available.

Turn R for 1km to **Finnsbråten**, *where accommodation is available if you phone ahead, as the huts are unattended and you need the key. [Finnsbråten, 2314 Espa, tel: 62.58.03.56, 61.33.69.00 or 91.74.37.12. E? Self-catering, CF, sleeping bag needed. Camping possible.]* Go through both gates. From here there is a waymarked *tursti* which connects you to a *grusvei* leading to **Lysaeter**, a farm at the southern end of **Granerudsjøen** *(another lake)* and then to

2.5km Granerud 353m (104.5/538.5)

Continue ahead, ignoring turnings, till you reach a junction at **Svea** and then turn L to

3.5km Spetalen 361m (108/535)

The name is believed to come from the word for 'hospital' or 'hospice', referring to a place which not only tended the sick but also looked after pilgrims.

Continue along the road you turned L onto (i.e. west), after which you have a choice of two routes:

a) the historic route, joining the other at Skaberud, between Espa and Tangen, 13km. Turn 2nd R *(1.5km after Spetalen)* and 1km later you will reach a junction. *The two routes join up again after 3km, but if you want to sleep in the hut at Romasetra (454m), owned by the same people as Hestnes gård (see below), take the RH option.* Continue for 5.5km (after the fork) until you reach a T-junction. Turn L and 2km later, at another junction at **Vensvangen**, KSO(R), forking R again 1km at **Gorovangen**, after which you KSO for 3km to **Skaderud**, cross the E6 and proceed as described below.

b) otherwise, turn third R after Spetalen and KSO, ignoring turns. Pass farms at **Prestsaetra** (3.5km), **Nilsberg** (3km) and 1km later, just after **Sørlia** and just before **Stor Re-vangen**, turn L down a lane which will lead you directly (1km) to

10km Hestnes nordre gård (118/525)

Simple accommodation here in a stabbur with CF, sleeping bag needed, camping possible. (Romasetra has similar facilities but, given its isolation, the owners will buy provisions for you if you give advance warning.) [Hestnes nordre gård, 2314 Espa, tel: 2.58.02.01, Shell petrol station nearby has basic shop.

[Mjosvang Pensjonat og hyttegrend, 2314 Espa, tel: 62.58.01.26, a guesthouse plus hut accommodation, is on the E6, 200m to L (south) of the petrol station.] Go under E6 (i.e. west) and turn R on the Fv 229. a quiet road with little traffic, alongside the *Mjøsa* to

3km Espa (121/522)

Shop.

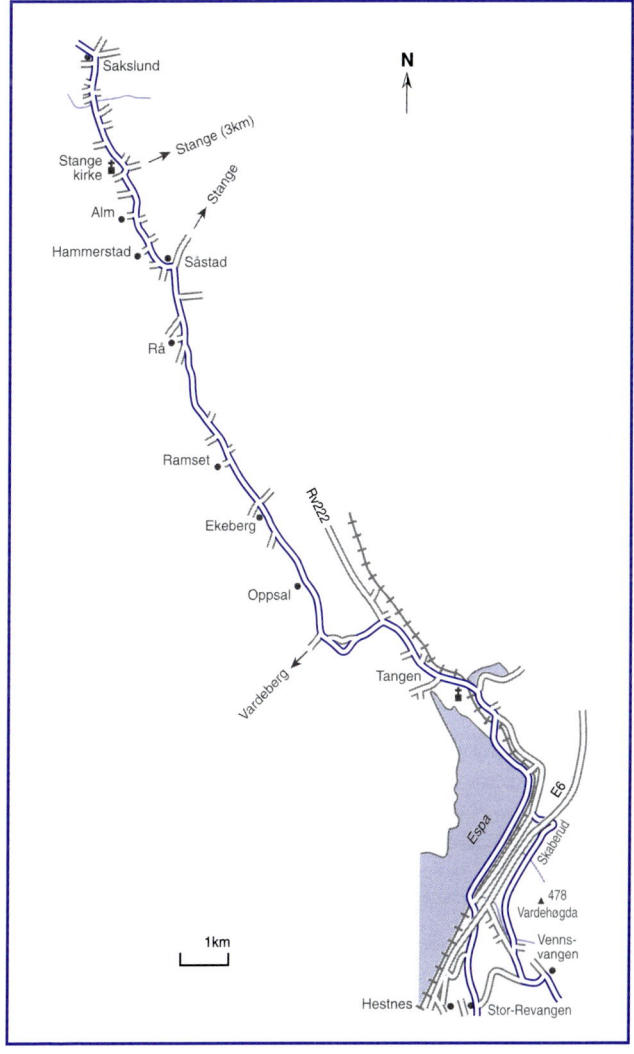

KSO. 1km later (signposted 'Hestnes Trappefabrikk') turn L, go under railway line and turn R alongside the lake for 2.5km. *(The route via Skaderud joins you after 1.5km.)* Return to road and KSO until you reach a junction and then turn L onto Rv 222 at

7km Tangen 160m (128/515)

Supermarket, PO.

KSO, passing church, railway line and river and 2km later turn L (signposted 'Varderberg 2') up Fv 204 – a *bygdevei* (BV) – with woods to either side. Just before a sharp LH bend after 1.5km *(with a black and yellow 'bend' warning sign)* turn R up an unmarked *grusvei*.

KSO ahead, quiet, undulating, pass junction at **Ekeberg** (271m) and continue to

8km Såstad 198m (136/507)

This area is more or less flat and there are some very large farms in this section.

Turn L and 200m later turn R and KSO to

2.5km Stange kirke (138.5/504.5)

Late 12th-century stone church containing two 16th-century St. James sculptures; visits early June to late August, Mon–Fri 10.00–12.00, Sun 10.00–13.00.

Turn R and then immediately L at junction onto **Vestbygdeveien** *(Fv 193; Hamar is 12km from here by road, 13 by PL)*. KSO to junction at

2.5km Sakslund 185m (141/502)

KSO(L) at junction.

The suggested route keeps you on the road here all the way to the turn-off (signposted) to the **Stange Brenneri** *(a distillery)* 3.5km later, though you can, in fact, turn L (5km from Stange church, just before road KM 5) to the **Atlungstad Ridessenter** *(a riding school)* and use part of the **Ottestadstien** (a local *tursti*). Veer R towards school and pass behind it and then turn R onto a *grusvei* which leads you to the bend in the road near the **Stange Brenneri**; here you KSO (or turn R if you have continued on the road – Fv 191 – **Sandvikavegen**). *After 1km the cycle track starts (and the Domkirkeodde and its glass casing around the remains of Hamar's medieval cathedral is visible ahead L for the first time, like a giant greenhouse on the other side of the water).*

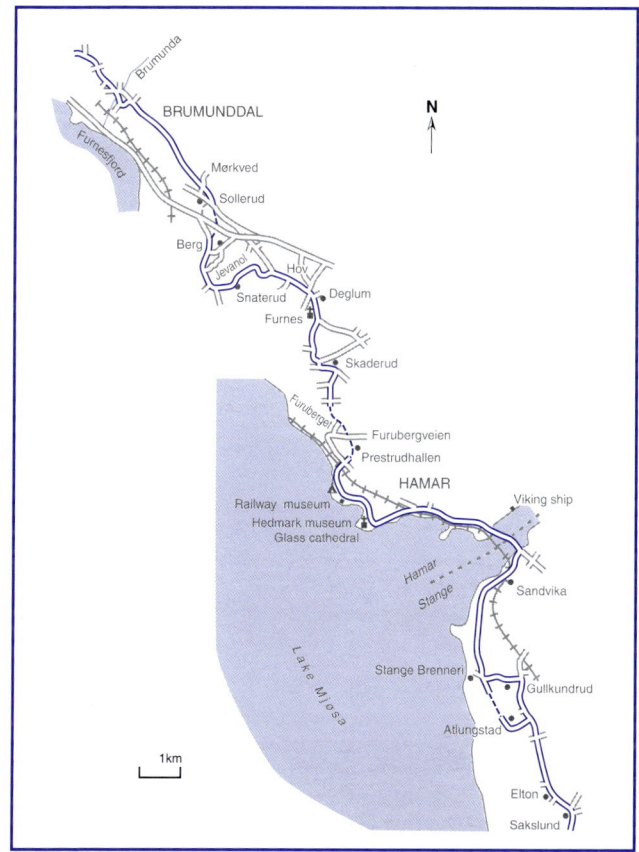

Accommodation available at Villa Rødhette, Buevegen, 2312 Ottestad, tel: 62.57.61.86, E?. CF, 1km from Stange bridge, follow signs for Sandvika.]

Go over the railway line and 500m later turn L onto the Rv 122 and the causeway and then the **Stangebrua** over the **Åkersvika** into Hamar. *The building that looks like an upturned Viking ship ahead is the exhibition centre; the youth hostel is opposite it, so if you want to stay* *there turn R down Åkersvikveien. [Vikingskipet Motell og Vandrerhjem, Åkersvikveien 10, 2300 Hamar, tel: 62.52.60.60, EE, CF.] Otherwise –* KSO, passing railway station (L).

11km Hamar 123m (152/491)

Population 26,000. All facilities, Tourist Office opposite railway station, trains for Oslo, buses for Gjøvik (frequent service); Skibladner, the world's oldest paddle steamer still in regular use, operates a daily service to Gjøvik end June to September, twice weekly to Eidsvoll and Lillehammer; 'Glass cathedral', railway museum, Hedmark Folk Museum, Kirsten Flagstad museum, Kunstbanken art gallery.

The only medieval town in Norway not on the coast, Hamar is made up, in fact, of two towns, the Hamar Kaupanga, or Old Town, to the north, founded by King Harald Hardråke around 1050, and the modern one to the south, dating from 1849.

The start of the route waymarked by the Riksantikvaren is the 'Glass cathedral', the ruins of the medieval cathedral now encased in a protective glass shell to prevent further decay and frost damage. This is situated, along with the remains of the Bishop's Palace, on the Domkirkeodde, a headland 3km to the north-west of the modern town centre.

From the railway station *(after collecting a street plan – 5 kroner – from the Tourist Office)* turn L outside into **Strandgata** and continue along **Storhamargata**. At the end *(old-style brick brewery to L)* go under railway line and continue on FP/cycle track ahead along side of lake which will take you to **Hamarkaupanga**. Just before you reach it turn R *(waymark tells you you still have 488km to go to reach Nidaros)*, turn L and then R between cathedral ruins and Bishop's Palace.

Just behind the museum is a replica of a medieval herb garden with some 300 different types of plants. It was inspired by a section of the Hamar Chronicle from the 1570s which describes how 'it was especially nice in summer, when we rowed out of Hamar, as the scent of all the plants was so lovely. Pilgrims who had been to Rome, to the Holy Grave [in Jerusalem] and many other places had diligently collected these sweet-smelling plants which they brought home with them. But best of all was a bush known as Angelthorn because it smelt so delightful'. This is one of the few extant references to contemporary pilgrims.

Ringsaker church (photo: Eivind Luthen)

River Lågen near Sjoa (photo: author)

Buildings in Meldal Bygningmuseum (photo: author)

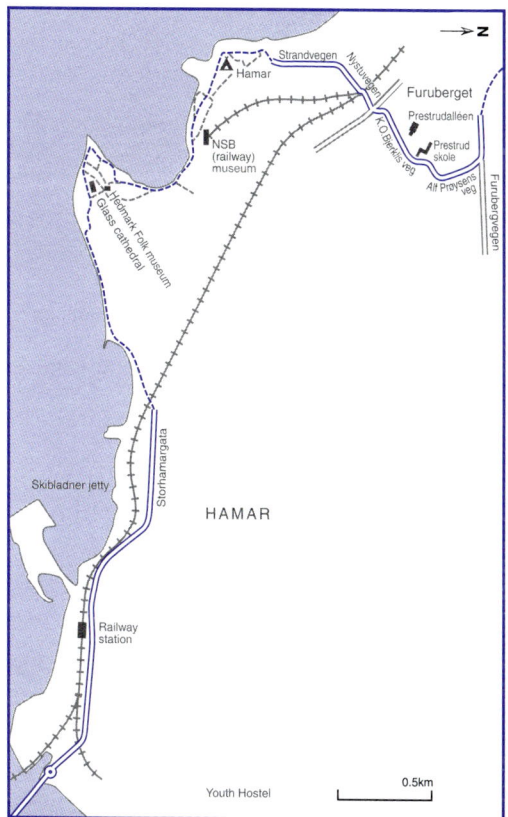

3km Domkirkeodden (155/488)

Turn L by museum café and pass amongst the reconstructed buildings of the **Hedmarkmuseet**, *a folk museum with some 50 buildings from the surrounding Hedmark district.* Veer L along lake side, veering slightly inland to pass the **Jernebanemuseet**, *the NSB (Norwegian State Railways) national railway museum,* and reach **Hamar NAF Camping** *(tel: 62.52.44.90).* Go through the site, following edge of lake, exit on other side and veer R to pass the LH side of its perimeter fence. Turn L along **Strandgata**, second R along **Nystuvegen** *(not marked at start but* *it is opposite the Torp legessenter, a doctors' surgery, 1.8km from start),* go under railway line and cross **Furubergveien**. *[Accommodation at Furuberget Bed & Breakfast, Furubergveien 154, 2300 Hamar, tel: 62.53.19.61.]*

Continue ahead up FP/cycle track to **Prestrudhallen** *(sports centre),* veering L behind it *(**Prestrud school** on R),* passing waymark that says 'Almuevegen'; *this is a reference to an old route dating from Iron Age times or earlier and which led directly to Furnes church.* Nowadays it is a small, clear FP that leads uphill between the school and the sports centre before it emerges on **Furubergveien** *(again, as this is a circular road).* Cross it, turn L and fork L into woods on other side. No waymark at start but KSO(L) inside.

After 700m pass waymark with 'Bydeberg/Forminne' *(pointing L and referring to the site of a former castle).* Fork right here. KSO, veering R downhill, turn R onto lane downhill past houses to a road junction at **Frøyset gård**, marked 'Hamar 5, Jessnes 3'. Turn L *(you have come from 'Steenskalkbr' and 'Vikerødgårdveien' and you have now passed from Hamar to Ringsaker kommune).* 400m later turn R up gravelled lane towards a farm (**Skarderud**), still on the old *almueveien*. Turn L and then veer round to R towards woods and continue ahead on forest road, ignoring turns. At a junction *(with the FV 72 – Furnes church visible ahead)* KSO(L) to

8km Furnes Kirke 235m (163/480)

Church built 1707 with stone from the ruined Domkirke in Hamar.

Opposite the church were Stor and Vesle Deglum with the site of a former church. Furnes was the first post-medieval church in Hedmark fylke to be built in stone.

Continue ahead past church, passing school (R) and KSO at junction (marked 'Berg 2.4'), where the road becomes gravelled. 1.5km later, at bottom of hill *(E6 visible ahead)* turn hard L into woods on forest road. Follow it round uphill and 250m before farm ahead turn R down grassy lane and KSO downhill for 1.5km, passing various farms (**Snaterud, Vesle-Ihle, Stor-Ihle and Jevanol**), rising slightly at end to reach junction with Fv 67, a gravelled road *(Furnesfjorden visible ahead).* Turn R and KSO for 1km.

500m later, just before fork in road (R to Brummundal, L to Berg) and at group of farms, fork L off road down FP amongst trees. This has two waymarks, a directional one and another marked 'Hulvei', *an old bridlepath which, with use, has become hollowed out (i.e. 'hollow way')*. Continue down this for 1km *(its various 'gates' may be difficult to negotiate with a heavy rucksack but it is a veritable carpet of wild flowers in the springtime)* and at its end, by a house, turn R up onto the road 10m above you. Turn L: this is **Kongvegen**. After 1km go under the E6 and continue for 3km more, passing **Mørkved Skole** (R), until you reach a junction by a petrol station (R) in

10km Brummunddal (173/470)

Population 7160. Small town with shops, banks,PO, café. Railway station (Lillehammer line), buses to Hamar, Moelv and Gjøvik.

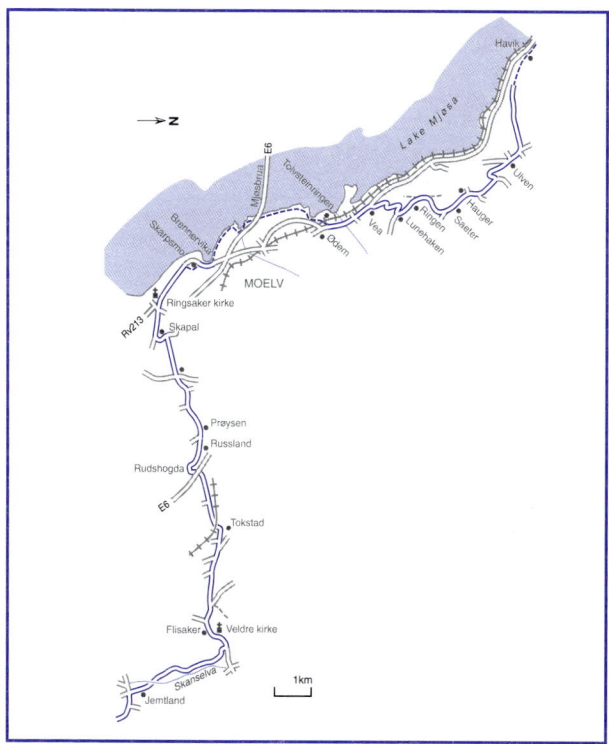

Turn L, cross the **Gammelgate** and continue ahead down pedestrianised street *(marked 'Gågate')*, along **Furnesvegen** *(blue pilgrimsleden sign at start)* and at end cross bridge over the river **Brumunda**. *It is thought, however, that originally pilgrims did not cross the river here, so far south as this, but higher up towards **Spikdalen** instead, a name which may be associated with 'Spedalen' or 'Spitalen' (i.e. 'hospice'), and that there was a 'hospital' here in the Middle Ages.*

Continue ahead on the other side of the **Brumunda**, veer R to go under underpass and on other side turn L behind building. Cross **Skolvegen** and continue ahead down **Fagerlundvegen**, passing fire station (L) and school (R). 700m after this *(racetrack)* turn R up a gravelled road marked 'Bilopphogerer' *(scrap yard)*, passing to L of farm (**Jemtland Vestre**). KSO for 3.5km, crossing the **Stanelva**, passing old quarry workings, a tip, the scrap yard, more woods and burial mounds (L), rising gently *(splendid views to rear over Furnesfjord just before the end)* until you reach the Fv 22 at **Byflaten**. Turn L for 250m to

6km Veldre Kirke (179/464)

The present church, still under construction in 1999, is of stave-church type design but of modern materials and with modern needs in mind, and is but one of several that have existed in Veldre. The first one, Flisaker kirke, was opposite, a wooden building dating from 1332. This was replaced in 1726 by another wooden building, which burned down in 1996. Note large burial mound (Kongshaugen) near site of Old Flisaker church which was demolished in 1776, some 30m in diameter.

From Veldre kirke to Ringsaker kirke, a distance of 12km, the two churches are linked by the Prestveg, an old road that takes its name from the fact that in former times (and until 1876) the prest (priest) at Veldre church lived at Ringsaker and had to make the journey between the two (presumably on horseback) almost every day. It runs in roughly a straight line, with only occasional interruptions due to modern intrusions.

Continue past church and cemetery and 1km later at road junction (marked 'Kvernstu 8.8') fork L onto gravelled road. *From here almost all the way to Ringsaker kirke you will see a series of information boards put up by the 'Prøysenvenner': Friends of Alf Prøysen, the author, of, among others, the Little Mrs. Pepperpot children's books, but better known in Norway as a writer using Nynorsk and dialect. These boards indicate places associated with different events and aspects of Prøysen's*

life, but they are in Nynorsk and so may be difficult to understand.
500m later fork L (marked 'privat vei') and KSO. Pass **Nordhaugen** *(L, childhood home of the painter Johan Nordhagen; this has been restored and is typical of many Ringsaker* husmansplasser *of centuries gone by).*

Sign indicating Prestvegen (Priest's Road) between Veldre and Ringsaker churches (Eivind Luthen)

1km later **Prestvegen** coincides with a tarmac road for 400m and then, at road junction *(marked with sign posts)*, it forks (not turns) L down farm road which becomes a grassy track. KSO, ignoring turns to L and R, gently downhill alongside old wall and cross the **Tokstadbekka** and then the railway line at

3km Tokstadfurua (182/461)

Place name refers to the (protected) 500 year old giant pine tree located here.

Continue on other side, more or less // to railway line, rising gently. KSO, ignoring turns to R and L, till you come to a crossing in a residential area. KSO ahead *(cul-de-sac sign)* to reach crossing with roundabout and continue ahead to cross the bridge over the E6 at

2km Rudshogda 257m 184/459

Not really a place as such but a junction, with motel, petrol station and shopping centre (with supermarket, PO, bank machine and cafeteria).

On other side of bridge follow road round to L (onto **Stolvstadvegen**), cross over, passing between building marked 'Landbrukssenteret' and the motel. Cross parking lot and, with statue of Alf Prøysen to R, go L up tarred slope and then turn (not fork) R on gravelled road marked 'Prøysen', leading into semi-shaded woodland.

Continue on this, passing the *Prøysenstua (1.5km), a house featuring his life and work, open June-Sept*, and continue for another 1.5 km until you reach a T-junction with a similar track and a large field in front of you. Turn L *(no waymark)* 500m later, at crossing by houses, turn L again onto wide, gravelled road. *(Here you leave the Prestveg – it continues straight ahead to Ringsaker kirke but the waymarked route takes you on a detour here to visit the Trollstein.)*

KSO for 1km *(you can see the tip of the church spire to R)* until you reach the Rv 213. Turn R. The *Trollstein, a stone said to have been hurled here by a giant from Biri (on the other side of Lake Mjøsa!)*, is 300m further on R at **Mariendal**, by the side of the road. KSO on road to

8km Ringsaker Kirke (192/451)

Church dedicated to St. Olav, built mid-12th century and restored and extended end of 13th century. Along with the Gamle Aker church in Oslo and the St. Nicholas church in Granavollen, it is the only church of this period and style preserved in such good condition. Open mid-June to mid-August, Mon–Fri 09.00–17.00, Sat 09.00–16.00, Sun 12.00-17.00; guided visits available.

Statue of St. James the Pilgrim (full figure) in Ringsaker church (Eivind Luthen)

Contains a magnificent altarpiece bequeathed to the church by the church's last Catholic priest before the Reformation (and who also became its first Lutheran minister). Made to order in Antwerp in the 1530s it contains nearly 100 carved sections, one of which depicts St. Olav. Others have representations of the six 'pilgrim' saints: St. Roch, patron saint of pilgrims, recognisable by the open wound on his leg; St. Nicolas, patron saint of sailors; St. Christopher, patron saint of travellers in general; St. Martin, patron saint of ferrymen; St. Gertrude, who *founded the Guild of St. Gertude to help poor people and pilgrims; and St. Ursula, a martyr, as she was killed in Cologne while returning from a pilgrimage to Rome. The church also has an original 12th-century Spanish statue of St. James the pilgrim, donated in 1999 and inspired by the sculpture of this saint on the outside of the church of Santa Marta de Tera in the province of Zamora (Spain).*

The prestegård (presbytery or vicarage) is a 250-year-old listed building and has two medieval cellars in its basement. It is planned to convert these into a chapel and pilgrim common room respectively and provide sleeping accommodation in a nearby building. At present it is often possible to sleep in the prestegård (phone in advance) if you are making the journey as a pilgrim. [Ringsaker prestegård, 2390 Moelv, tel: 62.36.45.58, EE, camping possible.]

After visiting church continue past it on cycle track and 900m later turn R *(signposted 'Moelv' for pedestrians and cyclists)*. Turn L at top onto **Skarpsnoveien** and return to main road again after 250m (waymarking to L indicates Steinsborget). Turn R along cycle track. 200m later, just before petrol station, there are three waymarks: a) *Mjøkastellet (remains of stone fortifications)*, b) *Helleriskringen* and c) (R) tells you to KSO on road.

400m later, opposite **Evjuvegen**, fork L off road down FP marked 'Moelvrunden', *a local walk waymarked in yellow which coincides with the* pilegrimsleden *for the next 5km.* This takes you along the edge of the lake, into **Moelv Camping** *[Steinvik Camping & Hyttegrend, 2390 Moelv, tel: 62.36.72.28].* Pass the campsite shop and continue out of the site again on the other side, along the shore, veering away from the lake to pass through the woods and a waymark indicating 'Gravrøyser' *(burial mounds).*

Veer R towards road at **Brennerivika** *(the harbour)* and cross FB over the **Moelva** *(river)* and continue on small tarmac road, passing the remnants of the jetty; *in the old days traffic crossed the Mjøsa by boat in summer and by horse/sledge in winter.* Continue until you reach the modern road bridge and fork L down FP to go under the

3.5km Mjøsbrua (195.5/447.5)

1420m long bridge over the Mjøsa.

Continue on small FP on other side, which becomes clearer and wider.

Veer R at fork, away from water. KSO(L) at next fork and at T-junction *(with handy seat)* turn L. Continue, veering L near a factory, to a crossing where you turn L downhill (gravel track) to do a 'loop', veering R at fork alongside water, then R at first T-junction and L at next. Cross minor road, pass in front of recycling depot *(railway line visible to R)* and continue ahead on track which veers L into woods and then R. Go through gate and cross the railway line (carefully). Continue ahead on other side to **Storgata** and turn L along its cycle track for 300m. Cross over to LH side of road to visit

2km Tolvsteinsringen (197.5/445.5)

Literally 'ring of twelve stones', the most famous historic monument in the area, a circle of twelve standing stones dating from the Iron Age (2000–2500 years ago). It was previously believed to be the site of a parliament or council but now it is thought to have been a burial place.

After visiting the site return to the cycle track. Cross bridge over a river, where you part company with 'Moelvrunden'. KSO along the Rv 213 for 1km to **Vea**. Turn R opposite nursery *(plantskole)* up a minor road *(marked 'Lundehaugen 1.3')* and go steeply uphill, climbing continuously for nearly 5km. Turn R at cross roads *(this is **Lundehaugen** – in the countryside signposts at road junctions often have the name of the locality on top)*, pass signpost to **Ringen** and KSO till you get to the junction at **Nordheim** *(nice views on a clear day but an exhausting 5km from Vea)*. Turn L downhill for 1.1km to the junction *(marked 'Brøttum Kirke 9.9')* at

5.5km Ulven (203/440)

Continue ahead but watch out very carefully for waymark to L here, which leads you onto a track into the woods. If you miss it, though, continue on road for 500m more, past a bend, to a junction with a coloured signboard marked 'Trettsveen'. Turn L and 800m later, opposite some houses, turn L down a clear grassy track between trees, and after 250m you will pick up the waymarks again, when the track comes from back L.

Continue ahead, gently downhill at first, then veering R descend more steeply when you enter the forest itself. Continue downhill to a farm and house, turning L and then R onto the Rv 213 at

Tolvsteinringen (circle of 12 standing stones) near Moelv (Eivind Luthen)

4km Havik (207/436)

Samuelstua Camping 300m further on on L. [2372 Brottum, tel: 62.36.03.90, shop.]

KSO (on road) for 3km with lake and railway line to your L. Turn hard L *(signposted 'Brøttum Stasjon')* and then hard R along gravelled road (the **Gamle Kongvei**) to

3km Brøttum Stasjon (210/433)

Trains do pass by but, like Bergseng Stasjon further on, they do not normally stop here any more. [Brøttum Camping, 2372 Brøttum, tel: 62.36.02.75, on Rv 213 near Brøttum church.]

Continue past station, veer R uphill and then L. KSO for 6km through undulating farmland and woods to

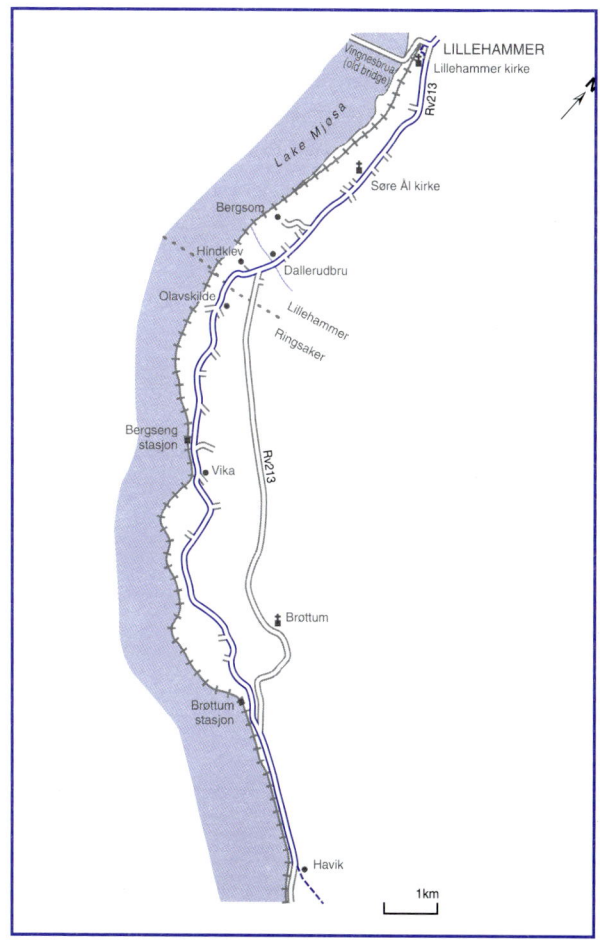

7km Bergseng Stasjon (217/426)

Continue on road behind station and KSO at junction (marked 'Hindklev 4.1'). After 1.5km pass **Hauknes** *and then, 1km later on R, reach the*

2km Olavskilde 219/424

Spring with healing properties, said to have appeared when St. Olav gave water to his horse.

Continue ahead and 800m later cross boundary from Hedmark into Oppland fylke.

200m later, when road (now tarred) bends R, fork L downhill on grassy track. Veer R alongside edge of first (small) field, R again along side of second (large) one and then L to cross field, heading towards the farm in front of you (**Hindklev**). [Accommodation: Hindklev gård, 2600 Lillehammer, tel: 61.25.06.24, E, CF.] Pass to L of it and then round edge of field to L, heading for corner of wood (to R ahead of you).

Inscription on Olavkilde near Brøttum (Eivind Luthen)

Continue, with wood to your L *(road over to R)*. Cross fence via stile, continue ahead and then turn R 100m later, veering L to take small FP passing to RH side of fence. Cross fence at end via another stile, turn L through gateway and then R into woods on grassy track. Go through gate and continue to cross 18th-century bridge (Dallerud Brua) over Smedbekken. Veer R onto farmroad leading to the Rv 213 and turn L along it *(cycle track starts after 1.5km)*.

Pass **Søre Ål Kirke**, *a modern church on the L (built 1964, note carvings on outside)*, **Sore Ål** and **Åretta schools** and go under the road *(you are on **Hamarvegen**)* by the underpass. Continue on FP on other side, cross **Åretta** *(river)*, continue between houses and turn L into **Årettaveien**. Turn R into **Moinichen Gate**, L into **Weidemann Gate**, passing Catholic church (L) and the Nansen School and then continue down **Bjørnsterne Bjørnsons gate** along LH side of sports ground. Cross road at end and go through the churchyard of Lillehammer kirke *(1882)*.

5km Lillehammer Kirke (224/491)

Population 24,000. Chief town in Gudbrandsal, all facilities, Tourist Office, regular buses to Gjøvik, Hamar, trains to Oslo and all points north to Trondheim. Site of winter Olympics in 1994. Lillehammer Kunstmuseum has best collection of modern art in Norway, home of Sigrid Undset, Maihaugen open-air museum, founded 1857, with over 160 buildings. Church dedicated 1882; open June–August, Mon–Sat 10.00-14.00.

[Youth Hostel at Lillehammer Skistasjon (above railway station), Jernbanetorget 2, 2600 Lillehammer, tel: 61.26.25.66, EE, CF. Accommodation also at Øvergaard, Jernbanegata 24, tel: 61.25.99.99, CF, in centre of town. 2 campsites: Lillehammer Camping, Dampsagveien 47, tel: 61.25.33.33, CF, by lake, to south of town; Lillehammer Motell og Camping, Sandheim, tel: 61.25.97.10, north of town centre.]

Pass in front of the church's main entrance and leave the churchyard on its opposite side *(large waymark indicates that there are now only 419km left to Nidaros)*. Turn R into **Langes gata** and then L into **Kirkegata** *(note statue of Tarn-Petter on corner, a poor man from Biri who became famous as a smith and clockmaker)*. Cross to RH side, pass **Kulturhuset Banken** *(built as a bank in 1894–95 but now an art museum; Tourist Office is up Bankgata to your R)* and continue ahead to **Stortorget**, *a square*, in front of the old **Norske Bank** *(built 1917, a* *listed property)*. Turn R up walkway between this and the **Lillehammer Kunstmuseum** and L into **Storgata** *(railway station and buses to L)*. Cross bridge (pedestrianised) over the river **Mesna** and cross a square (**Lilltorget**) diagonally *(the statue is of Ludwig Weise, one of the town's prominent citizens, and is by the same sculptor – Rolf Lunde – as the one of Tårn-Petter)*. Continue down **Gamleveien**, which you will stay on for the next 4 km. *[Lillehammer Gjestebu, Gamleveien 110, tel: 61.25.43.21, CF, has dormitory-type accommodation.]*

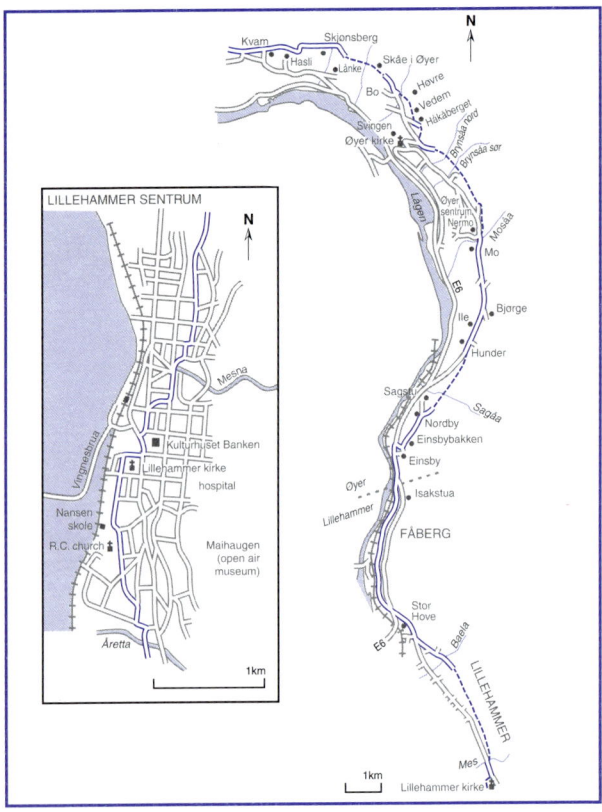

Cross **Smedstadvegen** and fork L ahead along cycle track between blocks of flats. Go under road and KSO on cycle track on other side. Cross **Fagabergvegen** by the **Gamlevegen** bus stop and continue ahead, out into the countryside now. Cross the river **Baela** and KSO until you reach the Rv 213 at **Storhove** and turn R along its cycle track.

Cross road via underpass, turn R in front of the **Høgskole i Lillehammer** *(a school)*, continue on cycle track, veer L downhill and then R to go through tunnel under the E6. Turn R on FP on other side, veering L downhill, go under railway line and then turn R on other side on small FP. Veer L and then R to continue on wide grassy track, passing waymark 'Gammelt Fergestad' by barn, *indicating a site to L below which was the old ferry crossing to places such as Fåberg church on the other side of the Lågen.* KSO(R) ahead up small FP which continues high up above the river. Go through gate into wood, forking R to continue alongside railway line.

Join wide grassy track coming from back L, turn R under railway line and fork L up bank, continue 20m alongside field and turn L through gate by HT cables. Cross stream, veering L downhill to electric transformer. Turn R, cross (disused) railway line and continue ahead on gravelled road (**Smerudstuguvegen**) to junction by bus stop in

8km Fåberg sentrum 230m (232/411)

Supermarket 300m to L by bridge.

Cross over and continue along the **Thomas Jørstads veg** *(signposted 'Fåberg Skytehall', a shooting gallery)*. Pass Fåberg railway station *(no longer in use)*, veer R uphill to farm machinery factory and 20m before road fork L down grassy lane ahead, veering L and then R below woods.

KSO in a straight line, // to road (above R). Cross FB over river and KSO. Just before fence turn R uphill, veer L up bank and turn hard R up second track in front of you to road. Turn L on road and then L shortly afterwards, returning to it 600m later. Turn L along road for 800m to a roundabout and turn R under E6 using cycle track.

Continue on cycle track *(direction 'Øyer S'; by now you have crossed from Lillehammer into Øyer kommune)*. 150m later turn hard R and then L up farm road, veering L uphill to **Ensbybakken gård** *(a farm)*. Veer round to R ahead and turn L alongside woods on RH side of fence on grassy track.

400m later, by house, turn L and then immediately R onto FP through open woodland. Continue for 400m then veer R onto farm road and turn L. 500m later, as road begins to descend, fork R onto FP leading into woods. From here the PL follows the **Tjodsvegen** *(literally 'the people's' or 'public' road), an ancient route which you will continue to meet, for longer or shorter stretches, for a long time to come. This next section has been waymarked with small wooden boards and a pilgrim logo.*

Continue ahead, cross the **Gjallarbru** *(bridge)* and then another stream, go through gate and continue ahead (R) on grassy track. Fork L 300m later by small house to cross field and enter woods again, crossing bridge over the **Sagåa**. Continue up hill ahead, after which path levels out, high up through open woodland. *This is a very nice section, with splendid views on a clear day. The gaudy building on the other side of the river is the Hunderfoss Familiepark. Øyer sentrum visible ahead. Waterfall to your R is the Kjaelighetsfoss.* Cross farm roads to reenter woods then, after 2.5km on **Tjodsvegen**, cross stile and veer L downhill to road (Rv 361).

Turn R uphill for 1.5km then turn L at junction (direction 'Øyer sentrum') and KSO, on the level for a while. 1km later, at **Kalbor** *(farm)*, the road goes into a tunnel. Do not go through it (even though there is a pavement) but fork L up to the side of its entrance and continue straight ahead above it for 100m, under a line of floodlights *(this is **Hafjell**, a ski station in winter). [Accommodation at Aasletten Pensjonat og Hytter, 2636 Øyer, tel: 61.27.76.12, CF.]* Continue to a U-bend on a gravel road. Turn L, rejoin the 361 below and KSO.

10km Nermo (242/401)

At junction just after crossing the **Mosåa** *(Øyer sentrum 2km, L, Nermo camping and caravan site L)* fork R up hill into woods, forking L onto the 'Trimløypen' *(a 'keep fit track'). This is a clear forest track, another very nice section, climbing gradually, following the line of the hillside all the time.* Cross a forest road after 1.5km and continue on other side.

KSO ahead, continuing to climb, until you reach a local road. Turn R uphill, then 300m later fork L between farms onto a small road, veering slightly L downhill all the time, in a roughly straight line, // to river. Road becomes a cart track after a while, passing between fields below rocky wall to R.

At end, turn L downhill alongside gulley, turn R between two clumps of trees towards dilapidated hut and go down clear FP to the R of it, through woods, downhill. This veers R and then L, descending steeply to cross FB over the **Brynsåa Sør** *(felled trees blocked entrance in 1999).*

Turn L on other side (this is **Tjodvegen** again), descending all the time. Join grassy track at its hairpin bend and follow it R downhill for 100m then fork R uphill to pick up another grassy track; this veers R, crosses a stile ahead (L), enters woods and continues ahead beside woods. It then veers R and then L uphill to cross first one and then another FB over the **Brynsåa Nord**. Continue ahead after the second one then veer R on small FP which follows round the line of the hillside.

Turn R through gate onto FP uphill, join farm road coming from back R, KSO in straight line to farm at top and go through its exit. Turn hard R up another farm road for 100m then L uphill up grassy lane alongside fence and woods, continuing to climb. Near the top of the hill (handy seat) is

4.5km Håkåberget 480m (246.5/396.5)

Named after King Håkon Håkonsson (1204–1263), who is believed to have fallen and injured himself here. Panoramic views on a clear day. (Waymark says 'Håkåberget'.)

Turn R up flight of wooden steps and cross stile into field. Continue along its edge to a farm; this is **Vedem** *(485m), where king Håkon Håkonsson has his* kongsgård *(royal court) and built his* veitslehall *(a banqueting hall; waymark says 'Vedem Veitslehall').*

Turn L on road and 500m later fork R through the farmyard at **Høvren** *(accommodation). [Høvren gård, 2636 Øyer, tel: 61.27.81.57 and 94.37.91.84, camping possible.]* Turn R uphill up stony track veering L and then R, uphill all the time. Turn L over stile onto grassy area through trees. 100m later turn L over another stile and then immediately R alongside old rocky wall, L at end of field and R along path between old walls. Turn R over stile ahead and then L alongside field. Cross stile, go along side of second field and cross two stiles at end by farm road. Turn R downhill then at bend continue ahead to cross FB over stream. Continue behind building, fork L down to stile and turn R up road (Fv 36). *The path from the western side of the Mjøsa joins you here from the left, though there is no marker post to indicate it, after which the* pilegrimsleden *continues as a single route.* Pass turning to **Bø** *(430m), L, the oldest farm in the whole area, from Bronze and possibly Stone Age times.* KSO at junction *(cul-de-sac sign),* still uphill, to

4km Skåe i Øyer 510m (251/392)

On your R (waymarked 'Kjørkbakken') is the site of a medieval church, said to have been built by St. Olav and mentioned in records as early as 1333; the monument marking it was placed there in 1959. An Olsokmesse is celebrated here every year on July 29th, St. Olav's day, attended regularly by some 200 to 300 people. Marker stone indicates that there are now 392 km left to Nidaros.

Ahead is Skåden gård, a farm with pilgrim (and other) accommodation. [Skåden gård, 2636 Øyer, tel: 61.27.81.60, CF.]

Turn to page 132 to continue.

Present-day pilgrim accommodation at Skåden Gård, Skåe i Øyer (Eivind Luthen)

Western (Cultural) Route

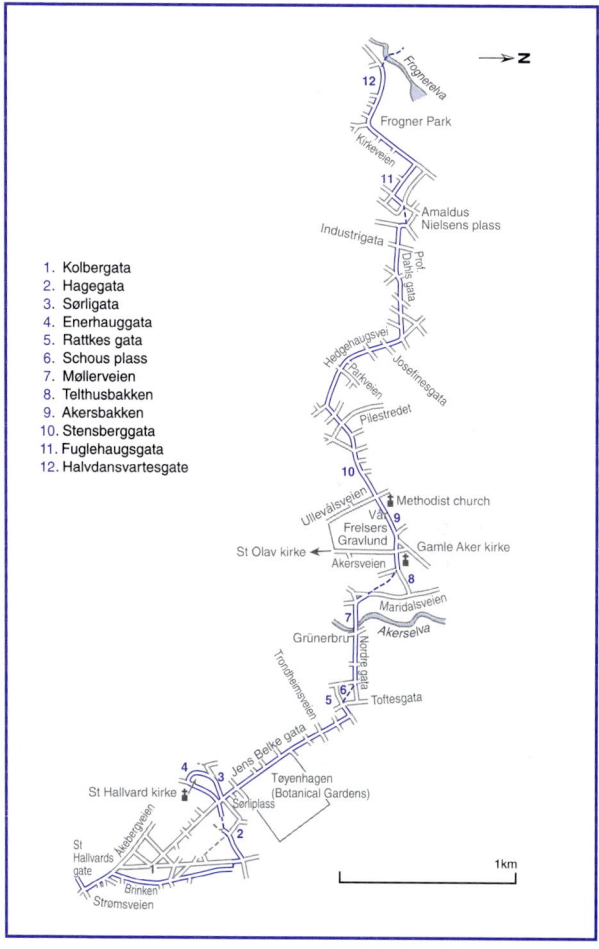

1. Kolbergata
2. Hagegata
3. Sørligata
4. Enerhauggata
5. Rattkes gata
6. Schous plass
7. Møllerveien
8. Telthusbakken
9. Akersbakken
10. Stensberggata
11. Fuglehaugsgata
12. Halvdansvartesgate

The western route *is* waymarked through the city of Oslo, but only very spasmodically. Regular, systematic waymarking does not begin until Jar skole in the suburbs, after crossing the Lysakerelva (river).

2.5km Galgeberg (2.5/640.5)

Veer L diagonally across the grassed area *(second waymark on building to LH side)* and turn L into the **Akebergveien**. Cross the road and turn 3rd R up the **Brinken** *(third waymark on LH side at start). This is a ridge-like road that was originally lined with 19th-century wooden houses; a few still survive today.*

KSO to the very end of the **Brinken** and a block of flats *(note houses by no. 59 – a group of older wooden ones, fourth waymark)* and turn L down a slope beside the post office into the **Kjølberggata**. Turn R, cross road and go down **Økernveien** ahead. Do not follow it round to the R (this part becomes the **Hagegata**) but KSO ahead down the **Sørligata**, passing between a building marked 'Universitetsforlaget' and a children's playground to the **Sørliplass**, *a six-point junction with a fountain and sitting area.*

Before you turn R down the **Jens Bjelkesgata** you are going to do a 'loop' ahead to pass the modern (Roman Catholic) St. Hallvard church and monastery. Continue ahead down the **Sørligata**, veering L into the **Enerhauggata** (the hill you are circumnavigating is the **Enerhaug**). Keep veering L to pass the modern (Franciscan) church and then monastery and return to the **Sørliplass**. From here turn L down the Jens Bjelkesgata, a very long street that passes in front of the University of Oslo's Botanical Gardens (R, *a good place for a stroll or a rest on a nice day)*, crosses the **Trondheimgata** and ends at a junction with the **Rathkegata**.

Turn L, cross the **Schous Plass** diagonally in front of the public library and go down the **Nordregata** *(view of the Gamle Aker church at end on R). (This area is known as the Grønnalokka, named after the man who bought all the land and sold it off for building.)* Cross the **Grunabrua** *(bridge over the Akerselva)*, go up **Møllerveien** on the other side, cross **Maridalsveien** and turn R on the other side. Go up some steps and a FP *(remains of waymark no. 5 on L at start): this is the Kjaerlighetssti.* KSO at top past allotment gardens (R) and turn L into **Telthusbakken** *(waymark no. 6).* Go uphill to the

5km Gamle Aker kirke (7.5/635.5)

Oslo's only remaining medieval church, dating from the mid-11th century, and its oldest stone building. Open Mon–Sat

12.00–14.00, Sunday services 09.00 and 11.00. Believed to have been dedicated to St. Michael.

To continue: KSO ahead along **Telthusbakken** past timber-framed house and join **Akersbakken** coming from back R.

Gamle Aker church, Oslo (Eivind Luthen)

Although you are walking the Pilgrim Road to Nidaros, to the shrine of St. Olav, you may have not yet visited his 19th-century Catholic cathedral church, a short, easy detour from here. To reach the church, instead of continuing ahead, turn L down **Akersveien** along the side of **Vår Frelsers Gravlund**, *the cemetery where, amongst others, many famous writers, artists and public figures are buried, much as they are in Hampstead Cemetery, Westminster Abbey or the Père Lachaise in Paris. Pass the St. Olav Bokhandel (no. 14, which has an extensive 'pilgrim section' in various languages) and at the junction with* **Thor Olsengata** *and* **Ullevålsveien** *reach the St. Olavkirke (contains a relic which is supposed to be part of the saint's leg, inside a raised steel arm in a glass case – and with a burglar alarm!). Note modern metal sculpture of St. Olav outside the front entrance, on the L, placed there* *in 1999. Masses Mon–Fri 08.00 and 18.00, Sat 10.00 and 18.00, Sunday: many services in many languages).*

Return to the **Gamle Aker kirke** and continue up **Telthusbakken**, continuing along the top (north) side of the cemetery on **Akersbakken** (which joins from back R). Cross **Ullevålsveien** and KSO along **Stenberggata**, veering R downhill to cross **Pilestredet**.

Continue along **Hegdehaugsveien**, a very long street, pedestrianised in part, and KSO, crossing **Parkenveien** and the **Josefinesgata**, and then, when it continues as **Bogstadveien**, fork L up **Professor Dahls gate**, another long street (not marked at start) and continue to its end. Cross the **Schives gate** and go down some steps into the **Amaldus Nielssens plass**, crossing the playground to the opposite LH corner.

Cross the **Tidemandsgate**, continue ahead along the **Fuglehauggata** *(waymark no. 7 on L at start)* to **Kirkenveien**. Opposite is

3km Frognerparken (10.5/632.5)

The official path does not take you into the park to see the Vigeland sculptures, so to visit you can either make a detour when passing in front of the main gates or, when you are inside, after crossing the Frognerelva.

Turn L along Kirkenveien to the Frognerplass and turn R into Frognerveien, pass the entrance to the Oslo Bymuseum *(City Museum, R)* and the Vigelandmuseum (L) and turn off the road R down a tarmac FP *(opposite the entrance to the Soltenheimgata on the LH side of the road, waymark on electric pole on L of FP)* and go downhill to cross bridge over the Frognerelva *(river)*. Continue ahead on other side, cross the Madserud Allé and, despite misleading waymark, KSO ahead down Jonserudveien. Turn R into the Arnstein Arnebergvei, veering L, and at end *(where it is closed for traffic)* veer L again to join cycle path ahead of you, passing between flats (L) and a building marked 'Oslo Fritidshuet Mads' (to R). KSO over stream, passing *Skøyen hovedgård (on your L), a group of old, now dilapidated farm buildings*, and veer L to junction at Øyre Silkestrå (an industrial complex). Continue ahead again, passing Skøyen church *(very modern, on your R)* and veer L *(small supermarket on your L)*. When you reach a waymarked junction KSO ahead on the level, through a complex of flats. *(The main road, away to your R below you in the valley, is **Hoffsveien**, which you will be crossing shortly.)* All this section, and from here until you reach Haslum church, is built up, most of it residential.

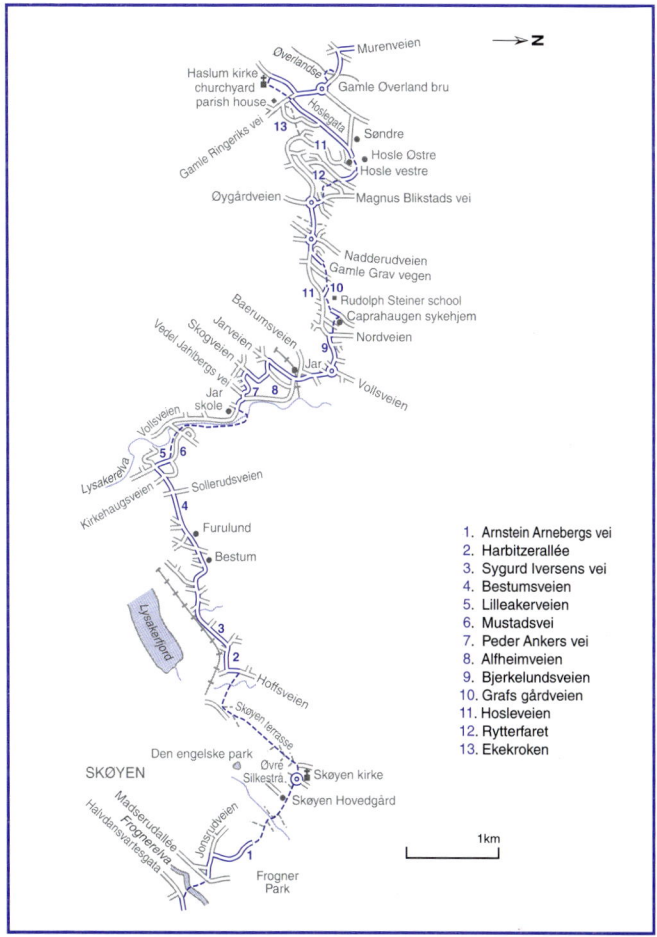

Murenveien
Øverlandse
Haslum kirke
churchyard
parish house
Gamle Overland bru
Hoslegata
13
Søndre
11
Hosle Østre
Gamle Ringeriks vei
12
Hosle vestre
Øygårdveien
Magnus Blikstads vei
Nadderudveien
Gamle Grav vegen
Baerumsveien
10
11
Rudolph Steiner school
Jarveien
Skogveien
Caprahaugen sykehjem
Vedel Jarlsbergs vei
Nordveien
Jar
Jar
skole
7 **8**
Vollsveien
Vollsveien
Lysakerelva
5 **6**
Sollerudsveien
Kirkehaugsveien
4
Furulund
Bestum
Lysakerfjord
3
2
Hoffsveien
Skøyen terrasse
Den engelske park
Øvre
Silkestrå
SKØYEN
Skøyen kirke
Madserudallée
Skøyen Hovedgård
Frognerelva
Jonsrudveien
Halvdansvilesgata
1
Frogner
Park

1km

1. Arnstein Arnebergs vei
2. Harbitzerallée
3. Sygurd Iversens vei
4. Bestumsveien
5. Lilleakerveien
6. Mustadsvei
7. Peder Ankers vei
8. Alfheimveien
9. Bjerkelundsveien
10. Grafs gårdveien
11. Hosleveien
12. Rytterfaret
13. Ekekroken

When you reach a junction with a turning place for cars go R down FP/cycle track between a large, older-style salmon-pink block of flats and the modern Alfa Laval factory and office building, cross the **Hoffselva** and veer R // to tram tracks to emerge on **Hoffveien** opposite a supermarket. Turn L and then immediately R up the **Harbitzerallé** by the side of the post office *(waymark on L)*. *All this may sound rather complicated but you are, in fact, going in more or less a straight line west, avoiding busy roads as far as possible.*

Enamel waymark (author)

Take the third turning on the L into the **Sigurd Ivesens vei**. After approximately 700m you reach a junction with **Bestumsvei** (coming from your L), which you now continue along ahead for some 1.5km, passing Bestum tram stop *(no. 10 takes you back to central Oslo)*, crossing **Vaekeroveien** *(supermarket on one corner, Fulurud tram stop, no. 10, on other)* and continue downhill until you reach the junction with **Lilleakerveien**. *All this section is through residential areas with increasingly large properties, many of them of older-type wooden construction. Watch out carefully for traffic in sections with no pavement.* Turn R here *(view of nearby sea to L)* and pass in front of a large shopping centre on the other side of the road. Go through its carpark, past the Mustad industrial complex and go under the new road (the **Mustadvei**).

6km Lysakerelva (16.5/626.5)

*On the other side you will see the river (the **Lysakerelva**) to your L (this forms the boundary between the city of Oslo and the kommune of Akerhus) and a big waterfall. From here the waymarking becomes regular.*

KSO ahead uphill (signposted 'Jar-om Fåbro-Pilegrimsleden'). *The cluster of wooden houses at the top is Fåbro (a gård).* Veer R uphill through trees, // to river way down below you to your L and turn L over modern FB to cross the river. Go through underpass ahead, veering R, which will bring you out on **Vollsveien**. Turn L along it (i.e. facing river) in front of

1km Jar skole (17.5/625.5)

From the school until **Jar gård** the most direct route is simply to continue along **Vollsveien**, but to avoid the traffic and use quieter roads you turn second L by a bus shelter *(war memorial and area with seats)* up the **Wedel Jarlsburg vei** and then immediately R up **Peder Ankersvei** *(the old medieval road to Jar)*. Follow it round uphill to L and at the top turn R into **Skogveien** and then L up an unnamed but waymarked lane (opposite house no. 8). Turn L uphill at end (**Altheimvei**) and then R along **Jarveien** to the junction with **Vollsveien** again *(shops, Jar tram stop down slope, no. 10 to central Oslo)* at

1.5km Jar gård (19/624)

Turn L over bridge over railway line, KSO up **Vollsveien** to mini-roundabout and then KSO ahead along **Bjerkelundsveien**. Turn third R up **Nordveien** and then immediately L up small side road leading to **Caprahaugen sykehjem** *(a hospital, some 700m from railway bridge)*, veering L. Go up steep FP to LH side of building and at top of hill turn L along flat, gravelled lane, which then becomes a FP/cycle track, leading you down into **Graf gårdvei**, just past the FB (on your L) over **Hosleveien** *(main road)*. KSO down **Graf gårdvei**, passing to L of a large older-type barn building with a cluster of other modern, wooden houses behind it; this is **Grafs gård** *(now a Rudolf Steiner school)*.

KSO ahead *(the road now becomes a cycle track)*, cross **Fagertunveien** and continue until you reach **Hosleveien**. Turn R along it, cross **Nadderudveien** *(petrol station and supermarket to L)* and KSO until you reach the junction with **Øygårdsveien**.

From here the offical path takes you onto paths and quieter roads until you reach Haslum church. If you are in a hurry, or in bad weather, a much shorter option is to continue along **Hosleveien**, passing a LH turn then a RH one until you reach another LH fork in an estate of houses (some 750m from the junction with **Øygårdsveien**). Turn L and then immediately L again up a cycle track through houses, cross **Ekrekogen**, continue ahead through more houses and emerge on the main road (**Gamle Ringerikeveien**) at **Haslum Skole**, almost directly opposite the entrance to the cemetery, in front of the **Menighetshuset** *(parish house)*. Turn R, cross over and go through the gates to the church.

Otherwise – turn R into **Øygårdsveien** *(supermarket on L)*, veer L into **Magnus Blikstadsvei** *(note metal sculptures of fox and geese at junction)* and then 50m later turn L up unnamed but waymarked lane behind a row of lock-up garages. This continues as a FP through trees, veering R. Cross **Rytterfaget** and KSO up FP on other side. Emerge onto grassed area, cross **Kalkbrennervei** and KSO on other side on unnamed but waymarked road into new housing estate. Turn R up lane by side of house no. 11, L alongside football field and follow lane round to L uphill, passing group of large farm buildings on L until you reach the junction at **Hosle gård** *(farm is to R)*. KSO ahead down gravelled lane, veering R *(note sign pointing to 'gravhaug' – a burial mound – on your L)* and at junction with **Ekrekrogen** KSO(R) ahead. This is **Hoslegata** *(not named)*, which leads you to the main road (**Gamle Ringerikeveien**) opposite the Haslum cemetery and crematorium. Turn L, cross road, enter its grounds and continue to

4km Haslum kirke (18/625)

Medieval church dating from late 11th or early 12th century, dedicated to the Virgin Mary, rebuilt and enlarged 1835 when sacristy was added. Contains an exact copy of a medieval wooden sculpture of the Madonna and child (the original has been removed for conservation), a limestone baptismal font and a 4m wooden relief sculpture with animal decoration over southern exit door. One of the churches bells dates from the 12th century. Open afternoons, Mon–Fri in July and August, and Saturdays if no weddings; service: Sunday 11.00.

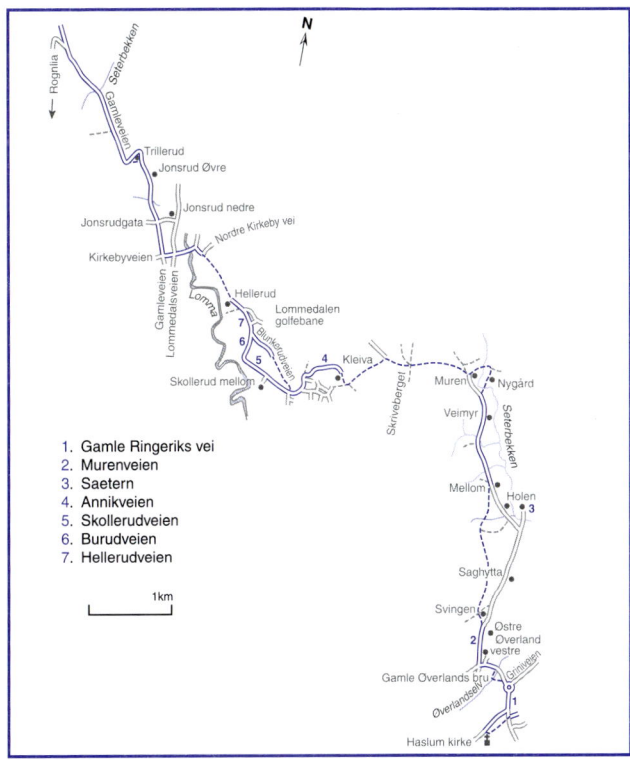

1. Gamle Ringeriks vei
2. Murenveien
3. Saetern
4. Annikveien
5. Skollerudveien
6. Burudveien
7. Hellerudveien

If you want to return to central Oslo (e.g. to sleep) turn L out of gate in front of church into **Kirkenveien** *and KSO downhill (1km, shops) to the T-bane station and take the metro into the city centre.*

Otherwise: turn R out of Haslum church gate into **Kirkenveien** and 500m later turn L into main road (**Gamle Ringerikevei**), crossing onto RH side to use pavement and then back to LH side again 200m later at roundabout. Almost immediately afterwards turn L down a FP by the beginning of the crash barrier. This takes you on a detour over the **Gamle Øverlandsbru**, *the medieval bridge over the Overlandselva, before veering R to return you to the main road again.* Turn L and 200m later, at bend in road, turn R into Murenvei, passing a small nature reserve on your L. KSO ahead uphill and veer L at fork (**Murenveien** continues R) and 200m later, at **Svingen** (a couple of red wooden buildings), veer L uphill to cross **Ankerveien** *(a long-distance FP)* and take the second R turn, a forest track marked 'Muren, Brunkollen'. Continue along this, climbing steadily. *Note that the* pilegrimsleden *coincides with other waymarked footpaths in this area, so as well as the PL waymarks you will also see the red flashes of another route (a horizontal stripe painted on trees some 6–7ft above ground level).*

Holen Skog (post waymark) (author)

When you reach a junction (4 paths) KSO ahead downhill, continuing to follow the red flashes. After some 2km from Svingen you will reach an area with newly planted trees and a waymark naming the place as **Holen Skog**, *the site of a medieval farm from the 11th to 12th centuries and Iron Age burial mounds*. Continue ahead to rejoin **Murenveien** by an isolated house (**Mellom**) and continue along it for 1km till you reach the turn to **Nygård** (R), with an information board at junction.

N.B. In bad weather or if it has been snowing omit the 'loop' via Nygård and continue for 400m more on the Murenveien to Muren itself (a cluster of houses). Otherwise, turn R and 200m later reach

6km Nygård (29/614)

A 200-year-old farm now owned by Baerum kommune. It is being restored as an outdoor centre and will eventually serve meals. (Only open on summer Sundays at present.)

Turn L in front of it and then continue across a field, alongside a wood (L) and then turn L up a forest track, veering L to cross a stream by stepping stones some 300m later. Continue to a group of buildings – this is **Muren**, the end of the **Murenvei** – and at a junction outside the farm take the second RH turn (two o'clock position), marked 'Skriverberget 1'. *This is another old historic route and is also marked with red flashes.*

Continue uphill through the trees till you reach the top *(the second waymark says 'Skriverberget' – literally 'writing mountain' – referring to the practice of passing travellers carving their initials and the dates on nearby rocks)*. Cross another long-distance path. Continue ahead, cross another FP and continue downhill. At junction take L turn alongside wood and continue down to **Kleiva** 1km later *(also marked in red)*. Here you will reach a gravelled road: turn R along it and follow it downhill through houses (it becomes the **Annikvei** but is unnamed at the start) until you reach the road (**Skollerudveien**). Turn R *(note unusual 'wire' tower on Lommadal church away in the distance to your L)*, and 750m later turn R up **Burudveien** and 500m later turn R into **Hellerudveien** which leads to a golf course.

Pass between the carpark (R) and the café-restaurant (L) and then, at the corner of the building marked 'Hellerup gård' *(an old farm)*, continue ahead in the same direction that you have been coming in on a clear track leading you downhill to a junction by a large wooden industrial building *(a lawnmower agent)*. Turn L uphill (the **Nedre Kirkebyvei**), veer R and then turn L at top down the **Kirkbyenvei**, crossing the river **Lomma** *(you are now entering Lommadal – i.e. its valley)*, cross the main road by the bus stop (**Lommadalsveien**), continue ahead up **Bjerkenveien** and *100m later turn R into* **Gamleveien**. *This is the 'old [i.e. main] road' to Bergen (though not a medieval one), taking you, in effect, all the way through the hills known as Krogskogen to the fjord at Sundvollen.*

Continue along it (100m after junction with Jonsrudgata is the entrance to the **Lommadal Ferienhus** *(accommodation may be possible)) for 1km to*

6m Jonsrud Øyre (35/608)

A group of houses. Here there is a gate across the road (locked for vehicles). You now leave Lommadal and enter Krokskogen (an extensive wooded area).

KSO ahead. After 300m, just before **Trillerud**, *an isolated house on your L*, there is a short-cut (steep) on your L, waymarked, which brings you out after the next bend and just before a second one. Turn L uphill *(Granbakken, a large house, is on your R 200m later.)*

300m later the waymarked route leads you off the road uphill to your L up a forest track *(waymark by electricity pole)*. This takes you uphill, turning R 500m later, onto a track through the woods, marked with red flashes, before returning you to the road again 1km after a junction (with **Rognliveien**) and 500m before the bridge at **Amtsbrua**, a total detour of 2.5km. *It is not all that easy to follow, however, and there are no distinguishing features to orient you as a lot of tree-felling has taken place in this area. The reason for the detour, as with others, apart from taking you off the road for a while, is to visit places with significant associations in Norwegian (though not necessarily pilgrim) history and follow the traces of historic paths.*

Otherwise – continue on **Gamleveien**, up and downhill, taking the RH fork at a road junction (the LH one is **Rognliveien**) marked 'Langbru 1.5, Kleivstua 13' and KSO till you go downhill to reach the bridge and a cluster of houses at

6km Langsbru/Amtsbrua (41/602)

This marks the border between Baerum and Hole kommuner. The original stone bridge, built in 1807, was restored in 1995.

Continue on the road, passing **Fredens Bolig** *(L), a religious community and Christian conference centre that provides self-catering accommodation but **only** for large, pre-booked groups.* KSO on road, climbing very steeply. You can, in fact, continue on it, up and down, all the way to **Kleivstua** (11.5km, i.e. ignoring the waymarks that lead you off the road from time to time, only to return again later), stopping for a short detour *(and back again – a few hundred metres only)* to visit the **Olavskilde** *(a spring)* just before **Midtskogen** *(LH turn at pilgrim waymark). If so, you will pass isolated houses and farm buildings from time to time and also information boards giving you details about the places you are in (Kjaglidalen), about the coal and charcoal industry that flourished in the area in the 17th century*

*(Køamile) – the last one closed in 1872, log transport, wild life, tree planting and members of the Norwegian Resistance in the Second World War. At **Frøshaug** (a farm which now belongs to a Norwegian Student Club) some of the huts in the area were used by the Norwegian resistance during the Second Word War before its members were captured, tortured and imprisoned in the Akerhus fortess in Oslo. The road gradually descends, though undulating all the time, to*

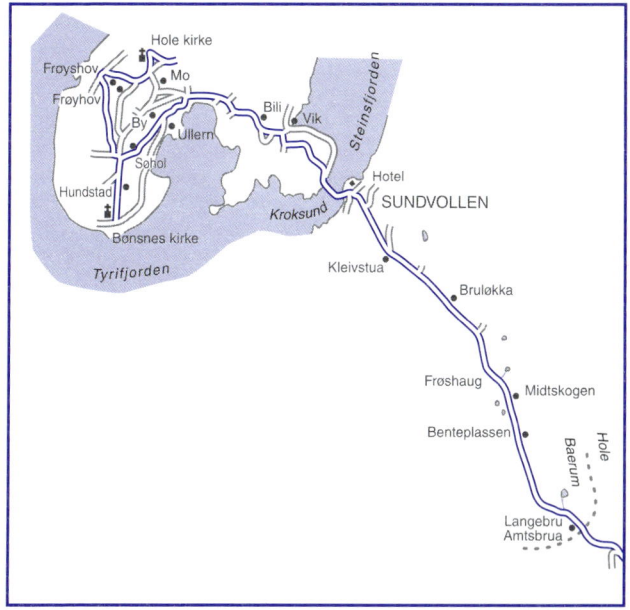

10.5km Kleivstua (51.5/591.5)

Family-run ski station, built in 1805. Café-restaurant.

*Optional detour from here (on a clear day and if you have time) to **Kongensutsikt** (the 'king's view'), a viewpoint 1.5km away (each way).*
    From here the shortest way (1.5km) down to Sundvollen is to turn L, pass behind large yellow building *(the café)* and turn R downhill down clear but very steep track. This takes you down to the road in the

settlement itself. (The alternative route down, via the road, is considerably longer (5–6km).)

1.5km Sundvollen (53/590)

Population 587. Small supermarket, 2 hotels. [Sundvollen Hotell, 3531 Krokkleiva, tel: 32.16.21.00, EE. There is also an hourly bus service to Hønefoss, including Sundays, which has a Youth Hostel: Hønefoss Vandrerhjem, Ringeriksgata 20, 3501 Hønefoss, tel: 32.12.29.03, EE, CF.]

Turn L by supermarket and then R down cycle track and go under main road. Turn R along cycle track as far as the **Sundøya Hotell**, go up path in front of its entrance and then down to cross the old bridge over the **Kroksundet** *(sundet = sound or straits); this was built in 1806 but is now used as a FP/cycle track, the modern bridge passing above it, immediately overhead.* At the end stay on the LH side till the end of the causeway, go up **Gamlevegen** ahead, veering R uphill and then turn L down **Karjolveien**.

Here the landscape changes, the mountains and forests giving way to undulating fields, with fjords in the middle-distance. It is often extremely windy in this area.

Follow this road up and down, veering R, L and R again to a 'stop' sign at a junction in

1km Vik (54/569)

Supermarket opposite.

Although from a map it may look as though you are approaching a centre of population of perhaps considerable size, here, as elsewhere, when you arrive it is all very spread out; the houses are scattered over the landscape and not all clustered together as they usually are in towns and villages in Britain, for example, except in relatively big places such as Gjøvik and Lillehammer. Vik is just such a case in point, in practice just an assortment of houses dispersed amongst the fields.

Turn L (use cycle track on other side) and at bend in road go up **Bratbakken**, which becomes a FP/cycle track uphill ahead 50m later. Go up it and follow it along until you come to a road. Turn R *(this is the main Vik–Gommes road)* and KSO along it. 2km later pass a junction and KSO. 500m later (this is **Mo**) reach another junction (marked 'Svendsund').

*To go to **Frøhaug gård** (i.e. to sleep) KSO ahead here. [Frøhaug gård, Hole, 3530 Røyse, tel: 32.15.71.09, meals available, camping possible.]*

Pilgrim path through Gjelleråsen woods (photo: Eivind Luthen)

Trollstein, near Ringsaker (photo: author)

800m later, at a T-junction (this is **Røyse***), go up its drive ahead of you.* From here you can then either backtrack to the junction and proceed as below or turn L (facing Frøhaug gård on the road, not busy), which will take you straight to Bønsnes church (3km).

Otherwise – turn L (signposted 'Bønsnes') amd then turn R 700m later at a farm road which brings you out, 1.5km later, on the road to Bønsnes. Turn L and at a junction 500m later *(signposted 'Bønsnes 1' – you can see the church ahead of you, perched up on a hill overlooking the fjord)* KSO to

8km Bønsnes kirke (62/581)

11th-century stone church dedicated to St. Olav (according to some sources he is said to have built it here as a thanksgiving for safe passage on his boat journey up the Tyrifjord). Not much is known about the church in the Middle Ages, though it was well visited by pilgrims going to Nidaros from the area around the Oslofjord (as were also Stein church, now ruined, Hole, Norderov and Haug churches), who could have sought overnight accommodation at the monastery on Storøya ('big island') just off Sundvollen. Bønsnes is not a parish church, however (it was closed after the Reformation), but is under the protection of the Riksantikvaren. The parish priest from Hole church is obliged to conduct six services a year there between May and October, the most important of which is, of course, the Olsokmesse on St. Olav's day. Inside there is a Baroque altarpiece and pulpit, a 12th-century wooden statue of the Madonna and child and a fully rigged Kirkenskiper (ship) hanging over the middle aisle. Open July 1st–31st, 12.00–16.00, guided visits possible.

From Bønsnes church retrace your steps to the junction at **Hunderstad**, pass junction (to R) where you came from, turn L at next junction (marked on top 'Klokkersvingen') up road signposted 'Røysetoppen' and turn R uphill 150m later. At top turn R down side of large wooden ski-jump and L 25m later onto forest track *(institutional building is now on your L; waymark may be missing)*.

Continue ahead, slightly downhill, and at crossing of four tracks 150m later turn L uphill, veering R. At top take middle of three tracks to R opposite farm (on L) and turn R uphill. Descend gradually downhill through pinewoods. Join farm road coming from back R and reach junction with two seemingly conflicting waymarks, one to R, one to L.

a) LH option is marked 'Frøyhovsgård', the purpose of which is to pass the largest burial site in the area.

b) Turn R and 300m later, at house, turn L onto forest road. Follow it downhill *(good views over to Krokskogen R)* till you reach a minor road *(Hole Kirke visible ahead to L)* and KSO(R) ahead. 300m later turn L at junction (marked 'Libakka'). (Turn R here – 500m – to return to Frohaug gård if necessary) and KSO(L) when road bends R to

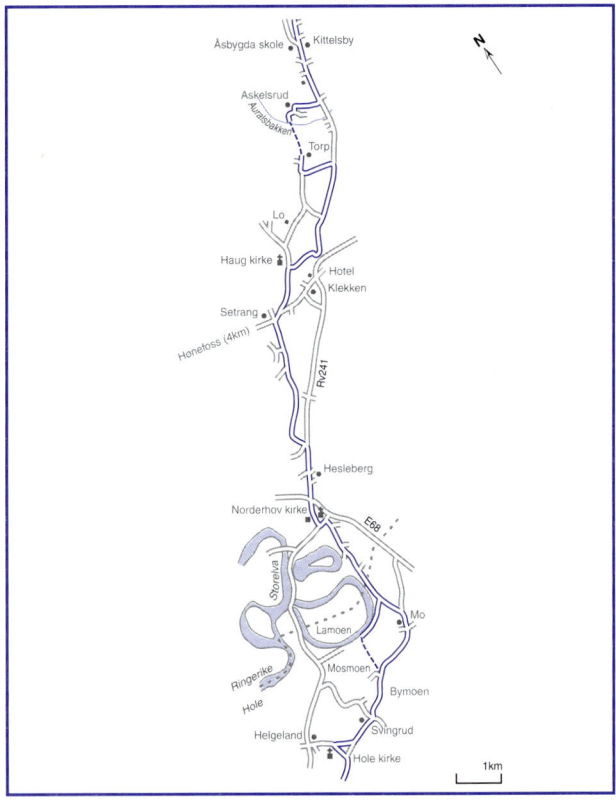

6km Hole kirke (68/575)

The original church dated from the 12th century and was replaced by another in 1660, which was destroyed by fire in 1943. The present church was rebuilt in 1951 on the remains of the medieval foundations.

Turn L in front of church onto gravelled lane and when this bends L KSO on FP alongside fields to road and turn L *(i.e. you have done a triangular 'loop' to visit church)*.

Continue on road, pass junction 1km later and KSO ahead *(direction 'Hønefoss')*. After approximately 1.5km (watch out carefully for waymark) you will be directed onto a forest track to L, to go through the woods for some 2km until you reach the **Storelva**. At present, however, it is very inadequately waymarked *(presumably recent tree-felling has destroyed them)* and there are no distinguishing features to orient you, so it is suggested that you continue on the road here to the next junction (**Mo**), turn L there *(the RH turn takes you to the main E16)* and in a little under 1km turn R onto the minor road you would have been on anyway and continue ahead for 2.5km to

6km Norderov Kirke (74/569)

Medieval stone church from mid-12th century – it is very prominently situated on a hill and you can see it well before you reach it. Church office next door. Ringerikes Museum opposite, while the brown house next to it, a listed building with cellars from the 12th century and the first floor from the 16th, is believed to have served as overnight accommodation for pilgrims. You are now in the kommune of Ringerike.

Continue ahead up road in front of the church (i.e. with it on your R), cross the main road by the tunnel and KSO on other side (use cycle track) up the Rv 241 marked 'Jevnaker' and 'Klekken', uphill for 1.5km.

After this (100m after a LH turn, **Tanbergmoveien**) the route should then lead you via a LH fork into the woods to follow the medieval road to Haug, first through the woods and then in a straight line ahead on a minor road to a road junction in **Saetrang**, 3.5km further on. However, since the waymarks are missing at the start and tree-felling has obscured the track it is not possible to follow it at present, so until the section is cleared and re-waymarked there is no option but to continue on the Rv 241 to Klekken. *(It is also not possible to rejoin it further on by taking future LH turns as these lead through private land.)*

When you get to the junction at **Klekken** turn L *(towards Hønefoss)*. [Klekken Hotell, 3500 Hønefoss, tel: 32.13.22.00, EE. Phone ahead as *they may have a special pilgrim price if they are not full. You can also take a bus from here to sleep in the YH at (4km, half-hourly service Mon–Sat, Sundays afternoon only).]*

After turning L at the junction take the first R turn (the *Øvre Klekken vei*), which takes you directly to Haug church (1km), visible ahead to R. *It is not really worth continuing to the second junction (Fløytingen), where you would have come from had you come through the woods, as you will merely be walking round two extra sides of a triangle.*

6km Haug Kirke (80/563)

Medieval stone church on hilltop with both Christian and heathen graves in adjoining cemetery. No specific opening times but phone 32.13.29.70 (Mon–Fri 08.00–15.00) or 32.13.21.39. (Mon–Fri 10.00–14.00) to visit. Supermarket and bank in 'Haugsentrum' opposite.

To leave: from church cross road and go up cycletrack marked 'pilgrimsleden' and veer to L behind playing field. Continue ahead *(no waymark)* across minor road *(sports hall on your L)* to road and turn R steeply uphill for 1km. At a LH bend and a cycle track coming from your R you will see a waymark telling you to continue uphill. (The road has now become the **Harehaugenvei**.) *Good views to L across to Hønefoss and beyond on a clear day.*

Pass **Hageringen** *(street on L)* and at very top of hill when road bends R turn L onto a gravelled road, just before a bus stop and a HT electricity pylon: this is still the **Harehaugenvei**. 250m later, at crossroads, KSO ahead down **Torpveien**, downhill. KSO ahead, downhill all the time onto clear forest track *(trees on LH slope have all been recently felled)* when **Torpveien** bends R, veering R and then L. When you are nearly at the bottom *(watch out carefully for waymark)* turn R to cross a stream, the **Aurbeck**, which is now only some 10–15m away from you, by a small wooden bridge.

Continue ahead on a level path, cross another similar stream by another wooden bridge and follow the track till you come to a T-junction some 800m later. Here a waymark indicates a 'short-cut' to, in effect, turn L here *(Askilsrud farm visible ahead)*. 20m later a waymark indicates a RH fork down a smaller track to cross a stream at the bottom and then cross a fence by a small stile into a field, continuing straight ahead along its LH edge to cross another similar stile onto a farm road. What you have done, in effect, is to avoid going through the farmyard, something you may need to do in practice if the stream is flooded.

Turn R very steeply uphill (this is **Askilrudveien**) to road (Rv 241) at top. Turn L along it (using cycle track) for 1.5km to

4km Åsbygda Skole (84/559)

School building is on L.

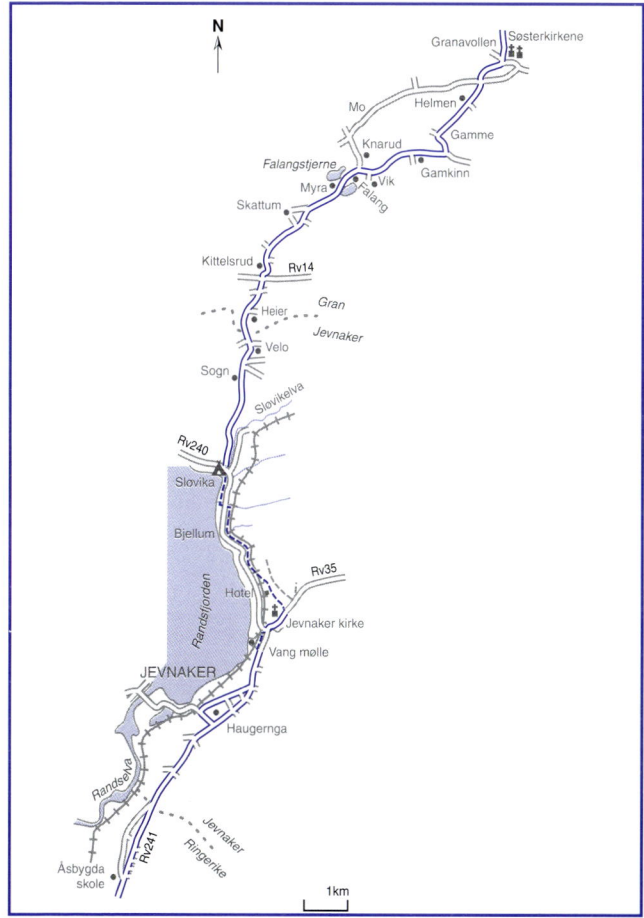

Go under road (when it bends to L here) and KSO ahead up Gamlevegen, a ridge-like road, continuing on it for 2km till you rejoin the Rv 241 at the boundary of the kommuner of Ringerike and Jevnaker (sign boards).

Cross road and turn L downhill beside small red house and 25m later turn R into forest. Just inside, on your R, is a waymark indicating the position of the medieval bridleway *(waymarked 'Ridevei')*, a ditch-like road // to 241.

Veer L and then turn R onto wider forest track, returning you to the 241 400m later. 150m later waymark with 'Sternringen' (on front) and 'Mosmoen' (on side) indicates a FP that follows alongside the road but just inside the wood. *(Here you will find the first of a new type of mini-waymark.)*

You can continue on this till the entrance to **Jevnaker** *(by its entrance board, views over Ragnafjord to L); if you want to go (off-route) into the town (famous for its glass works – guided tours available) follow road round sharply to L.* Otherwise continue ahead on **Gamlevegen**. After 1km a waymark directs you L, down the **Haugegata**, alongside a field; *the 'Haugerenga' referred to on the waymark is the area in which there is a* gravfelt *consisting of four burial mounds and the remains of a stone circle.*

No waymark at end so you can either continue to main road *(especially if you are hungry – snack bar/fast food outlet opposite and petrol station to L has small supermarket inside)* or turn R instead down **Wangvegen** right to its end, where it bears L and joins main road further along. Or you can simply stay on **Gamlevegen** as it rejoins the main road anyway at bend later on.

KSO on road and 2km after the **Haugerenga** fork R up a farm track then KSO, returning to the road again. KSO until you reach the junction of the Rv 242 and the Rv 35, just below Jevnaker church, now visible ahead of you on the hill. To your L, at the bend, is **Wang Mølle**, *an old watermill, now rather dilapidated.* Go uphill (on the Rv 242) to

7km Jevnaker Kirke (91/552)

A very large 19th-century white wooden structure with three storeys of windows, looking more like a big house than a conventional church. The original church on this site dated from late 11th/early 12th century.

From here the path takes you on the old road up to **Øvre Wang**, *a former ski resort,* before bringing you down to cross the railway line

1.5km later. After this you continue between the railway line and the road (now the Rv 35) until you cross over onto its LH side 2km later. Here you fork L through gap in fence behind trees and continue down a grassy track to the fjord. Veer R round edge of fjord to campsite, crossing the stream over a plank 'bridge' and enter

3km Sløvika Camping (94/549)

Campsite with huts (CF), open in summer, shop (sells food). [Sløvika Camping, 3520 Jevnaker, tel: 61.31.55.80 (office), 61.31.56.80 (shop), EE.]

Continue ahead through campsite, pass in front of owner's house *(the road is over to your R all the time)*, go over the **Roen bro** *(the bridge over the Sløvikelva, built in 1840)* and reach the road. Cross it (by the bus stop) and go up minor road opposite, climbing continuously. *This is still 'Den bergenske Kongevegen' (the old 'Royal Road').*

After 2.5km, just past **Rodstein** *(a milestone, name indicated on waymark – another cluster of houses)*, KSO ahead up a grassy bank at a junction to short-cut a bend in the road *(handy seat at end)* then turn L and immediately R up road again. Up to this point it is (unfortunately for pilgrims) tarmacked, but hereafter it has a fine gravel surface, like a farm road. You are now at **Sognstoppen** *(285m, i.e. the 'top of the parish').*

After 200m turn L for another short-cut, turning R immediately behind electricity poles, up grassy track. Emerge on road by junction to **Rund** *(390m, L)* and turn L and then fork R immediately up a grassy slope between a house and the road for another short-cut. On returning to road again note waymark pointing to 'Rudstoppen. Gravhaugen' to L. *This is only for your information, though, telling you that the burial mounds are there so do not turn L but continue on road, entering the* kommune *of Gran a few metres later, though there is nothing official to tell you so.* KSO.

After **Heier** *(400m), the cluster of houses ahead,* you are (finally!) at the top of the hill, after which you start to descend, slowly. As you go down to cross the Fv 14 (road) you can see where you are going to, ahead. Cross the Fv 14 just below the cluster of houses at

7km Kittelsrud (101/542)

Continue ahead and then short-cut the next bend by continuing ahead, first up a gravel track and then a grassy slope, rejoining road at top of hill. KSO.

150m later fork L off road down grassy track alongside woods, veering L *(view of Grymyr church at the edge of the fjord to L ahead)*. Turn sharp R at small red house (**Svingen**). KSO at junction with another track, return to road and turn L. Continue down to **Falang Bru** *(a stone bridge dating from 1834)* where you will see two lakes *(Falangstjernene, i.e. 'tarns')*, one to R and then one to L of road. 200m later you come to a fork, **Falangsvegen** (L) and **Gamkinnsvegen** (R). Fork R uphill, pass **Gamkinn** and 2.5km later reach a junction. Turn L up **Gammevegen** and KSO. KSO(L) at fork; *here you have your first view of Granavollen's two 'sister churches' – a sort of 'Feginsbrekken' or Mountjoy.* Pass **Helmen** *(another cluster of houses)*, but before you get to the Fv 33 turn L just below brow of hill, passing to R of two white houses, down to road. Cross over and continue up **Vollgutua** on other side up to the two churches in

9km Granavollen (110/533)

Small community known for its 'sister churches', built side by side: Mariakirke, built 1100, and Nicolaskirke (now used as the parish church), built 1150. There are various explanations as to why two such prominent churches were built so close to each other both in time and space: they were built by two sisters; as churches for a religious order; a name given to them because they form a pair together... The other prominent building is the medieval Steinhuset, though again there are different theories as to its original use: Cistercian monastery; meeting hall for parish priests in the area; episcopal residence when the Bishop of Hamar was travelling through his diocese... Marker stone tells you there are 533km left to Nidaros.

18th-century Gjaestgiveri (guesthouse) opposite church [Granavolden Gjaestergiveri, Granavollen, 2750 Gran, tel: 61.33.00.73, often closed in July]. Ringvold Pensjonat [Ringvoll, 2750 Gran, tel: 61.33.00.74] also has accommodation. Otherwise – to sleep – you can continue for 2km to Tuv.

To leave: facing churches (and with back to Gjaestgiveri) turn L and 800m later reach road (Fv 34). KSO ahead (**Kongevegen**), passing **Tuv**, a farm. *[Gården Tuv, Granavollen, 2750 Gran, tel: 61.33.11.65, EE, CF; rooms plus pilgrim loft, camping possible, also meals if booked ahead.]*
    Continue ahead, KSO(L) at fork, and 1km later at **Alm** KSO. *[Turn R at Alm to sleep at Stastad Pensjonat, 2750 Gran, tel: 61.32.82.90, located near Røysumlina.]* You are still on *Kongevegen, which will take*

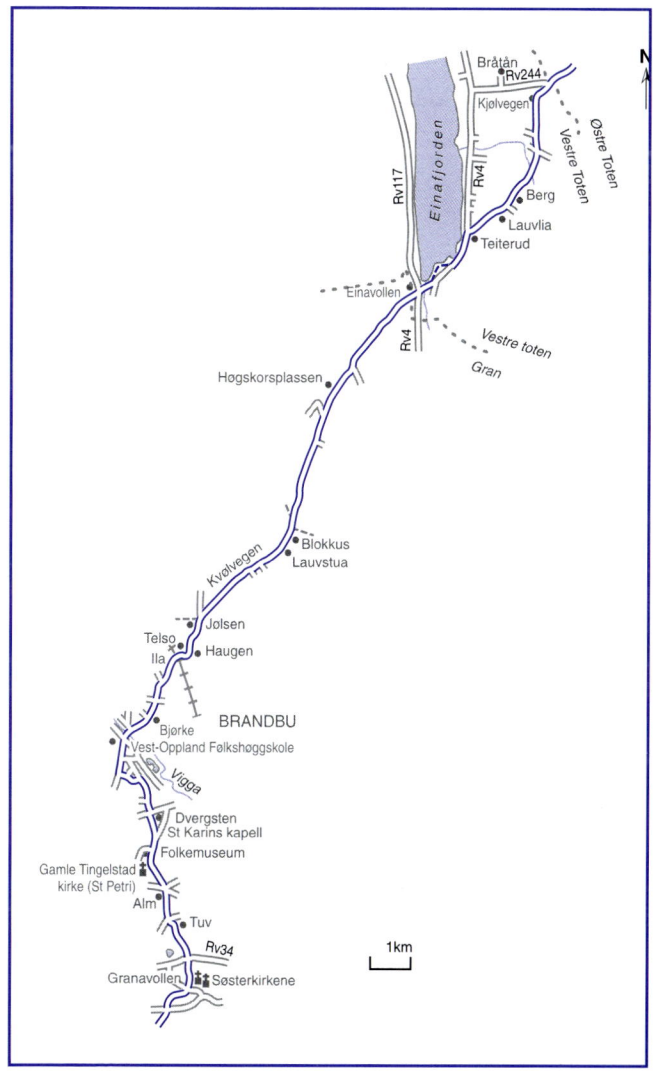

you all the way to Brandbu, after which you continue on Kjølsvegen (i.e. a network of old roads, one after the other). View of Old Tingelstad church (St. Petri) ahead, perched on hill top. KSO to

4km Gamle Tingelstad kirke (114/529)

12th-century Romanesque village church dedicated to St. Peter, built on hilltop in local stone. Splendid views all round. The tower (wooden) dates from 1820, but originally, like the Maria and Nicolas churches, it had a tall spire before it was struck by lightning: note weather-vane, from bow of Viking ship.

Inside there is some of the oldest church furniture in Norway, and it is one of few churches retaining its original interior. Information board in English and Norwegian. To visit: June, July and August, open every day (ask in Hadeland Folkmuseum). At other times ring ahead. New Tinglestad church can be seen to west in valley below.

Gamle Tingelstad church (St. Petri) (Eivind Luthen)

Pass to RH side of church (i.e. with church on your L) and 500m later reach **Hadeland Folkmuseum**. *Worth a visit, and contains a copy of the Dynnastein, a 10th-century rune stone prepared by a mother as a memorial for her daughter, including amongst its images the three wise men (the original is in the Oldsaksamlung, the University of Oslo's Historical Museum). Open June, July, August (brochure in English and Norwegian).*

300m further on, at crossing, KSO *(unless you want to visit the ruins of St. Karin's chapel, 500m to east: turn R if so)*. At bend 50m later KSO (not marked) and continue on farm track. *From here to Brandbu the route runs in a straight line, in effect; useful map of local walks on board on R to give you an idea of area – look for 'Gamle Kongenveg' for your route.*

200–300m later – note burial mounds on R . *This area was well populated in Viking times as it was both fertile and near water (their main means of transport).*

At the top of the hill you have a view of Brandbu below. (On R of track note milestone marked 'MILSTENBAKKE 7 mil fra Kristiania'.)

20m after milestone cross road, KSO on farm road coming from back R. This becomes **Brurbakkvegen** and leads you down to the Rv 240 (the **Grinakerlinna**). Turn L here and 200m later turn R (by driving school and sign to Vestoppland Folkhogskole) down **Augedalsvegen**. KSO along it, veering sharply R near end to cross main road by underpass. Turn L along cycle track, veering R at end *(supermarket on L)* to cross the old **Augedalsbrua** *(bridge)* into the centre of

3km Brandbu (117/526)

Population 1950. More shops, PO, bank on R. Brandbu Hotell opposite (at junction).

Cross road and continue ahead up *Kjølsvegen, which will take you all the way to the fjord at Einavollen 13km later. Its name, 'keel road', refers to its use as an overland short-cut for carrying ships in Viking times.*

KSO uphill and after 7km reach **Blokkus**, *a farm. Snow is not cleared from here onwards in winter or spring. The highest point on route is 600m, after which you descend, until you reach the road (Rv 4) at southern end of the Einafjord.*

13km Einavollen (130/513)

You are now in the kommune of Vestre Tøten.

The next 2.5km is very fiddly as the route weaves about a lot to avoid walking on the very busy Rv 4.

Pilgrim path in Toten (Eivind Luthen)

Turn L along Rv 4 on inside of crash barrier and then go up some wooden steps onto a small FP above the road and // to it, before veering L into the woods. Follow the track down to the fjord, veering R, and return to road 1km later, shortly after passing behind a small snack bar *(open in summer)* at a bus stop. Turn R up farm road *(not waymarked)* and then L and L again through a complex of holiday cabins, veering sharp R at end and then turn L downhill to cross a stream by a wooden bridge. Continue uphill towards two telephone poles ahead by wood, following small red marker posts, and turn L inside edge of wood at top. This brings you out on the road again by another bus stop at a spot marked **Teiterud**. Fork R immediately up a gravelled road and follow it uphill. At **Berg** *(a farm)* pass to L of buildings (waymark on barn) and shortly afterwards *(spot marked Kjølvegen as you are now on this road again)* veer R and KSO. This brings you out, after 3.5km more, at the Rv 244, just past the boundary between Vestre and Østre Tøten (to L on road).

Turn R along Rv 244 for 2km to just past **Tandsaeter** *(i.e. a saeter or summer farm)* and then turn off road down path between the trees, alongside a stream. However, if you want to sleep in **Engen Kloster** you can KSO on the road here for 2.5km. *[Diakonisseklosteret Engen, 2847 Kolbu, tel: 61.16.74.70, EE. Simple accommodation (CF) in Norway's only Lutheran convent, established in 1987; four sung services a day, open to all. Essential to phone in advance.]* Alternatively, you can turn L after **Dyste** (see below).

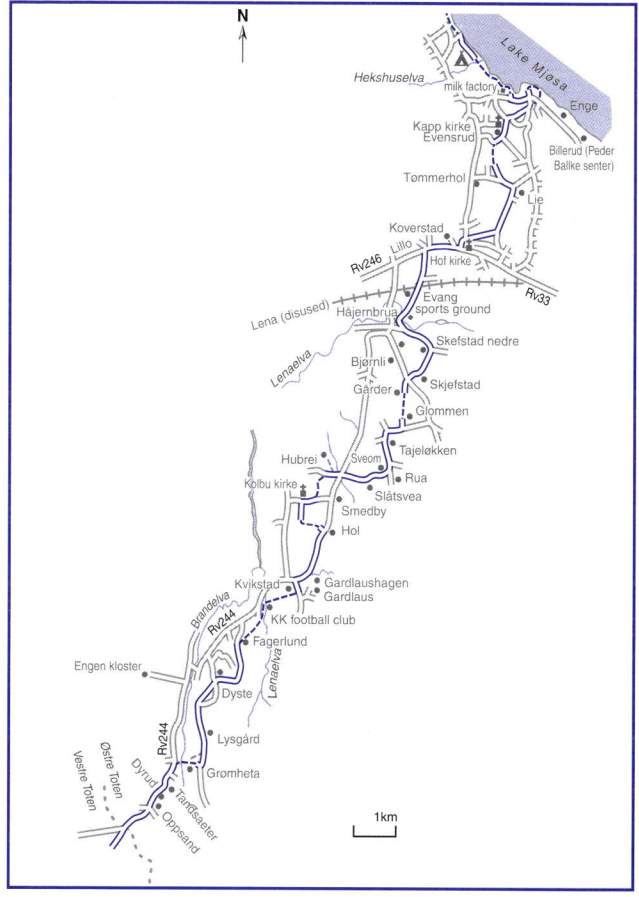

Tøten kommune is too high up to grow corn but produces a lot of potatoes, and as it is also too high for common pests very little chemical treatment is needed either. Carrots and strawberries grown on a large scale in this area.

Go up the hill on the other side of the valley and turn L towards **Grumheten**, from where you will continue on farmroad along the ridge for 2.5km (KSO at **Lysgård**) until you come to a T-junction *(the building opposite the bell tower is marked with the place-name)* at

10km Dyste 400m (140/503)

In front of the two large yellow houses on the left are the remains of the altar from the medieval stave church, pulled down in 1780 because it was unsafe. A wooden statue of St. John and sculptures of other saints from the original church are now in the Oldsakssamlung in Oslo.

[You can also turn L here if you want to sleep at **Engen Kloster** *(the three white buildings with modern, free-standing bell tower visible to L across road in valley)*; after turning L turn L again at petrol station *(supermarket opposite)* and L again on the Rv 244; 400m later turn R uphill marked 'Engen'.]

Turn R here if you want to sleep at **Holthe Gård**, *situated 800m to the east. [Holthe gård, 2847 Kolbu, tel: 61.16.72.10, CF.]* To continue: turn R and then immediately L onto farm road with open fields to both sides. After LH bend turn R alongside fence 200m before farm buildings *(notice says 'Hunder lekker. Velkommen!' ['Dogs playing. Welcome!'] !)*, and when fence turns L KSO ahead across field *(waymark ahead)*, in the direction of the river in the valley ahead. On other side of field veer L on FP, // to field at first, then veering R downhill to a large field. Turn L along its edge and KSO for 1km *(Kolbu ahead on R)*, the river to your R getting gradually closer until you reach Kolbu football club (R) *(marked 'KK 1935 – Kolbu Kameratene')*, shortly before a road.

Turn R between the club house and the pitch and on the other side make your way carefully down through the trees to the river bank, zigzagging L in general, and go through small gate. Ahead of you you will see a wooden bridge (suitable for tractors): cross it, veer L uphill, and at an isolated group of trees by telephone pole continue L along LH side of next field, passing to L of following telephone poles to start with. *This section is fiddly to find too, but in general you are making for the farm ahead of you –* **Kvikstad**.

Turn R at end of field along its edge and 100m later veer L and then

R and go up a mound ahead, veering R to barn. Turn L there along cart track to farm (**Kvikstad**), veering L between barn (brown) and house (white) and then turn R out onto a minor road.

Turn R, then 150m later *(marked 'Fjellby, 1.3')* pass through farmyard and 150m later turn L down grassy lane alongside stream. At end *(farm above you ahead)* turn L over stream then R through field and cross stream again at end.

Continue ahead, passing first to L and then to R of hedge. Join farm road coming from back R and KSO to Rv 244. Turn R and KSO for 1km.

In **Hol** pass burial mound (R, *waymarked*) and then watch out carefully for waymark to L to take you directly to Kolbu church, across the fields *(its green-tipped spire is visible away to the L)*; this brings you out on a track leading down the side of the parish office (R), opposite the church. However, if you miss it, it is not a great deal out of your way to continue to the next road junction and turn L there, to

7km Kolbu kirke (147/496)

Built in 1730 to replace earlier church, with interior decoration by Peder Balke, though this is no longer there.

To continue: with your back to the church turn L (i.e. R if facing it) down gravelled road and 300m later turn R across a field. Turn L along edge of second field, R along farm road and return to the Rv 244.

Turn L 250m later then second R by a garden centre, up a gravelled road. 500m later at T-junction (**Svem**) KSO ahead down cart track through field, veering L, then L again after 500m to join farm track coming from back L. KSO along it.

500m later (farm), after track has become a gravelled road, reach a bend under telegraph wires. KSO ahead along track veering L *(road visible ahead)*. KSO, continuing as gravelled road, to road. Turn L (this is **Tajeløkken**, *splendid views all round on a clear day*) and KSO, following road round for 1km.

At a crossing on the brow of a hill at **Glommen** *(ahead you can see a more main road and forest behind)* turn L down a farm road between buildings and KSO. *From here to Håjenbrua (3km) it is all downhill, straightforward and is a very pleasant walk in good weather, with views over to Lake Mjøsa to the R. (The factory you can see ahead is at Lena.)*

After 1.5km, when you reach a road, cross it and KSO down gravelled road, downhill again, veering R. At a large farm with several barns and houses turn L opposite large red barn with bell tower on top, downhill all the time. When you reach a T-junction at the bottom with a gravelled road, turn L and follow it round until you reach the Rv 244. However, a few yards before it, turn hard R down a gravelled road, passing behind a potato factory (marked 'Norske Potetindustrier Tøten'), veering L. 300m later turn hard R and zigzag down L to cross the

8km Håjenbrua (155/488)

Old stone bridge (1860) over the Lenaelva.

Continue ahead on other side, forking L and L again uphill on farm road. *(Hof church is visible ahead to R.)* When you reach a junction by the factory you have seen ahead of you for several kilometres already *(the path you are crossing is the old railway line but its tracks have now been removed);* KSO ahead, veering R and then L. At end veer round to R at junction with Rv 33 at **Lilo**. Cross road carefully and turn R *(waymark, with an arrow, simply says 'Nidaros'!)*. 500m later turn L uphill then R through carpark to

3km Hof Kirke (158/485)

Along with Balke church, Hof (dedicated to St. Andrew) is the only church in the area in continuous use since the Middle Ages. The first (wooden) church was built sometime after 1021; the present stone building dates from between 1175 and 1200, though it has been enlarged and restored several times, once following a fire in 1508. Several Iron Age grave mounds in its immediate vicinity and several of the buildings in the prestegård nearby are listed. A stone waymark informs you that there are now 474km left to Nidaros, though this is a somewhat optimistic assessment. Information board with useful map. Church open daily June 15th–August 15th, 10.00-19.00.

Pass along lane with church to R and then you will see two sets of waymarks:

a) ahead (marked 'Nidaros');

b) forking R, marked 'Balkekirke'. This leads to another church 8km away, hard R, beyond **Billit**, *i.e. south-east of where you are now. Balke church contains an altarpiece with a painting of St. James (patron saint of pilgrims) standing on the R of the Virgin Mary (to whom the church is dedicated). To visit: phone ahead (tel: 61.16.40.32). A wooden* kalvariegruppe *from the church is now in the Oldtidsammlung in Oslo University's Historical Museum; Christ* *was originally flanked by six other figures, of which four remain, all of them with extraordinarily expressive faces.*

Hof church (author)

To continue to Kapp, Gjøvik, etc.: continue ahead (marked 'Nidaros') through the Hof Prestegård, in front of the house and out the other side onto a farm track between fields. 600m later turn L at T-junction with similar track, KSO(L) at fork and then KSO, ignoring turnings. Pass a first set of farm buildings, but at the second *(Lie, in effect a classic gård with all the buildings round a central 'square' or tun)* pass to L of barn and then KSO(L) ahead. 250m later turn R, veering R *(view of Lake Mjøsa ahead)* and reach the entrance gates to a private house with a turf roof. Watch out carefully for waymark and pass to LH side of their boundary fence alongside field for 20m then turn L along edge of a second field, veering R. Half-way down turn R along wide grassy track (*unwaymarked*), L at end, cross farm road and continue down LH side of long barn. 500m later veer R by houses (Evenrud), pass to RH side of barn and follow lane downhill to road and

7km Kapp kirke (165/478)

Population 1495. From here you do quite a long 'loop' to avoid the main road, taking you down to the lakeside.

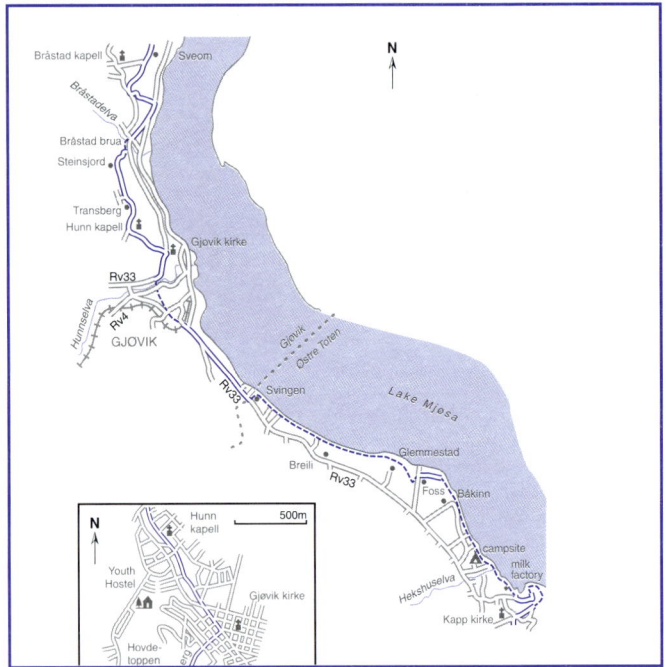

Turn second R here (down minor road marked 'Skriverberget'), then turn L and cross a road down the side of an old people's home, a single-story complex marked 'Kapp eldresenter'.

If you want to sleep in the **Peder Balke Senter** turn R here along road for 1.5km and the centre is on the LH side. You then retrace your steps to this point to continue. *[Peder Balk-senteret, Billerud gård, 2858 Kapp, tel: 61.16.90.75, E. Guesthouse used by church study groups, choirs, walking groups, etc.; pilgrims interested in patchwork will* *appreciate the – literally – hundreds of items used in the centre's soft furnishings.]*

To continue: go towards lake, almost to water's edge, veering R and returning to the road 200m later. Turn R on road then 500m later turn R again beside a supermarket and 250m later L onto a FP/cycle track that veers tround to R near the water.

Pass behind the **Kapp milk factory** *(an older-style brick building)*, turn R and then turn R down LH side of fence along side of field. *(The island to your R is Helgøy i.e. 'Holy Island'; Hamar is across on the other side of the lake.)* Cross the bridge over the **Hekshuselva** *(river)* and continue through the **Hekshusstranda campsite** on the other side. *[Hekshusstranda Camping, 2858 Kapp, tel: 61.16.91.57, shop.]* KSO(R), veer L uphill in woods (i.e. to skirt private property), veer R behind large concrete building. Turn L at junction and then R at next one (well waymarked).

In this area you will see more of the by now familiar black plastic 'caterpillars' (hay bales), many of them some 100m long.

KSO ahead at crossing, KSO(R) at fork, and when you come to the end of a series of holiday huts/cottages continue ahead on a FP (marked 'Tursti') which veers R to take you below the edge of the woods by the lake. *Nes church visible on opposite side of lake.*

Shortly afterwards the path veers L for a while and then turns R into the woods (i.e. path follows lakeside more or less but with an indentation to go round private property).

At the end of the woods (more holiday cottages) turn L onto farm road (this is **Foss**).

When you reach a farm (**Glemmestad**) veer L to pass through farmyard and turn R between fields. Cross two stiles, enter woods and KSO, veering R. After 400m turn R downhill in roughly a straight line, veering L to cross a wooden bridge over a stream some 50m from lake. Continue on FP through trees, // to water. *(Gjøvik visible ahead.)*

When path veers L towards field turn hard R back to path // to water again. When you reach a forest road on L veer L and then turn R onto small FP a little farther away from the lake.

When you reach the next house turn L up small FP *(watch out for mini-waymark)* and veer R, crossing stream and then stile, before returning to path // to lake.

After crossing two more stiles turn L up a wide track *(from where you can see Nordli church above you to L beyond the road)* and then R along edge of field on a cart track, before the waymarks return you to a FP in the woods 400m later. This takes you gradually back to the lakeside. Veer L uphill to cross bridge over stream and stile, cross field, another stile and another bridge. Continue ahead along RH edge of field, veering L uphill beside fence, and cross stile in top LH corner.

Cross bend in gravelled road in front of house and fork L into woods and at end turn R into field and follow its RH edge. *(Road to L is getting closer now.)* Continue ahead through woods but do not follow track right down to water's edge – KSO on higher FP // to lake. FP gradually becomes a wider track, then meets another one at a T-junction. Fork R downhill to lakeside again and turn L along it. Pass behind a house, cross a field and a bridge over a river. Pass behind other houses, pass a jetty, continue on beach and watch out carefully for waymarks to lead you onto broad track further away from but // to water.

Pass junction with track coming from back L *(a big building up on the road has 'Bruktbiler' – 'used cars' – painted in large letters on its red roof)*. KSO. 500m later, at bigger group of houses where woods end, turn L into field, R along its edge and then turn L uphill alongside stream to the Rv 33 in

9km Svingen (174/469)

Suburb of Gjøvik.

Turn R at top *(kiosk opposite)* into **Østre Tøtenveg**, just before the boundary between Tøten and Gjøvik *kommuner*. Continue on road but watch out for traffic as the cycle track doesn't start for 2km yet (till **Bondelia**, *school up on L*).

Shortly after entering the city boundary (industrial estate to L) reach a large junction. KSO, in the direction marked 'Sentrum', still on the cycle track. When this veers L, away from the road, continue on it, pass under railway line and go up slope between factory buildings to **Ringvegen** (ring road). (This is not marked here, but the road ahead of you is **Alfarvegen**.)

Turn R and take the second turn L up **Kirkbyvegen** and at end veer slightly R by bus stop to cross road and go up **Jonas Liesgate** for 20m then continue L up **Kapperudsvegen**, *a long road*. Continue right to the end, passing the waymarked 'Øvre Gjøvik' *(Upper Gjøvik)* and crossing the **Alf Mjøens Veg** until you reach **Teknologivegen** opposite a school. *(Top of Mustad factory visible through trees.)*

Cross over and continue down **Brufosstien**, veering R past sports field and then cross a foot/cycle bridge over the main road (Rv 4). Veer R down to cross FB over the **Hunnselva** *(the old building next to it is* *now the Gjøvik Musikverksted)* and continue ahead up a flight of steps which brings you out on the road above. Cross it to the **Hans Mustad plass**, *where there is a large concrete statue of the industrialist (1837–1918) who made his fame and fortune from the manufacture of fishhooks before diversifying later into other areas.* Turn hard R into **Hans Mustad gate** and KSO along it for 1km until you reach the crossing with **Hunnsveien** *(church opposite).*

3km Gjøvik (177/466)

Population 26,000. Old industrial town on the Hunnselva, where Mustad opened his first factory. Ski centre with Olympic ski-run. All facilities, Youth Hostel [Gjøvik Vandrerhjem Hovedtun, Parkveien, 2800 Gjøvik, tel: 61.17.10.11, EE, CF, see below for directions.] Tourist Office (opposite railway station), trains to Oslo. Frequent daily bus service to Lillehammer stops in Biri, Vingrom (both centre and church) if you need to adopt the 'bus method' for accommodation.

If you decide that you would prefer to continue after Gjøvik on the eastern bank of Lake Mjøsa along the historic route you can go from from here to Hamar (from where the route has also been waymarked since 1997) either by bus or, preferably, on the Skibladner, *the world's oldest paddle-steamer still in operation, which runs a daily service from Gjøvik in the summer months.*

If you want to visit the town, turn R here and follow Hunnsveien downhill, to the shops, railway station, Tourist Office, etc.

To continue: turn L up **Hunnsveien**. (If you want to go to the Youth Hostel, signposted as 'Hovedtun', fork L shortly afterwards into **Prost Blomsgate** and then turn L by an open-air skating rink/diving pool/ice rink up **Parkenvegen** and you will see it on your L.)

Continue up **Hunnsveien** past the cemetery and the *Hunns Kapell (supermarket to L)* and when you get to its end turn R up **Transbergveien**, climbing very steeply uphill. At the top is the

2km Transberg Gjestegård 310m (179/464)

Formerly a café-restaurant, now a hostel for asylum-seekers. Splendid views all round.

Fork R off road down cart track, veering L, and then turn R onto forest track downhill. At white house KSO and at bottom (1.5km later, when road bends round to R) KSO ahead down FP into woods, // to cycle track to R at first. Veer L, in general, downhill, though this section is not well waymarked, until you reach a farm at the bottom and a T-junction with a farm road. *(Waymark to L, marked 'Gammelt Brosted', shows position of former bridge over the Bråstadelva.)* Waymark to R indicates a R turn, after which you turn L onto the road to cross the road bridge over the river. You are now on **Trondhjemsvegen**: KSO at its junction with **Bråstadsgutua**.

2km later and 50m before you reach the Rv 4 turn L up a steep gravel track, beside a stream. At first building at top turn R, then immediately L behind it and then R uphill up wide grassy track through fields. *(Handy seat half way up, with splendid views.)* Pass waymark 'Gravrøyse' and enter woods, veering R uphill round its edge, then veering L into woods. Continue to a four-point junction and (at waymark) fork L along forest track. When you come to a clearing and a track joining from back L KSO downhill *(view of lake ahead)*, veering L.

Cross stream *(a mini-waterfall in bad weather!)* by small house and garage and KSO, veering L. When you reach a crossing in the woods shortly before the track you are on veer L (and by now you can hear the traffic again on the Rv 4 below) fork L.

When you come to a clearing with a house immediately below you to R and a view of the main road and a cafeteria by the lake and houses nearby to it watch out carefully for mini-waymarks as you may find it difficult to follow the path. In general, you are going in more or less a straight line ahead, // to lake, but felled trees make it hard to see very clearly exactly where you are going. Continue ahead, veering very slightly R to enter woods again, where the path goes downhill, veering R to bring you out at the edge of a field. Turn L. Cross bridge over stream ahead and cross next field, going towards top LH corner. Continue on track just inside wood. Cross a grassy area and go down slope towards corner of field below (but remaining above it) then continue ahead to L of line of trees bordering second field on their R *(farm away to R below, near lake).*

At the end turn R and then L onto what is now an obvious track, // to road away to your R. When this turns R downhill over stream, turn L. KSO, first on a path through newly planted trees, then on clear track through forest.

After passing a small yellow concrete building (L) (road close by below you now) and a junction – KSO. When you reach a farm road coming up from back R (**Slettum**) KSO ahead // to the Rv 4 all the time; KSO ahead at next junction and when road bends L KSO(R) down forest track. After farm it becomes gravelled: KSO.

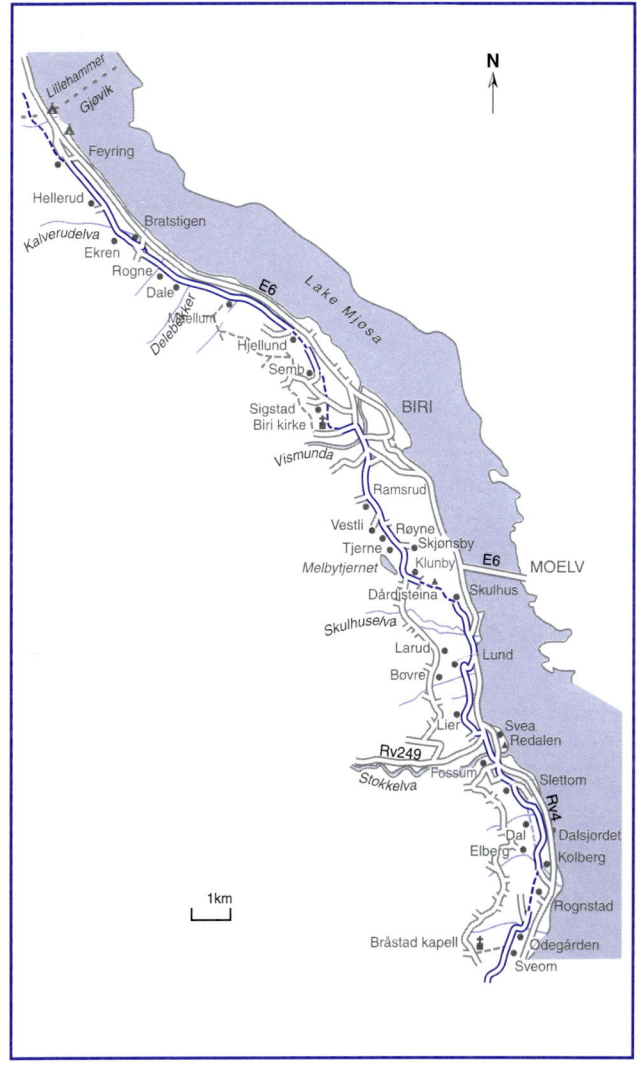

When you leave the trees you can see Ringsaker church (white) across the lake on the other side, by the water's edge, on the historic route via Hamar. Farther to the north is Moelv and then the Mjøsbru, the 1420m long bridge linking the two sides of Lake Mjøsa.

Continue until you join a minor road (**Kollsvegen**) coming from back L and then turn L to cross the bridge over the **Stokkelva**. Turn L along the Rv 249 on other side *(entrance gateway to campsite R)*. *[Sveatranda Camping, 2824 Redalen, tel: 61.18.15.29; campsite with huts as well.]* KSO till you reach a junction where the RV 249 turns L *(shop on R)*. This is

11km Sveen (190/453)

KSO ahead on road. 400m later turn L up flight of wooden steps up bank and fork R up small FP uphill into woods. This takes you in more or less a straight line, climbing steadily all the time. Just before the top, turn L and reach a much wider path. Turn R along it for 300m and join a forest road coming from back R. KSO. KSO(R) at unmarked junction, cross large field on rough cart track, following a series of concrete irrigation points and veer R, just before you reach the woods, downhill. KSO at next junction and continue until you reach the Rv 4 in

3km Smedmogrenda (193/450

Continue ahead along **Smedmovegen** *(marked 'Blindveg', i.e. 'no exit')* and 200m later turn R downhill to cross the old bridge (beside the new one) over the **Skulhuselva**. (You are now on **Skulhusvegen**.) Turn L on other side alongside river and KSO(R) at fork. KSO(L) at junction with **Skulhusvoa**, uphill towards woods.

400m later, opposite house no. 103, fork L into woods up clear forest track. KSO(R) when ground levels out a little and then continue uphill ahead, passing waymark marked 'Dårdi Stein', after which you veer R. *The origin of its name is uncertain but tradition has it that the stone moved when the bells of Ringsaker church were rung.*

Continue to climb steeply. Just before the top, when you emerge from the woods, a small notice marked 'Utsikt' ('viewpoint') indicates a hard R turn up a small FP. If you take this, retrace your steps to the main path again afterwards. At top, veer R round edge of field, passing **Kleivstuggua** *(a small house)* to road at

3km Klunby (196/447)

Turn R on road then turn R off road onto area of cleared trees, veering L uphill. 200m later go through small gate and pass to LH side of fence along side of field and cross stile at end. Veer L along to RH side of another fence and reach another stile. Cross it and continue, veering R *(view of small lake, Melbytjernet, ahead across road)*. After this it is not clear from the waymarks what you should do, but make your way across the field or along its edge to road (100m) and turn R. KSO, ignoring turns, downhill, for 2.5km, passing several farms.

At the bottom, 200m past sports ground, is the **Domsteinslett** *(Domstein Plain)*, with an information board in both Norwegian and English, explaining that these were rings or squares of stones, graves from the period of the birth of Christ to 700 AD. The body of the dead person (who would have been an important one) was first cremated and then the remains collected and buried with a ring of 7, 9 or 13 stones.

Turn L here into **Snippvegen** and turn L at the end into **Birivegen** in

3km Biri (199/444)

Shops, bank, PO, café, campsite (in summer) and Gjestgiveri.

Continue ahead to cross bridge over the river **Vismunda** and then turn L by police station up Øverbydsvegen. Just before **Biri church** (1km) fork R up gravelled lane to house then continue ahead up wide grassy track between trees, which brings you to the church. Continue along RH side of church yard and continue ahead, passing to L of **Sigstad Gård** *(stone waymark informs you that there are now 424km left to Nidaros, though this time the calculation errs on the pessimistic side)* between fences and then turn R at next set of buildings onto gravelled road leading to woods. 500m later fork R onto local waymarked forest path (marked 'Skrinnhagen 1.6'), leading through recently planted trees to FB over small lake. Do not cross there, however, but continue to small hut and ford stream (waymark on other side) and turn R down grassy track.

300m later turn L onto similar track, which leads to a road. Cross over *(from here the pilgrimsleden coincides for a while with a local FP marked in red and blue)* and continue along wide FP uphill along side of field and up bank to farm (**Semb**). Turn R downhill along farm road alongside woods on a ridge with open vistas over to the lake. *(Handy seat half-way along.)* Veer L to continue higher up into woods (still // to lake) along line of telegraph poles and veer L again, turn R downhill on small FP alongside stream and then veer slightly L. Cross farm road and continue ahead on other side *(here the local walk turns L uphill)*, veering slightly L and then turn L uphill to telegraph poles, continuing on path underneath (i.e. in same direction as) them. Cross FB over stream and a stile and continue ahead *(lake is over to RH side all the time)*.

When you get to a fence at the end of wood (house ahead) turn R and immediately L alongside fence along LH edge of field, cross stile at end and veer R through trees. Turn L along LH edge of lower of two fields (waymark ahead at end). *Brøttum church is now visible part-way up hillside on other side of lake.*

At end of field veer L uphill (crossing fence if necessary) up cart track coming from back R. Cross another track 200m later and KSO on clear forest track.

400m later, in clearing, turn R downhill on FP and then L 100m later onto another one which picks up the line of telegraph poles again. Cross FB over stream and then turn R, pass pond (on L) and turn L alongside field (house to R) and continue to farm road. Turn L (no waymark) and 250m later cross stream and turn L onto **Biristrandvegen**.

7km Maellum Gård (208/435)

KSO for 2.5km to **Bratstigen** then fork R (between red barn and small grey house) down grassy lane between fences (the old road) and go through small gate, continue on FP between trees, veering R and then L along edge of field to minor road. Turn L uphill and return to **Biristrandvegen** 400m later. *(This section is simply playing 'hide and seek' with the road.)*

Turn R for 300m and just past supermarket fork R down slope to continue between wood to bridge 300m later over the **Kalverudelva**. Turn L on other side of bridge up gravelled lane, veering R, and continue ahead up FP (// to road) and then on minor road coming from R and turn R between buildings to mound marked with waymark 'Kalverudbakken – Husmannsplass'. Continue ahead to rejoin road, via 'kink' in old road, at a road junction at

4.5km Hellerud 203m (210.5/432.5)

A group of buildings, one marked 'Strandheim', another 'Nordgaard'.

Cross **Åsroveien**, continue up gravel track and pass between farm buildings and return to road again 1.5km later.

Turn L up farm road *(farm is **Feiring**)* by house no. 802 (waymark missing), pass under telegraph wires and turn R along side of hill on small FP. Go through gate, KSO ahead in straight line to a second gate, pass to RH side of house and turn R down gravelled road, veering L to junction 150m later. Turn L uphill and then take lower of two RH turns, downhill to farm. Continue ahead on gravelled road coming from your R, continue ahead, passing between farm buildings (mini-waymark) to next farm (**Bjørnstad**, 169m), signposted 'Birisentrum 14.3, Åsroveien 2.8', where river runs into small lake.

Continue ahead in a straight line through farm buildings and KSO ahead on gravelled lane *(Lillehammer visible ahead on east side of lake, Vingrom church on west)*. Veer L uphill by barn and then fork R immediately down clear FP (marked 'Pilegrimsleden'), passing small lake on L. Continue through woods, passing waymark 'Kullgrop', keeping gulley to L and cross FB over the

2.5km Bjørnstadelva (213/430)

> *Boundary between Gjøvik and Lillehammer kommuner. [Two campsites, both by the Mjøsa, on other side of E6: Stranda Camping, 2823 Biristrand, tel: 61.18.46.72, CF, shop; Furuodden Camping, 2823 Biristrand, 61.26.21.10, shop, CF.]*

Turn R on other side, uphill. Turn L along field in front of houses (this is **Sveen**, 191m) and turn L up farm road, veering behind barn and then continuing straight ahead to a forest track leading into woods, where you fork R through gate 20m later onto small FP downhill. Veer R and then L, track becoming wider, leading down to pass behind a farm (**Audenhus**). Cross gravelled road and continue ahead on FP through trees, cross stream, continue on track coming from back R. Take L fork uphill, turn R on gravelled road coming from L and turn R again by house no. 215. Pass above farm and turn R at T-junction. Veer L round enclosure for horses and KSO(L) at fork, passing another farm, veering R and then L. KSO ahead at crossing *(Vingrom visible to R below)*, veering L through farmyard at **Jevne**; *Bohemian glassblowers settled here with their families in the 1770s and set up a thriving glassworks which lasted until 1835, accounting for south German names in the area.* Turn R onto farm road. Follow this down, veering R, to reach the Rv 250 above

3km Vingrom (216/427)

The path does not actually take you into the centre of Vingrom but if you want to buy food (supermarket) or take a bus to Lillehammer (to sleep) turn R downhill and R again (400m each way). [Bakke Camping, 2607 Vingrom, tel: 61.26.21.49; campsite with huts as well.]

Otherwise – to continue, cross road and fork R down small FP,

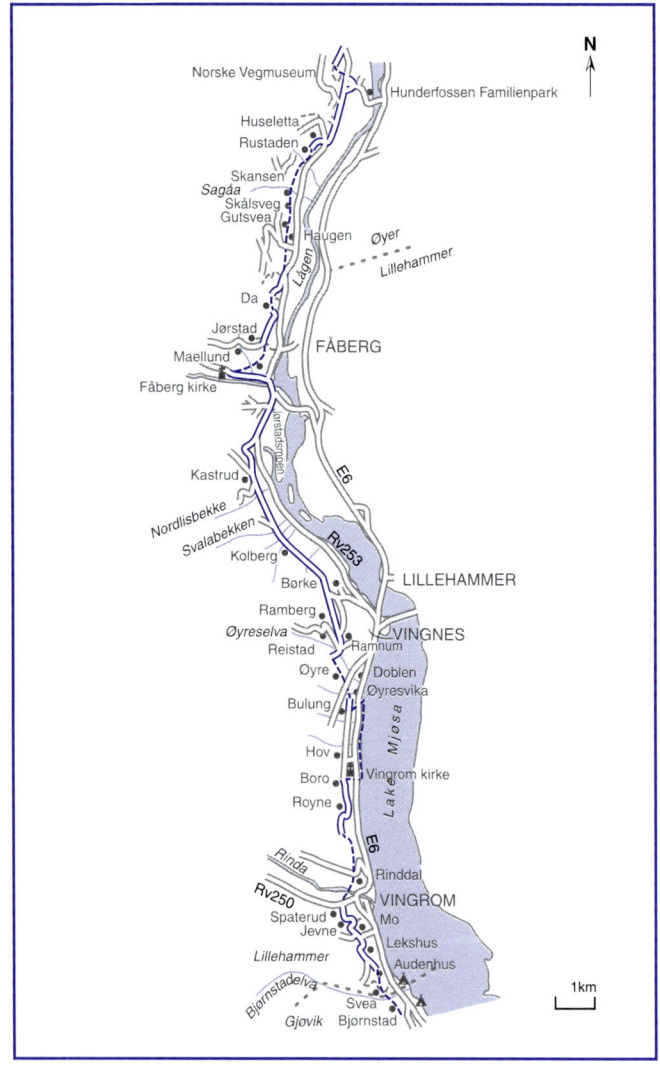

N

Norske Vegmuseum

Hunderfossen Familienpark

Huseletta
Rustaden

Skansen
Sagåa
Skålsveg
Gutsvea
Haugen   Øyer
                   Lillehammer

Lågen

Da

Jørstad

Maellund   FÅBERG

Fåberg kirke

Kastrud

Nordlisbekke
Svalabekken
Kolberg

Børke   LILLEHAMMER

Ramberg
Øyreselva   VINGNES
Reistad   Ramnum

Oyre   Doblen
             Øyresvika
Bulung

Hov   *Lake Mjøsa*

Boro   Vingrom kirke

Royne

Rinda
Rv250   Rinddal   E6
             VINGROM
Spaterud   Mo
Jevne
Lillehammer   Lekshus
             Audenhus
Bjørnstadelva
Gjøvik   Svea
             Bjørnstad

1km

veering L to join wider track; fork R downhill and then veer R along edge of field. Cross a minor road and contine to cross FB over river **Rinda**; *the bridge is very solid but may in fact be difficult to climb up onto – and off again – with a heavy rucksack as it does not actually touch the ground on either side of the river.*

On other side take centre of three RH options and 20m later turn L and then R onto track coming from the L. 50m later veer L round side of hill (up and down), enter woods and 150m later turn L uphill through gate, veering L all the time to the top (**Rindal**). Turn L onto the road and then turn R between buildings, veering round to road at the top at a bend.

Continue downhill for 250m then, after a road fork to L, fork L uphill on a small FP into woods. When you reach a gap by some houses turn R on the level then continue uphill and turn R onto much wider track through woods. Pass waymark with 'kilde' on it to R *(reference to a spring)* and continue through woods, undulating. At end KSO on FP to L of fence above house. *Lillehammer is now visible on other side of lake, though the waymarked route on this side of the Mjøsa does not take you there but continues past it on the western bank.*

Join gravelled lane coming from back R, and 250m after house fork R into woods on a clear FP; *the object of this detour is to visit a place marked 'Røyne', the site of a settlement from the 14th to 17th centuries.* 200m later there are two waymarks – one says 'Røyne', the other indicates a LH turn back onto the lane at a gateway. Turn R onto it and follow it downhill (1km). Just after it joins another track coming from back R there are two more waymarks together again: a) *'Røyne/Kirkested' indicates the site of its 15th-century church*; b) indicates a RH turn across a field down to the road where you turn L to

4km Vingrom Kirke (220/423)

Church built in 1908. Buses to Lillehammer (otherwise you will find it easier to wait till you reach Jørstadmoen).

a) Turn L along road to visit church.

b) To continue: turn L and then immediately R to cross the E6 via underpass, turn L and walk along the side of the lake (with the E6 on your L) for 2.5km. The path is partly a vehicle track, partly small FP. When you get near the end look ahead, L, and you will see a long expanse of white fencing; the break in the middle is where you will shortly turn uphill off the road.

To recross the E6 turn L under the second underpass. Turn L on other side initially and 200m later turn R steeply uphill on gravelled road through residential area.

From here you climb up to pass behind the 'lump' you can see on the skyline to go directly to Fåberg Kirke. (So if you want to walk into Lillehammer, to sleep, for example, KSO on the road here, turn R to cross the first road bridge over the lake, turn L up cycle track at end (the **Vintabrøita**) and R under the railway line to Lillehammer church. After that you may find it easier to continue your journey along the east side of the **Lågen**; if not, recross the old bridge and retrace your steps. Alternatively you can wait until *** below.)

At the top turn hard L onto another road and 150m later turn R through a small gate, turn R initially and then veer R up FP through trees. Pass above farms (on your R) and then turn L up flight of steps by fence to farm road. Turn R along it and KSO ahead (L) at bend in grassy forest track uphill. 250m later fork R onto path through woods, turn R down edge of field and 20m later L down clear FP. Go through gates, cross FP and turn L uphill on other side (**Øyresvegen**).

Turn R at junction opposite house no. 155, L into **Saksmundalsvegen** and 200m later fork L down **Ravnumsvegen**. (From **Heimtunvegen**,*** to the R at this junction, there are hourly local buses into Lillehammer; you could therefore wait till this point to enter the town and return retracing your steps the following morning, except for Sundays.) KSO along **Ravnumsvegen**, for 1km, ignoring turns. Turn L at end then KSO(L) along **Kasterudsvegen** for 4.5km *(view of Lillehammer Olympic ski-jumps opposite)*. As you walk you can see up the valley to where you will be going next, continuing ahead at road junction, until you reach the military base at

9km Jørstadmoen (229/414)

Population 551. There is also a regular bus service from here into Lillehammer.

Turn L along the Rv 253 and KSO for 1.8km (shop part-way along on L). Go over wooden bridge, turn R under Rv 255 and L on other side to cross metal bridge over the river **Gausa**.

(However, if you decide now that you would like to continue on the other (eastern) bank of the **Lågen** you can do so from here by keeping straight on ahead at this point for 800m and crossing the road bridge over the Lågen at **Fåberg** *(supermarket on other side)*. Continue on road for 300m to where the PL coming from Lillehammer crosses it, from the **Smerudstuguvegen** (on your R) over to the **Thomas Jørstadsveg** *(marked 'Fåberg Snyttehall')* to L and continue as described on page 79.)

Otherwise – after crossing the **Gausa** – turn L up the **Garverberget** for 1km towards

3km Fåberg Kirke (232/411)

Unlike most of the churches you have seen so far this one is bright red and rather squat; it was erected in 1727 to replace a 12th-century stave church. Next to it there is a tall rune stone dating from 1050; a panel painting of St. Peter from its medieval altarpiece and its main door are now in the University of Oslo's Historical Museum.

At bus stop opposite church fork R up a FP uphill marked 'Kultursti' – i.e. a local footpath, this one waymarked with an animal logo – and which you follow for the next 3km. Fork R up gravelled lane and continue ahead up small but clear FP, veering R through gate up along side of hillside in the direction of the **Lågen** to east *(i.e. the water to your L is now a river; Lake Mjøsa ends at Lillehammer)*.

Pass large burial mound (R, 'Gamleveifar' waymarks) and **Gamlegården Jørstad**, *site of Iron Age farm with seven buildings – an administrative centre where the 'ting' or parliament was held.*

Join gravelled road coming from back L and KSO at **Søre Jørstad** *(buildings moved here in 1710)*. Go towards farm but turn L through small gate before entering yard, pass to L of buildings alongside fence and under HT cables, veering L downhill to wide gravel track leading into woods.

At fork – both options gated – take LH track and continue until you reach a farm (**Dal nedre**, 301m) and a road. Cross over and fork L uphill on other side. Go through two gates, pass information board about **Dalsgårdene** *(i.e. farms; Fåberg sentrum visible across Lågen to R)*. Reach another farm, continue ahead, passing to R of it and then continue up FP uphill into woods. Continue along LH edge of field below (**Dal øvre**), veering L and immediately R through gate marked 'Lukk Grinda' ('close the gate') uphill up grassy track veering R to information board about Viking farms at Dal and continue ahead on FP.

500m after farm, in a depression with very large square boulder to R, the 'Kultursti' and the *pilegrimsleden* part company and you continue through the woods for 3.5km to **Huseletta** *(a farm)* in roughly a straight line all the time – but watch out carefully for the waymarks.

Fork L and continue through the trees to pick up a FP (mini-waymark) which continues directly ahead to R of tractor track, becoming clearer as it enters woods, climbing steeply. Cross stile at top, veer slightly L uphill again at clearing and when it starts to descend fork R back into the woods again. Continue to climb steadily, veering L all the time, before turning hard R to pick up track coming up from below, which you turn R along (no waymark) downhill. Join a gravel track coming from L and then turn L up another one, 60m later.

Continue along it, KSO ahead when track joins from back R and in small clearing 500m later with LH fork, KSO(R) ahead back into woods, track becoming clearer as you go. At fork by farm (R, **Skansen**) fork L onto FP, join track coming from R 100m later and KSO, in more or less a straight line all the time. Cross wide bridge over the **Sagåa** and KSO.

Pass two small holiday cabins, cross gravelled road 400m later, cross FB over **Kroktjernbekken**, pass waymark 'Husmansplass' and 100m later fork L at junction. KSO at crossing and continue ahead, gently downhill all the time. KSO(L) at junction and veer L ahead uphill in clearing. Enter woods, veering R downhill to join track coming from L (uphill). Turn R downhill, veering L.

Cross stile, continue ahead towards farm road *(the farm to R is* **Huseletta***)* and KSO downhill ahead through wood to the road (Fv 253). Turn L along it for 1km. There is, in fact, a small FP running // to it, a few metres to your L and waymarked, but unless there is a lot of traffic it is easier to walk on the road. When this path returns you to the tarmac turn R (or cross over if you were on the FP) down side of wood and 100m later turn L onto wide track through them, returning you once more to the road opposite the **Hunderfossen Bob-og-Åkebane [bob-sleigh] Stadium** opposite.

Continue on wide track just inside wood to R of road and shortly afterwards fork R down wide track that veers R to another road opposite entrance to the **Hunderfossen Familiepark**, *a theme park with somewhat gaudy buildings that is one of Norway's most-visited attractions*. Cross over onto FP into woods, leading you into the grounds of the museum adjoining it, the

7.5km Norske Vegmuseum (239.5/403.5)

Road museum, open all year from 10.00 to 15.00 except Mondays (longer hours in summer), free admission, café.

The next section is very fiddly, designed simply to keep you off the tarmac at all costs for 2km. You may, in fact, find it just as easy to simply continue on the road after leaving the museum grounds – not much

Detail from altarpiece in Ringsaker church: nativity scene (photo: Eivind Luthen)

Buildings in Meldal Bygningmuseum (photo: author)

Stabbur, Frøhaug gård (photo: author)

traffic – and stay on it for 2km until you turn R off it at **Rybakken** (the first time you turn right, so you will see the waymarks).

Otherwise – veer R past museum's entrance and then pass to L of it on path marked 'Friluftmuseet'. At the very end pass to L of the **Høydalsmo Vegstasjon** (a red building) and return to road (on your L).

Cross over, fork L into woods and 40m later fork L up FP to skirt large field ahead. *Øyer sentrum is now visible on the other side of the river.* Keep to LH side of fence, after which you continue up forest track. Reach waymark with 'Edellovskog' on it and continue ahead (L) on FP // to field, going through gate, turning R, crossing stile and continuing down edge of fields to cross stile into wood and turn L inside. *(In this section you leave the* kommune *of Lillehammer and enter that of Øyer.)*

200m later reach farm road and continue (L) along it, then turn R and pass to L of barn. Join a gravelled lane coming from back R and KSO, // to road below. Go through gate and KSO in straight line, becoming a FP, and after 1.5km cross stile and turn R back to road.

Turn L along road for 500m, passing **Rybakken hut** and **caravan site**. Turn R along gravelled lane between woods and 100m later fork L onto a clear FP which undulates through woods. At crossing 800m later (near railway line) fork (do not turn) L onto FP which continues in more or less a straight line uphill *(Øyer church visible to R from clearing).*

100m before you reach a scrap yard (visible through trees ahead) turn R onto FP downhill, veering L and then continue ahead (L) onto farm road coming from back R. Turn R 300m later to cross road bridge (use LH side) over the **Lågen**.

7.5km Tingberg (Øyer kirke) (247/396)

Continue on pavement on other side, down slope ahead (not R), turn L on road *(petrol station opposite has food shop)* and then turn R *(café on road to L)* up road *(marked 'Øyer Kirke, Skåden Gård 4, Hoven 3.5')*. Turn L up **Klokkerstien** *('Sexton's path')*, veering R uphill and then, by house no. 12, go up steep bank (short-cutting bends) and turn R along lane at top, veering L and then R, emerging on road at

1km Øyer kirke (248/395)

Original stave church was burnt down in 1722 and the new building aleady in place by 1725. Inside, the altarpiece, pulpit and ornamental work in the choir are by Bjørn Bjørnson Olstad, one of the first to work in the acanthus style.

Turn L over bridge and fork L up farm road to **Svingen** *(a farm)*. Then

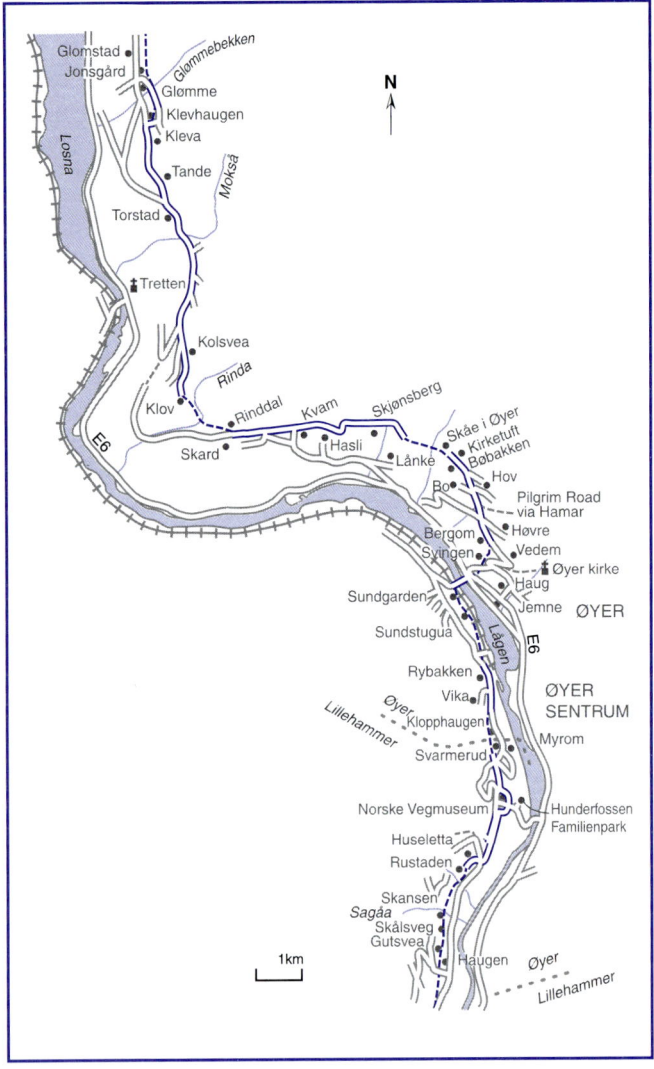

turn L onto BV and follow it for 1km. *On the way you will meet the pilgrim road coming from Hamar along the east side of the Mjøsa, which joins the road you are on at a farm (R) just before the turning (L) to Bo, though there is no sign to indicate this.* Pass the site of the medieval church at *Skåe* and reach the farm at Skåe i Øyer.

Skåe i Øyer to Hjerkinn

3km Skåe i Øyer 510m (251/392)

See page 82 for description.

Continue through the farmyard and out the other side along grassy lane (R) ahead and go downhill. Fork L before bend to cross bridge over river. Turn L on other side, veering R round side of hill (**Lånkahaugen**); this is **Tjodvegen** again. *Waymark at crossing at top indicates 'Gravfeld' and 'Lånkahauget'; this area is rich in Iron Age burial mounds and there are 15 between here and Skjønsberg.* KSO to end of wood and go through gate.

Cross field ahead and continue along top side of several more until you reach **Skjønsberg** *(490m, a farm 2km from Skåe)*. Pass to L of it and veer R onto farm road which leads to a local road 200m later.

800m later, at bend, KSO down grassy track ahead, leading to woods, returning to road shortly afterwards. Turn R downhill and shortly before junction at bottom fork R up clear track uphill into woods, following the line of the hillside. Cross track coming up from road (L) and continue on other side, through woods. Cross field above **Kvam** *(358m; in the 16th century there was a two-storey building straddling the route, believed to have provided shelter for pilgrims)*, veering R in direction of the two prominent hills ahead of you.

Ford stream and continue alongside LH side of fence. Cross stile and KSO on grassy track coming from back L. Continue uphill alongside river and 400m after changing sides turn hard L up FP, veering R, then 200m later fork L uphill up another FP (you are still on the **Tjodveg**).

Pass to L of farm *(**Rindal**, 430m)* at top, after which you descend. Turn R on track coming from L. Fork L onto small FP veering R through trees then turn L to pass to LH side (i.e. below) farm (**Kløv**). Cross road and fork R over FB back into woods again, alongside old wall, till you reach a farm road (just below **Kølsvea** – farm). Turn L.

Tretten visible to L below. The river Lågen has now emptied into a lake, the Losna, before becoming a river again after Fåvang.

KSO(R) along another road coming from back L and reach a local road. Turn R uphill for 1.5km to

9km Kjørkehaugen 505m (260/383)

Large mound to RH side of road, surrounded by trees, with prominent base of ruined church. A listed site, protected by a wall, with bell tower over gate, altar. There was a church here till it was moved to Tretten in 1720; the original one was wooden, while the medieval stone church was superseded by another wooden one in 1580s. Monument put up in 1954. Prestegård *is on LH side of road.*

Continue on road for 500m then fork R down FP, just after farm road on L. Turn R 300m later to farm (**Tårstad**), turn R up farm road to local road, cross over and continue up gravelled road to **Tande**. Turn L just below it, to pass to L of it onto cart track. KSO(R) at fork then continue ahead up through open woodland and fields for 1km to **Klaer**. Pass through farmyard, to L of barn ahead, and KSO to road junction (400m).

Turn R (signposted 'Østfjellsvegen' – the second time you have seen this) and 100m later, by cattlegrid, turn L onto FP into the woods. This goes in roughly a straight line (not too badly waymarked), then downhill, before veering R and then L to cross Glommabekken.

Veer L up bank on other side, continue on FP to RH side of fence, cross stile, turn L onto grassy track and then R up towards fence below very large rocks. Path takes you up over rocks and ahead onto gradually clearer track (// to lake to R below). Go through stile, continue along flank of hill, then veer L via another stile into woods, veering then forking L, leaving woods at end via stile.

Accommodation is available here at **Glomstad**, *a farm 200m below the route to the L, and a small sign board points you to a second stile to L, which you cross and turn R down side of field and through trees. [Glomstad Gård og Penjonsat, 2635 Tretten, tel: 61.27.62.57; meals available if reserved ahead.]* Otherwise, to continue, KSO ahead, veering R past stone sheep pen to cross another stile into the woods. KSO ahead, ignoring turns, cross stile at end, continue ahead to cross forest track, cross another stile and veer L and then R downhill alongside trees and reach gravelled road via cart track. This is **Enge**.

Turn R and cross old bridge over river *(impressive waterfalls in spring)* and fork L *(RH option marked 'Veslesete-vegen')*. Continue through farm and 100m later, at **Vedem** (491m), turn L over stile by concrete silo and veer R down hill on farm road. This is the **Kongveien**. **Mageli Camping** *visible to L below. [Mageli Camping, 2635 Tretten, tel: 61.27.63.22.]*

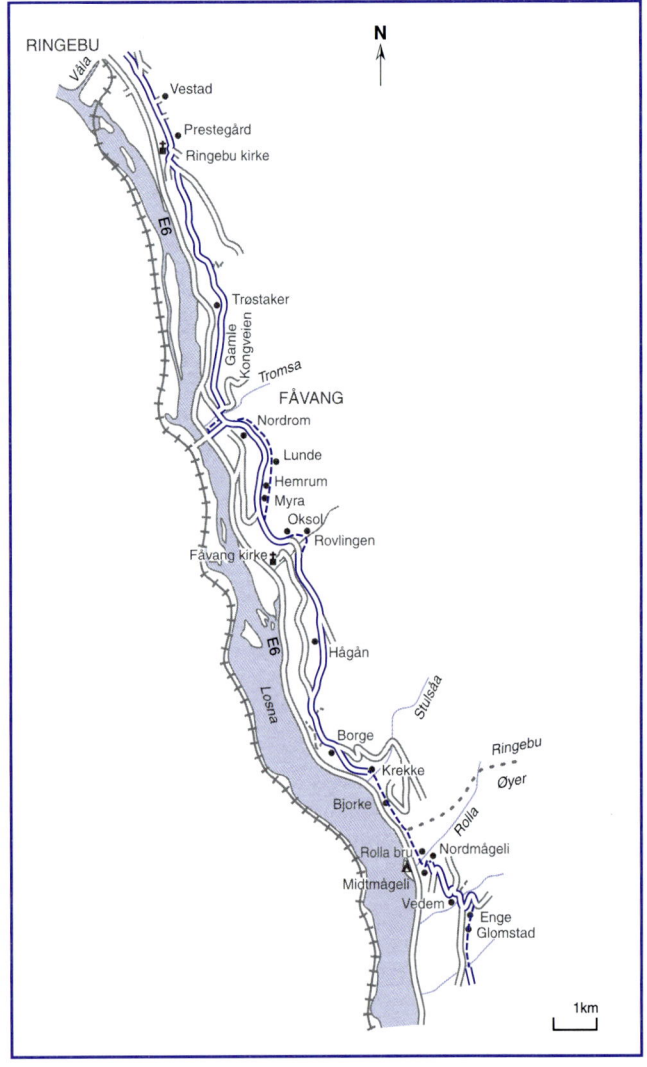

Rollabru, bridge near the border between Øyer and Ringebu   (author)

KSO, zigzagging L and then R downhill. Near end, level with campsite below, veer L downhill towards road by second farm (**Nord-Mågåli**), cross it and continue through field to another stile. Continue steeply downhill in second field, veering R towards two very large rocks in a depression. *(Campsite office is directly below you now)*, veering L through stile and R to cross the bridge over the river **Rolla**.

4km Rollabru 225m (264/379)

Listed stone bridge, built 1829 to replace former wooden one.

KSO on other side, ignoring turnings to L and R, climbing steadily. *This is the old Kongvei to Trondheim*. After 1km (not marked) you leave Øyer and enter Ringebu *kommune* at a height of 300m. At first the track is quite wide but it becomes increasingly narrow, reduced to a very small FP as you continue downhill. *Very few waymarks.*

300–400m after crossing stile turn R onto much clearer and wider track alongside fence *(road nearby below L)*, crossing a forest road coming from back R and fork R ahead uphill again.

When you get near a farm (below L, **Bjørje** – 2km from Rollabru) pass above it, forking R uphill up FP and then forking L. From here for the next 2km you skirt several farms, passing above (to the R) of them on a combination of (well-waymarked) FPs, grassy tracks and farm roads, crossing the FBs over the **Stulsåa** and three stiles along the way. When you reach a local road at **Borgen** turn hard R then then up FP (the **Sminhaugen**) and then L again at clear forest track // to river. Take the middle of three tracks/options at junction, R at next and continue to climb in step-like sections a sort of wide, rocky 'staircase'. Cross tall ladder-stile (1km) later at farm and turn L up along fence. *(N.B. similar but not identical waymarks are for another local walk that does not coincide with pilegrimsleden all the time.)*

200m later reach farm road, turn L and 200m later fork R between farm buildings uphill, veering L round side of hill and onto FP through woods. Cross stile at end, pick up track (R), pass below farm buildings and continue ahead (R) up grassy lane leading to farm road. KSO ahead downhill for 100m then fork L over stile onto banked-up lane leading down to a local road by a farm (**Amrud**). Cross road and go down FP, cross stream and turn L along it. Continue on old walled lane leading to woods and then open woodland, reaching farm road from back L 1km later. Continue ahead to local road and turn R (the Fv 375) for 2.5km, a quiet rural road with little traffic. Pass **Bråstad** and several other farms along the way.

When you reach a double road junction (both with signposts) continue ahead (marked 'Fåvang 5'). *Its heavily restored stave church, brown with a white spire, is visible below L.*

From here decide what you want to do next as the waymarked route takes you off the road, for the sake of it, it would seem, passing to the R above three farms (Hemran, Lunde and Nordrom) to approach the bridge over the river Tromsa from above. The first detour off the road is steep but easy enough to follow while the second is extremely fiddly, with constant changes of direction and is not well waymarked either.

For the first detour turn R off the road 100m after the junctions with the signposts, steeply uphill and then turn L along a grassy lane coming from field on R. Cross stile with field at end, continue along its RH edge to cross another and turn L to cross bridge over a small river *(R turn is to **Røvlingen**)*. Continue ahead (R) for 200m back towards the road to Fåvang but then turn R uphill up a ladder into the forest and then R through trees on a very small FP at first which becomes wider and clearer as you go. Cross stile at clearing and veer L downhill to return to the road *(only some 800m after you first left it!)*.

Continue a short distance and after a bend by a 60kph sign you will see a waymark telling you to turn R up a very small FP uphill. As indicated, this is so complicated as to not be worth the trouble, so it is suggested that you continue on the road here *(very little traffic)*, downhill all the way into the centre of

15km Fåvang (279/364)

Population 696. Two supermarkets, PO, bank (with cash dispenser), café and other shops, railway station (Oslo–Trondheim line). [Accommodation available at Tromsnes Gård, a historic farm to north of town centre, 300m off route: Tromsnes Gård, 2634 Fåvang, tel: 61.28.22.76.]

The road you came in on (**Fåvangvegen**) brings you into the town's square, with the shops. To return to the waymarked route turn R up **Fossvegen** (signposted 'Tromsbrua 0.3'). Veer L uphill and 300m later cross the new wooden bridge *(built in 1997) high above the river Tromsa, with a dramatic waterfall to your R. This bridge replaces a much older one, in the same position, built as early as 1799, and main road traffic used it until as late as 1860.*

Continue ahead to the road on the other side, KSO ahead and continue up **Kongsvegen**, which you stay on for the next 7km, all the way to Ringebu stave church. Pass waymark indicating burial mounds 20m to L and KSO to top of hill. Then, when the road bends round to the R (to become the **Furubakken**) KSO ahead down a forest road; this is Gamle Kongsvegen, 7km of easy walking to Ringebu stave church.

Pass a shooting range (R) and a waymark 'Kollgrup' *(indicating a place where charcoal used to be prepared)* and KSO. After 3km you will pass close to **Trøstaker gård**, *where accommodation is available: turn L at U-bend, though if you miss it it doesn't matter as there is a sign some 200m later. [Trøstaker Gård, 2634 Fåvang, tel: 61.28.26.72, EE, CF.]* After crossing the stream by **Brandstadmoen** (R) fork L. Veer R to cross bridge over the **Brandstadelva**.

7.5km Ringebu stavkirke (286.5/3567.5)

The only stave church on the pilgrimsleden. Built and rebuilt several times, the first church to be mentioned in records dates from 1360, though archaeological investigations undertaken at the time of major restoration work to the church in 1980–81 not only unearthed the largest collection of 11th- and 12th-century coins in Norway, many of them thought to have been donations left by pilgrims, but also revealed that the original building probably dates back to the early 12th century. Inside

Ringebu stave church (author)

The church is open to visitors every day from the beginning of June to mid-September and guided tours are available. 200m to the L of the church (as you arrive) is Gildesvollen (waymarked), a meeting hall for the 13th–14th century builders' guild.

Turn R in front of church and continue on road *(the prestegård is now Ringebu Samlingen – café, gift shop and one or two farm buildings to visit)*. Short section on farm road after **Vestad**, *with good views out over the Gudbrandsdal (valley) ahead – both of where you are now and where you will be going.* Fork L downhill at junction 2km after leaving church and cross bridge over the river **Våla** in

3.5km Ringebu sentrum (290/353)

Population 1305. Ringebu Hotell, cafés, supermarket with cafeteria, banks (and cash dispenser), PO, other shops, railway station. [Ringebu Hotell, 2630 Ringebu, tel: 61.28.26.10, 27 beds plus 18 more in annexe, also has 4- and 5-bedded rooms, available per person; café, restaurant.]

KSO on other side of bridge *(turn L for shops, etc.)* and turn R at *Ringebu Hotell (signposted 'Folldal' and 'Enden')*, using cycle track; this is **Kjønnåsvegen**, though it is not marked at the start *(Kjønnas is the area between the Våla and Frya rivers)*. Continue to top of hill and then, 1.5km from town centre, turn L down **Midtvegen**, *a local road, 3km of easy walking with woods on either side.*

KSO(L) at fork (you are now on **Slettavegen**) and continue to another road 3km later. Turn L and 100m later fork R onto gravelled road (signposted 'Kjønnås sag' – a saw mill) then fork R 100m later last the sawmill (on your L). KSO(L) at fork below house, veering L past farm and then veer R to turn R onto a local road leading uphill, forking and then veering L all the time to cross the stone bridge 18m above the river **Frya**.

6km Fryabrua (296/347)

There has been a bridge here since medieval times, on the boundary between the kommuner of Ringebu and Sør-Fron. Impressive waterfalls to either side, in a sort of chasm.

Turn R on other side on FP alongside river, veering L across field to cross stile into woods. Turn L up clear forest track. Cross a local road through its U-bend and KSO ahead when it veers L downhill. Cross a

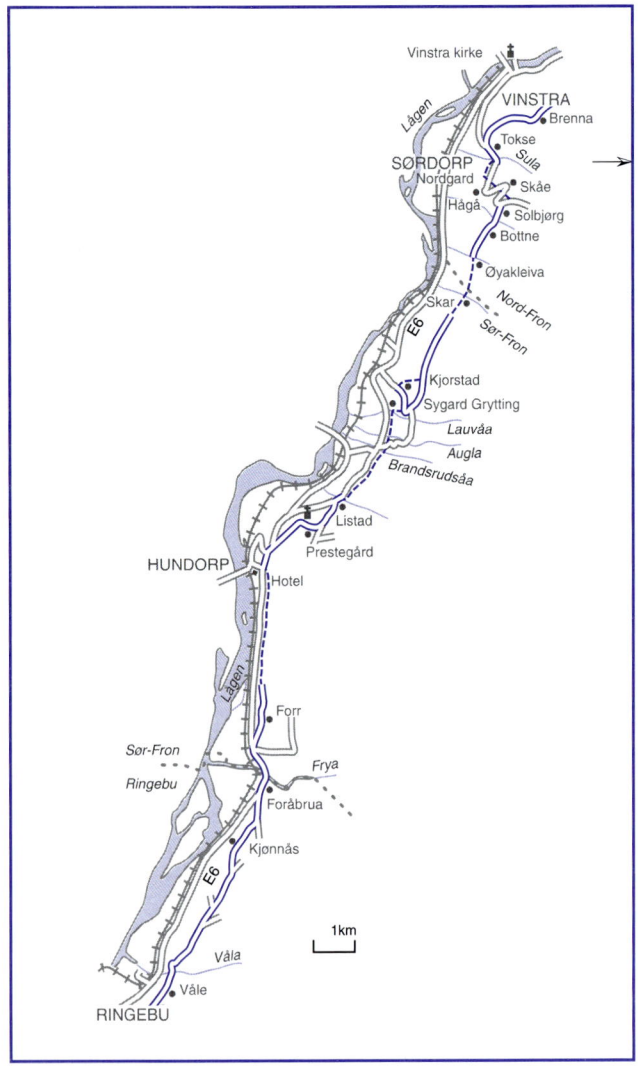

road and continue over FB to fork L back into the woods again, across open woodland alongside old wall to R. *(By now the huge concrete factory building to your L is on other side of road below.)* Reach a farm road, turn L down through residential area and turn R at junction.

KSO for 500m then a minor road joins from back L at **Forr** (a large farm complex). KSO for 2km, and when you reach a farm the road becomes a grassy track.

When you reach the E6 500m later continue ahead uphill, alongside fence (// to road), do a 'loop' over stile and continue ahead, passing waymark with 'Hakkemett' *(a place taking its name from the whitish material that comes out of the slate bed-rock)*. 100m later, by wall, veer R up onto slightly clearer track, still // to river, and follow this, crossing FB over stream and picking up a cart track coming from above back R. This takes you back to the E6.

*(If the weather is very bad (wet and slippery underfoot) you may prefer to continue (very cautiously: unfortunately there is no other alternative) along the E6 to **Dale Gudbrands gård** as the path that follows is very steep, narrow and crosses several gulleys; it has been waymarked for the purpose of keeping you off the main road, but is both strenuous and possibly difficult under foot in or after heavy rain.)*

Otherwise: continue on a clearer track close to the road, climbing very steeply all the time. *Hundorp visible across the river to your L.* Track eventually levels out a little then continues as a narrow FP across hillside, crossing a succession of gulleys till the track widens out again and leads you down, via a stile, to the E6 again.

Cross it carefully, cross stile on otherside and veer L round edge of field, R along the side by the railway line and R again, turning L through gate up towards the hotel. *On your L you pass a large burial mound, Olavshaugen, one of the seven still existing from pre-Christian times (one can be visited inside, though the contents of all of them are now in the Historical Museum in Oslo). There are also several stone circles in this area.*

6km Hundorp: Dale Gudbrands gård (302/341)

A tiny place but rich in history, a chieftain settlement from Viking times and the spot where, via the intervention of St. Olav, Christianity came to Gudbrandsal, when one of his men took up his club and smashed the image of the god Thor to pieces. The Dale Gudbrands gård (i.e. the farm and all its buildings) was used as a school until 1987 but it is now a cultural centre belonging to the local community, with exhibitions, courses, accommodation and meals. [Hundorp, Dale-Gudbrands gård, 2647 Sør-Fron, tel: 61.29.71.11, EE; as well as the hotel rooms the management also provides simpler accommodation for pilgrims in one of the other buildings.]

Turn R (in front of hotel) to E6, cross over and continue along inside of fence on other side before turning R up local road to

1.5km Sør-Fron kirke (303.5/339.5)

Octagonal stone building, 1792, also known as Gudbrandsdal's 'cathedral' as it is the valley's largest church.

Sør-Fron octagonal church   (author)

Turn R up walled lane beside church to the *prestegård (the original buildings date from late 14th century)*. Turn L onto a minor road and L again on local road downhill to the E6 again. Turn R and immediately R onto a minor road: waymark says 'Bautastein', *indicating a stone monument believed to be one of the two large rocks hurled down the mountain by the troll woman Ulvei; when she heard the bells of the former Listad church ringing (site indicated to R, marked 'Kyrkjetuft') she took aim but missed her target*. The minor road continues as a cycle track for the E6, till it peters out by the **Brandsrudsåa** *(river, shop to L)*. Continue (carefully) along E6 for 150m more then fork R uphill and along LH edge of field. Turn R alongside fence to skirt house and pick up clearer FP behind it. Continue ahead, crossing three stiles, along top side of large field, passing waymark 'Rolstad/Kyrkegård' *(site of former church)* 200m to L, towards brown and white farm complex: this is

4.5km Sygard Grytting (308/335)

Very ancient farmstead with a medieval 'pilgrim loft', the only one still extant of many that formerly existed along pilegrimsleden. It has been restored and is now in use as simple overnight accommodation for modern pilgrims. [Sygard Grytting, 2647 Sør-Fron, tel: 61.29.85.88; hotel-standard accommodation also available.]

Turn R up steps and continue up LH edge of field, to L of giant burial mound, the **Kjemphehaugen** ('Giants hill'), with the **Lauvåa** to your L, turn L over FB and R to road.** *Before you continue any further, however, read the description of the next section and decide what you would prefer to do.*

The waymarked route indicates that you should turn left next, downhill again, to **Kjørstad nordgård** (farm), losing all the height you have just gained. You then turn R up a cart track, cross a stile and continue up a steep wide track between fences, passing a waymark part-way up marked 'Kyrkestad', indicating the site of a former church, 50m to L. This is the object of this exhausting detour (no remains in sight, however), after which you turn L into the woods++++ (see page 144) (the hill is the **Høgberget**) onto a path marked 'Styggdalen' *(the RH option indicates 'Sugardslonnin')*.

Sygård Grytting: farm with medieval pilgrim loft (Eivind Luthen)

However, if you turn right instead of L when you reach the road** and continue on the level for 200m more you will pick up a FP through the woods which you would otherwise join at ++++. *This will save you nearly half an hour and what will seem like a useless detour in the shape of an inverted 'N', unless you are particularly interested in former church sitings (but with no ruins extant, though important Roman burial finds were made in the 19th century, revealing gold jewellery and other items in bronze).*

In either case, once you have entered the woods continue on small FP at first then pick up wider track turning R uphill, climbing steadily. Just before track ends abruptly (1.8km) in a ravine watch out carefully for waymark and turn R very steeply up a small FP uphill *(slippery in bad weather)* for 20–30m till you reach a forest road and turn L *(good views)*.

Continue along forest road, passing signpost (this is **Styggdalen**) marked 'Skar 5' ahead (and 'Kilevegen 1' – where you have come from). Next signpost is at **Tryymmshaugen** (Skar 1.5, i.e. 500m later). After this the track levels out a bit, but 500m later watch out for waymarks and bright red paint blobs that mark the track from here to the abandoned farm at Skar. Turn R uphill here, then veer L to follow small FP to RH side of fence all the way (well waymarked with red paint) for 500m more to Skar. *(The track you were on does, in fact, continue through the fields to Skar, but there is presumably some reason why you can't simply continue along it instead of having the tiring job of picking your way along narrow uneven paths.)*

6.5km Skar 600m (314.5/328.5)

Abandoned farmstead on a 'mountain shelf' with fine views out over the valley. They are indications of very ancient settlements in this area and people were still living here until 1955.

Deserted croft at Skar (600m) (author)

Continue on RH side of fence but now on a much better path, passing the border between the *kommuner* of Sør-Fron and Nord-Fron *(don't get too near the edge if you don't like heights)*, veering R and then L on a forest track. 600m later reach the remains of another abandoned farm at **Oyerkleiva**. Continue ahead on wide grassy track, ford stream at bend and then turn L (diagonally) up hill, along the cliff side to the top. *(The path was originally only very narrow but has now been widened to allow tractors to pass; it is, although it may not look it, just as wide as the one you were already on.)* After that you begin to go downhill to R, with woods to either side, descending for several kilometres. Turn R up farm road above **Solbjørg** and KSO(L) along another one coming from R, passing over a cattlegrid. Descend, passing farms, to a junction with a Fv (marked 'Haugen'). Turn L for 100m then hard R down banked-up grassy track, passing below (to L) of small house (**Staom**), whose many hairpins you will short-cut. This goes down to a road (waymark says 'Helleristinger'). Cross it and continue in line you have been coming on, down a similar track veering L and hard L over a stile and continue downhill.

Reach road again, turn L for 100m then fork R through (purpose-built) gap in crash-barrier down FP and turn R down it to road. Turn R for 50m then L *(in front of you is Nordgård Hågå, the farm where the historical Peer Gynt is said to have lived, the model for Ibsen's (and Grieg's) 'Peer Gynt' character. The farm is a listed (*fredet*) monument but is privately owned and is not open to visitors.*

Turn hard R over stile, veering L down tracks through fields that become clearer as you go. Reach road again via stile, turn R *(waymark 'Kyrketuft 200m' points L to probable site of old Sødorp church)* and at bend turn L to cross road bridge over the river **Sula** at

6.5km Vinstra (Sulabrua) (321/322)

Vinstra sentrum – population 2354, shops, etc., railway station – is away downhill to the L but the PL does not go into it. [Amundsen Gjestgiveri, 2640 Vinstra, tel: 61.29.00.45; near river Lågen and centre of Vinstra.] You are now at the half-way point between medieval Oslo and Nidaros.

Turn R 100m later up gravel track by farms at **Tokse** *(this was for centuries the local* **ting**, *offical assembly place for the whole settlement)*. Reach junction with new forest road, turn R onto track and L onto grassy track uphill. Pass to L of houses, cross road and continue ahead to R of buildings up gravel lane which becomes grassy track and leads into the woods again.

Cross road by more houses, continue into woods and turn R downhill onto lane that passes farm and then continues as small track through the trees, veering L at fork.

Continue uphill, cross gravelled road and zigzag R and then L onto a more level path (**Tjodvegen** again) for a while before climbing again and undulating higher up. Ford stream, KSO veering R uphill at junction, after which track levels out again, high up above the river.

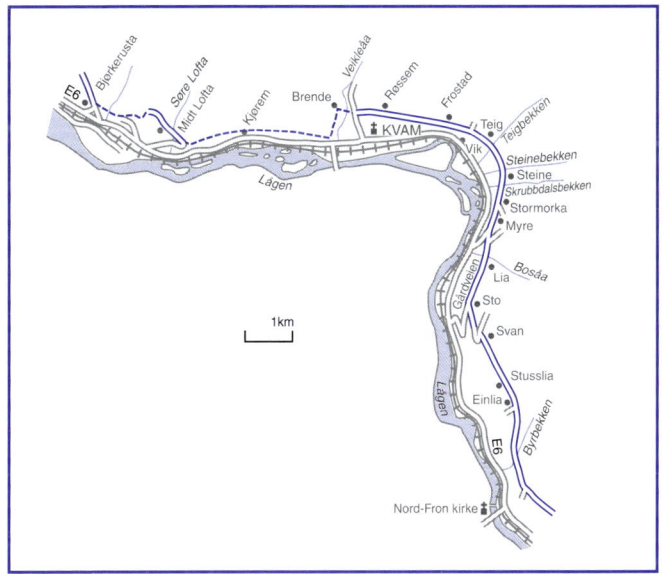

When you reach a gate pass to RH side of fence to skirt another abandoned farm (**Støslia**), returning to original track 400m later by another gate. KSO and from here all the way to Kvam the walking is very easy, downhill for the next 4km and then mainly along the level.

Continue downhill, reach a road just after **Svam** (a farm), cross over and continue down wide grassy track for 1km till you reach **Gravdalsvegen** *(self-service toll-booth marked 'Bom' in shelter hut to R of road)* at a junction with a local road. KSO(R) for 200m then fork R into woods on grassy track just after cattlegrid, easy walking again, just above the road, passing to RH side of fence to skirt farm then returning to track. Go through gate, continue and cross FB over the **Bosåa**. KSO, downhill more than up, to the road again 1.5km later.

Turn R, KSO(L) at fork and continue on this road for the next 5km. This is **Gårdvegen** or *'farm road', so-called because of all the farms it passes as it circles its way (on the level and veering L all the time) all round the valley in front of you to Kvam (whose name comes from the word for 'bow'); after Hundorp the Gudbrandsal valley became* *increasingly narrow but here the landscape opens out for a while, like a large bowl.*

After 4km you pass a waymark 'Kyrkjetuft/Vik', *indicating, to the L, the site of the former Vik church. (Gården Vik is one of the oldest farms in Kvam.) Stave church built in 1574–75 and in use until 1776, when it was dismantled. St. Olav is said to have been born at Vik, though several other places claim the same fame too. A cottage known as the Olavs-stua was here formerly, but it has now been removed to a museum. An iron sword (in good condition because it was well buried) was found here and is now in the Vitenskap Museum in Trondheim.*

1km later pass waymark 'Eldre Veg' ('Older path'). When you reach a junction KSO(L), turn R onto **Leikavegen** opposite a garden centre.

(The waymarked route does not take you into the centre of Kvam, but if you want to go there, perhaps to sleep or eat, KSO(L) here along **Kvernevegen** *and turn L again on main road (i.e. going back on yourself – unavoidable as there aren't any other linking paths available to the public from* **Gårdvegen***).)*

Otherwise, to continue, turn R again (off **Leikavegen**) up RH bank of the river for 200m before turning L over the FB to cross the **Storåa** (literally 'big stream') in a gorge at **Kveiholen**. *The modern FB is built on the foundations of the original stone bridge. Ruins of a cornmill and gate-saw mill in use well into the 20th century.*

13km Kvam (334/309)

Population 792. Supermarket, bank, railway station (Oslo–Trondheim line), Kirketeigen camping and huts by church, cafeteria, motel and other shops. [Kirketeigen Ungdomssenter og Camping, 2650 Kvam, tel: 61.29.40.82, campsite and hut accommodation; meals available for large groups if booked ahead.]

War Museum (Krigsminnesammlungen), 54 Commonwealth war graves in cemetery by church (after the Battle of Kvam April 1940).

Church is open for visits Tues, Wed, Thur, Fri 11.00–15.00 in mid-July to mid-August.

From the bridge over the **Storåa** – turn L on other side towards farm and pass it to L over stile, along river for 500m. *From here to Otta the whole section is somewhat fiddly as the PL avoids the E6.*

Turn R to road junction, KSO ahead for 200m uphill, fork L (downhill) then fork R (**Steinråket**) and after first houses fork L to cross stile into field. Continue alongside wall at end, cross farm lane and continue over another stile (almost) opposite, turning L through two more fields. Turn R and L through woods and L to cross another stile onto track close to (and // to) the E6. Cross another stile, turn R then L through woods along hillside, skirt farm and veer R uphill to road at a fork. Take second L (upper) forest track then 100m later turn L onto small FP and continue along hillside for 1km under line of electricity cables.

Turn R uphill onto forest road, veering L, then turn L and immediately R *(waymark says 'Vassveite' – ancient water supply ditch)* on clear FP through trees. KSO ahead, ignoring turns, for 900m till you come to a cart track crossing it at right angles; turn R here, steeply uphill, veering L and then R and turning L along another forest track. This dwindles to a FP through increasingly rocky terrain for a while so watch out carefully for waymarks. Join a wider FP (coming from L) and follow it uphill, forking R just before a farm (**Søre Lofta**) and join a local road coming from L. *(Here you are at 400m above sea level.)* KSO(R) along it and 700m later, at second farm (**Midt Lofta**), fork left downhill (confusing waymark, placed on R at entrance to woods in fact indicates a LH turn here) then turn R into woods towards a gate.

Do not go through gate but turn R alongside fence and continue between fence and woods and then on FP downhill all the time through rocky woodland. Cross FB over river after 1km and KSO. 500m later fork L, FP becomes wider, veering L under HT cables 400m later to reach a road by a farm.

6km Bjørkerusta (340/303)

The next section takes you up to the viewpoint (at 500m) under the Kolloberg. However, in icy weather or if it is very misty it is suggested that you turn L here and return to the E6 as far as Varphaugen, despite the busy traffic.

Otherwise – turn R on small local road, semi-shaded, no traffic at all, and KSO for 1.5km, mainly climbing. Then when road bends R (towards a red hut at Dalum) KSO ahead on wide grassy track. *This is the point at which you cross from Nord-Fron into Sel kommune.*

Approximately 1km later, as it becomes a FP and starts to go steeply uphill, you will see a mini-waymark with its face towards you; this position normally indicates a turn to the L or R but you should, in fact, KSO here, picking up another waymark 200m later on. Continue ahead to descend through rocky woodland, watching out very carefully for the waymarks. Veer R ahead when FPs divide (very small by now).

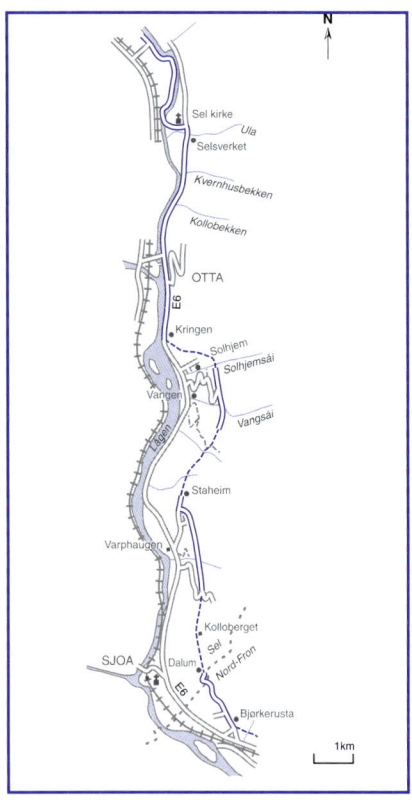

Veer R uphill along base of rocky cliff face (this is **Kolloberget**), climb up steep bank which is a sort of natural 'staircase' with stone steps and then make your way to a notice board ahead presenting information regarding **Heidal**, *a side valley of the Gudbrandsdal with many listed farms still in use. It is also well known nowadays as rafting centre.* This is the 'viewpoint', though there are quite a lot of trees around you, obscuring the view somewhat.

After this make your way downhill in the direction indicated by the waymark (i.e. a continuation of the line you have been coming in). It is not as difficult as it probably seems initially, but be careful as you pick your way amongst the boulders, especially if you have a heavy rucksack. The 'steps' become clearer and you gradually pick up a clearer FP as you go (though no waymarks for a while), losing height all the time, though you are still high above the river (and **Sjoa** to the L by now). *Allow plenty of time in all this section – strenuous, and the terrain is slow to walk on as well.*

KSO ahead, descending all the time, and then the path widens out into a rough forest track just before you reach a junction. Turn R uphill here and at bend KSO(L) ahead *(waymark may be missing – the next one is some 800m later)* on FP along flank of hillside, through open woodland *(good views)*, descending steadily. FP becomes a wider track. KSO at each of two crossings on FP through trees, veering L downhill to road. Turn L, veering R and fork L through trees to E6 by bus stop at

5km Varphaugen (345/298)

Storrusten Gjestehus and camping on other side of road (hut accommodation as well). [Storrusten Gjestehus og Camping, Varphaugen, 2670 Otta, tel: 61.23.52.20.]

The place takes its name from the custom amongst travellers of placing a large stone on the hill as a symbolic casting off of their sins and the hope of a safe journey ahead.

Turn R on track, cross stile ahead and then another and turn R on local road.

KSO for 1km, ignoring turns to L or R. Road undulates through semi-shaded woodland with little or no traffic. When road bends R KSO(L) ahead on forest road, continuing to ignore turns.

500m later, after track climbs, veer R *(place has nameboard 'Ormsteinflote')*. Fork L part-way up very steep hill onto FP beside it, veering L, gradually becoming a wider, banked-up stony road, following the course of another ancient route. 100m later waymark points to a splendid viewpoint, L; this is

4km Ståheim (349/294)

Panoramic views (and good place for a rest). Large (modern) wooden cross on spot and notice board informs you that there was a church here, pre-14th century, the oldest in the whole area. Otta visible ahead below.

Continue ahead, continuing to climb steadily for 500m more till you reach the bridge over the **Skarvåtå** (the **Skarvåtåbru**). *Spectacular waterfall to R in springtime.*

100m after crossing bridge reach a T-junction of similar tracks *(R to Guedden)*. Turn L, zigzagging downhill for 1km then continue straight ahead, downhill all the time, for 1km and then, as track bends hard L, turn R to ford river **Vångsåi**. The 'platform' or crossing area is level and fairly wide but there is no bridge here. *A waymark on the other side indicates that you should cross, but you will have to decide whether it is safe to do so, judging by the quantity of water tumbling or cascading down from the falls on your R. If you decide to cross it you continue ahead on the other side, gradually downhill.*

Viewpoint at Staheim (author)

If, on the other hand, you feel it is unwise to attempt to cross, turn hard L downhill to return to the E6 and continue along its cycle track. You can pick up the waymarks some 600–700m later, however, by turning R up a minor road signposted 'Solhjemvegen', and at bend 100m later go up bank, L, to join a grassy track and turn L. The next waymark is by a group of standing stones that look like gravestones by a farm (**Solhjem**), 200m later.

When you reach this point, by whichever method, pause and decide what you want to do next, reading the next section of the text and looking at the landscape before you make up your mind. It is 3km from here to Otta, two of which are on the cycle track between the river and the E6. If you are tired or if the weather is bad it is suggested that you continue on the cycle track from here. If you look ahead, you will see that the river curves round a large hill in front of you, which has a spring (waymarked 'Kjelde') part-way up.

The waymarked route turns R from where you are standing now, over a stile, and then L to skirt a farm (keep close to buildings as there is a large gravel pit behind the farm) and cross the river **Solhjemsåi** *(by a substantial bridge this time)*. You then cross another stile and continue through fields to pass above the other buildings you can see ahead of you, after which you climb very steeply up a narrow FP leading you to the spring. *(The water is very cold but good to drink; good views back over the valley on a nice day.)* After this both the waymarks and any obvious track disappear, but the route takes you up over the hill and then back to the E6 by the **Kringenstøtta**, *a memorial to an uprising in 1612. The object of the excursion, apart from passing the well, is the view.* If you decide to take this option you then turn R along the E6 cycle track.

6km Otta (355/288)

Population 1616. All facilities (supermarket, shops, banks, PO, cafés, railway station, Tourist Office); popular ski-resort in winter. You are some 350m above sea level here but the next 15km, from here to Nord-Sel church, is a flat, easy walk.

When you reach the first (now pedestrianised) bridge over the river **Lågen** you can either turn L to go into the town centre or KSO to continue, crossing the E6 via underpass and KSO on **Kongsvegen** on other side. Pass waymark 'Rodestein' *(a milestone)* 1 km later. Continue on road – very little traffic – crossing **Kollobekken** and **Kvernhusbekken** and recrossing the E6 by the place-name board for **Selsverket**. Stay on cycle track and cross bridge over the **Ula** *(the buildings on the other side are on the site of Selkobberverk, one of Norway's oldest coppermines, recorded here from 1647)* and continue to

4km Sel kirke (359/284)

Church built 1742 but it had no bell until 1752; this is still hanging (and used) in the present church. Waymark informs you that there are now 284km left to Nidaros. [Sandbumoen campsite and huts.]

Turn L in front of church and then KSO(R) at junction and cross bridge over river **Lågen**. Turn L on other side onto a gravelled road and KSO alongside river. Pass end of old bridge; *much of the Nobel prize-winning Sigrid Undset's (1882–1949) trilogy* Kristin Lavransdatter *is set in this area.* KSO until you reach the name board for **Jørundgard**. Fork L and then turn hard L immediately towards its entrance buildings and pass between them.

10km Jørundgard Middelaltersenter (369/274)

Loft building, Jørundgård medieval centre (author)

This is a reconstructed 12th-century farm, built initially as a film set in 1991 for Kristin Lavransdatter. *It was no mere temporary cardboard installation, however, but was established with the idea of it becoming a permanent farm after the filming was over.*

There are 14 buildings of different types and uses (animals, storage, living accommodation) as well as the stave church, burnt down in a spectacular scene in the film but now rebuilt again. It is interesting to have a look round, now that you have already seen or passed many old farms, and see the layout and functioning of a typical large farm from the period, all the more so if you have already read Sigrid Undset's trilogy. Some of the houses have medieval beds and it is possible to sleep there if you telephone in advance. (Very simple accommodation, somewhat draughty, and tall pilgrims may not be very comfortable.) Jørundgard is now an open-air museum cum educational centre, with concerts, talks, children's activities and a working farm; café open in summer. [Jørundgard Middelaldersenter, 2664 Sel, tel: 61.23.37.00; open early May to end August.]

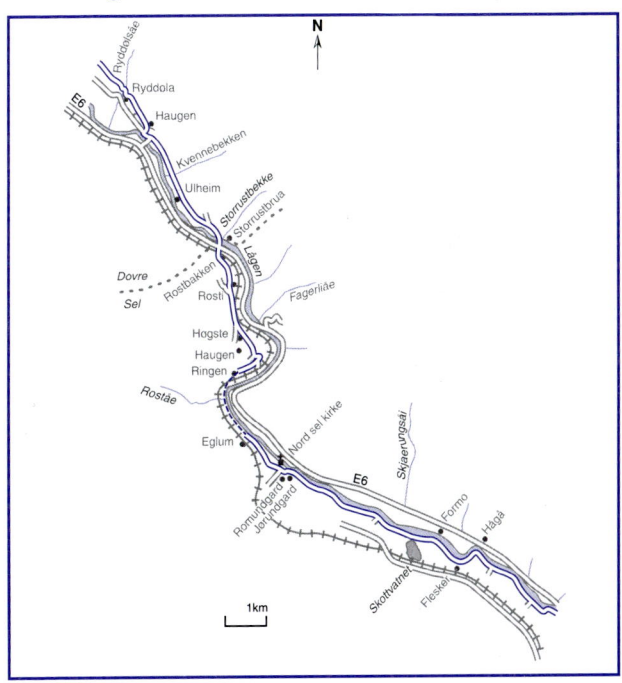

To continue – pass entrance to grounds, KSO(L) at junction and turn R onto minor road, ignoring turns, to Rv 435. On L at junction is **Romundgård**, *one of the many listed (but still working) farms in Gudbrandsdal.*

[Simple accommodation at Nerøygården, 2664, Sel, tel: 61.23.30.68, 1km from Jørundgård on Fv 438 in direction of Vågå.]
Turn R to

1km Nord-Sel kirke (370/273)

The present church dates from 1932, with an altarpiece from the original building. (31 British war graves in cemetery, after the battle on April 28th 1940.) Statue of Kristin Lavransdatter outside church gate. A nice section from Nord-Sel, which is also quiet, as river drowns the noise of the E6 on the other side of the valley.

After visiting the church KSO and continue ahead up lane to its L, passing waymark 'Kyrkjestad' *(pointing R, to site of original church)*. KSO(L) ahead at junction, passing **Lårgård**, *another listed working farm,* and KSO, // to river (R) below you, through residential area.

After farm *(***Eglum***; railway line visible to L)* the road becomes a clear grassy track, climbing gradually. When you reach a fence warning you that the railway line is ahead, turn R down FP through trees, along hillside (railway line to L, river to R). *This section is also somewhat fiddly as you are having to avoid the railway tracks.*

When you reach a wooden fence the path veers R towards the river and then up a flight of solid wooden stairs and then a second set of steps. Not all that well waymarked, but enough if you are attentive, watching out for a turn to L and then to R to pass higher up alongside fencing immediately below railway line.

After 1km the railway line goes into a tunnel and the FP becomes clearer. When you reach a fence with another railway notice take the higher of two small FPs, as you will have to use the railway bridge *(in a separate pedestrian section)* to cross the river **Rostäi** 200m later; this path takes you uphill first before bringing you down to the LH side of the railway line and its fence via a sturdy staircase of steps. Cross in front of a spectacular (in spring time) and very long waterfall on the river **Rostäi**.

Continue alongside fence and FP becomes increasingly clearer and wider to become a semi-shaded forest track, climbing most of the time to

Statue of Kristin Lavransdatter, Nord-Sel church (author)

3km Ringen (373/270)

Site of abandoned croft; altar with cross above it and biblical text on stone slab. A St. Olav's well is believed to have existed near here, but its location is uncertain.

Continue up hill. Forest road joins from back L: KSO, mainly climbing. You are now at some 500m above sea level. Turn R onto farm road coming from **Høgstei**, L, and KSO. Pass farm and join bigger local road coming from back L. KSO downhill.

Just before **Rosten** *(a farm with a large number of buildings and its name on a board)* KSO(R) at fork. Pass **Rosten**, turn R at junction and then L to go under railway line to the E6 (2km after Rosten). Turn L along it for 200m, crossing the boundary from Sel to Dover *kommune*, and then cross the road carefully and turn R (between two bus stops, one on either side of the road) by house onto lane and KSO ahead, veering L to cross the river **Lågen** via the

5km Storrustbrua (378/265)

The bridge was restored in 1996, using traditional techniques.

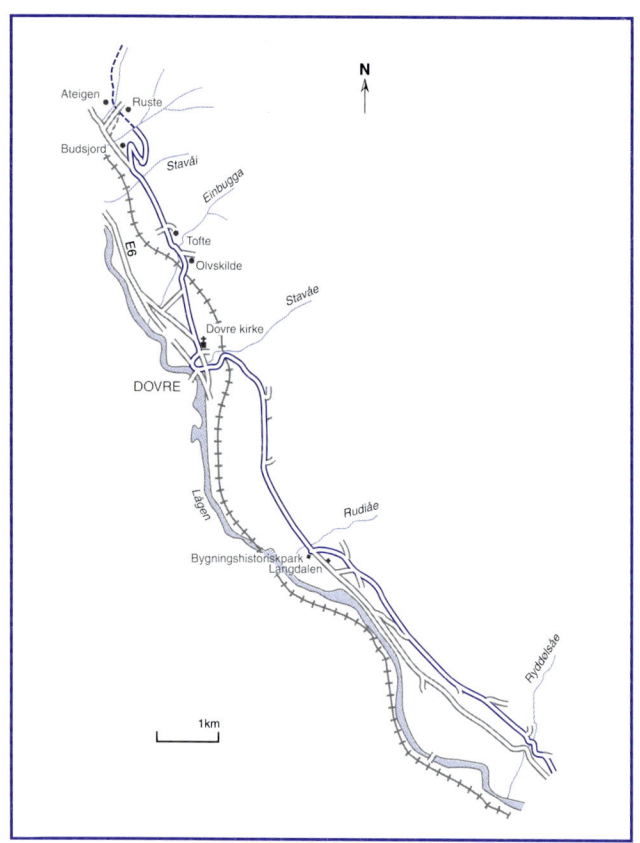

Cross it, veering R and then L onto local road. KSO, mainly level, past farms.

3km later, at **Haugen** [*Vollheim Camping and huts at junction*], KSO ahead (a minor road by now), passing waymark 'Haugen' ('Hill') on R. KSO uphill (the Fv 491). 2km later cross the river *Ryddøle* and then 200m later turn hard R uphill through trees, veering R to local road. KSO(R) along it, veering L (i.e. north) all the time along hillside.

After you reach a vehicle turning circle 1–1.5km later the track becomes rather overgrown, but KSO ahead up an old banked-up road

Storrustbrua over the river Lågen (author)

(**Kongsveien**). After a while it reduces to a small FP for a while, 500m before joining a wider (still overgrown) track coming from bottom L. KSO(R) uphill ahead, after which the track levels out and, as it descends, becomes clearer until you reach the road (Fv 491) at **Langdalen**.

Turn R. From here you continue on the road all the way to Dovre. After crossing the **Rudiåe** pass the **Bygningshistoriskpark**, *an open-air museum,* on L. *View over the (widening out) Dovre valley, church and route ahead.* Road veers L and downhill as you approach Dovre.

(However, if you want to go straight to Budsjord (to sleep) you can turn R before you go down into Dovre itself (i.e. staying more or less on the level) – signposted – and follow the road on the level along the side of the valley.)

Otherwise – continue downhill. KSO(L) at junction, cross railway line, veer L and R down to junction (the road you are on has become the **Stasjonenveg**). Turn R (**Kongsveien**), *cross the Stavåe* and 300m later reach

15km Dovre kirke 482m (393/250)

PO, cash dispenser, cafeteria, supermarket (all near church). Accommodation. N.B. Make sure you buy food here, as although there are some places that serve food there are no more shops until Oppdal. [Accommodation 1km from route at Toftemo Turiststasjon, 2662 Dovre, tel: 61.24.00.45; ski station dating from 1820, now restored: rooms, huts, camping possible.]

90% of the land in Dovre kommune is over 900m. The present church was built in 1736 and is unusual in its exterior, being completely faced with slate slabs (the biggest building in Norway of this type). There were, however, at least two other churches prior to this, the last of which dates from some time before the Black Death in 1349. That was a stave church and was located higher up, about 30m from the Olavskilde at Bergsgrenda, which you will pass as you climb up out of the valley. This was pulled down in 1736, and some of the materials used in the construction of the present building (also in wood) and the chalice, platen baptismal font and other equipment still in use today was also brought down from there. The present Dovre church was inaugurated on July 29th 1736 (St. Olav's day), and although its is not dedicated to a particular saint, as it was built after the Reformation, the two church bells have inscriptions and symbols connected with St. Olav. Church open July1st to mid-August, 10.00–14.00; at other times phone verger, tel: 91.32.77.60. Part of the duties of the parish priest in Dovre involves attending to the needs of pilgrims, and pilgrim days are held in the summer at the Eystein church in Hjerkinn. The only wood-carving school in Scandinavia is here in Dovre.

If you look up the Vangveg while standing by Dovre church and follow its line in your mind's eye up to Budsjord and over the top, it is 10.5km to the highest point at Allmannrøyse, after which the route descends to Fokstugu. You will be going in virtually a straight line all the time.

Go up **Vangvegen** (to L of churchyard) and KSO for 1km. Go under railway line, turn L, turn L along Fv 491 and immediately to your R there are two waymarks: *a) indicates a spring, the Olavskilde; b) points to a Kyrkjetuft (site of Dovre's former church) 30m inside field.*

150m later, at junction, turn L over road bridge over the **Einbugga** *(signposted 'Budsjord 2').*

Reconstructed stave church, Jørundgård medieval centre (photo: Eivind Luthen)

St James the pilgrim on façade of Nidaros Cathedral (photo: Eivind Luthen)

Olavkilde at Bergseng (above Dovre)   (author)

700m later pass waymark 'Tofte' *(one of the oldest farms in Dovre).*

1.6km after bridge fork R up **Gamle Kongeveien** (signposted 'Budsjord 0.6'); *this was a bridleway originally, but in the early 17th century it was made suitable for horse and cart traffic. It begins here and is the one the pilgrim road follows. (The other route starting here – the Gautstigen – is the oldest public transport road in Dovrefjell, taking a longer route to Hjerkinn; today it is a popular walking route in the summer months.)*

4km Budsjord 630m (397/246)

Historic bishop's farm, dating from the 14th century, now a museum with 17 buildings from different periods still intact, including the furniture. The farm also has simple but very nice pilgrim-only accommodation in a small house that used to be a bakery (sleeping bag needed). Some meals available on request (apart from breakfast), camping possible. Very 'pilgrim friendly' owner. [Budsjord Gård, 2662 Dovre, tel: 61.24.04.88, EE. Phone in advance.]

Fork L downhill for Budsjord. Otherwise: continue uphill and 100m later fork R up track, crossing stream. *(Track is waymarked with blue crowns too – for the Gamle Kongveien. Very well waymarked as far as Fogstugu, with PL logo stencilled on stones as well (farm below to L.) The route is not difficult to follow but watch out carefully for these waymarks.*

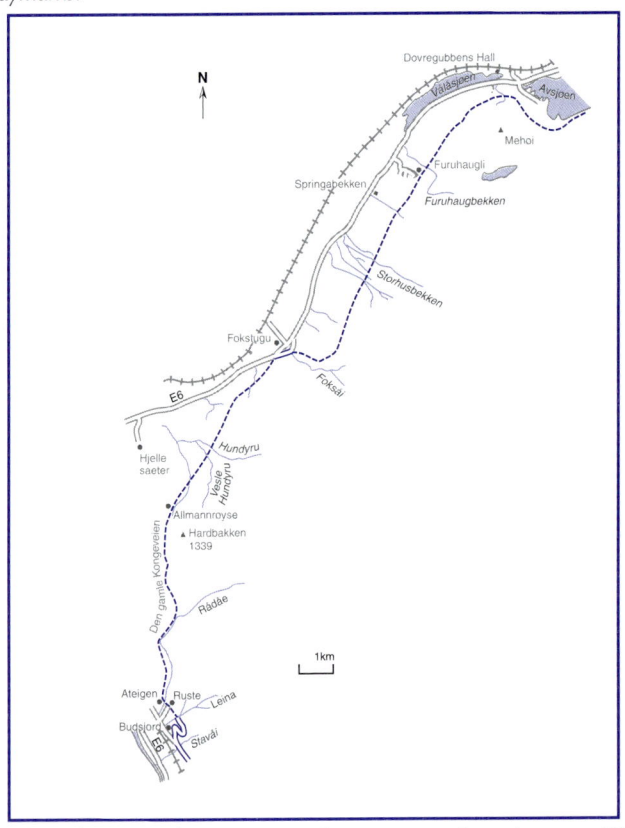

Go through gate and veer R to another stream and another gate. KSO towards farm 100m above to L. Go through another gate, pass to R of farm buildings and continue ahead on farm road. 300–400m later go through small iron gate and pass to R of old buildings with grass roofs. Turn hard R and then L up a stony lane (i.e. suitable for tractors) and KSO(L) at fork to pass to L of isolated small house.

Continue ahead, in roughly a straight line, apart from gentle zigzags, the track becoming more defined as you walk. When you reach a fork take the smaller RH option (a short-cut for bends). Track becomes a drove road.

2km (from Budsjord) pass waymark 'Ståkån' and 1km after that you are above the tree-line. Track goes alongside the river Rådåe for a while. Ford it and 3km later pass waymark 'Bønnealter', *referring to a stone, believed to have been one of two on either side of the path, where pilgrims paused to pray for help on the journey ahead and to give thanks for having got safely thus far, possibly as a symbolic casting off of sins too, since it was also customary for travellers to place a large stone on hills for this purpose, in the hope of a safe journey ahead.*

The climb becomes more gentle after this, up to

6km Allmannrøysa (403/240)

Optional detour to the top of Hardbakken (1339m, the peak to your R) on a nice day, with good views over to Rondane, Jotunheimen and Dovrefjell. After this it is 6km downhill to Fokstugu, a beautiful descent if the sun is shining.

[From Allmannrøysa you can go straight to the hut at Hjelle Seter if you want to sleep there – the route is indicated down to your L. If so, however, you do not need to retrace your steps the next morning but can continue north on a farm road to just before Fokstugu. *(Seter visible below, with other buildings.)* Hjelle Seter, 2660 Dombås, tel: 61.24.16.95.]

After 1km (after Allmannrøysa), when you are about level with an isolated house over to your L, the path splits. Take the RH option (well waymarked). When you reach a river (the **Veslehondyru**) you can either ford it or, if it is too deep, go 100m to L to cross it via a broken but passable FB (remembering to turn R to return to the path, once you are on the other side).

Ditto with a second river (**Hondyru**), except that the bridge has now disappeared. *If you do have to wade across (knee-deep), though, choose your spot carefully: remember that the current is quite strong and will force you downstream, possibly to a place where the other bank is not so easy to land on. Stick useful. Keep your boots on, too (or change into other stout footwear), as with a heavy rucksack you could easily overbalance with bare feet.*

Allmannrøysa, Dovrefjell (author)

The track gradually descends (it has become a FP), very wet and boggy after rain or when the snow has melted. Gradually the scrubby trees return and you descend, passing under electric cables. Reach a wide earth road // to the E6 and turn R along it to

6km Fokstugu 938m (409/234)

Farm here is one of the highest in Norway in use all year and the site of the Fokstugu Fellstue. Several saelehuser, overnight shelters or hospices for pilgrims and other travellers, are known to have existed on the Dovrefjell and the surrounding area since the 14th century, though their exact location is uncertain. These were replaced later by the government-built fjellstuer (literally 'mountain room', as that was all that the original ones consisted of), and there were four of them, at Fokstugu, Hjerkinn, Kongsvoll and Driva, until all of them were burned down by the Swedish army in 1718, along with some 20 to 30 houses in each of the four places as well. All were rebuilt at different times, and of the remaining three Fokstugu accommodates self-catering groups and individuals, while Hjerkinn and Kongsvoll are now hotels; Driva Fjellstue, now deserted, but which you will pass later on the Vårstigen, will give you an idea of what they were all like in previous centuries.

Fokstugu is also the location of the Fokstumyra Nature reserve, with marsh habitats rich in bird life. There is a 6km marked trail which leads round the reserve and which is accessible to the public between May 1st and July 8th, beginning at the house immediately north of Fokstugu railway station.

To sleep in Fokstugu turn L by hut. [Fokstugu Fjellstue, 2660 Dombås, tel: 61.24.14.97, EE, CF, no meals.] Otherwise, it is 7km further to the huts at Furuhaugli.

To continue: cross bridge over the **Foksåe** and turn R up FP uphill on other side.

According to your tastes – in nice weather, if you like open landscapes – the section from Budsjord over the Dovrefjell to Fokstugu and Hjerkinn and from the Vårstigen up to Drotningsdal and then down Vinstradal to the Driva Kro and Motell on the E6 before Oppdal is probably the best part of the whole walk.

Go uphill, veering L, pass under electric cables *(well waymarked with cairns and Olav stencils)*. *('T' waymarks are those of Den Norske Turistforening (DNT), a walking organisation which also runs mountain huts.)* After you reach a plateau the path veers L again. 500m later turn L at a 'proper' PL waymark, continuing high up but more or less // to E6 and railway line below to your L (2km after Fogstugu). The FP is not always very distinct but there are plenty of cairns.

Pass information board about **Fokstugumyrin** *(i.e. marsh – cf. English 'mire') and its bird life. (There is a series of such boards (all with bilingual text) between here and Hjerkinn, explaining different aspects of the flora, fauna, geology, building, etc., of the area; they are referred to in the text that follows as they also serve as reference points for way-finding in bad weather.)* Path goes in more or less a straight line.

After 6km you lose height and the path becomes drier. *From the top of the hill (as you go to the L) you can see the Furuhaugli huts (accommodation) and the beginning of the* **Vålåsjøen** *(lake) ahead to L. [Furuhaugli Turisthytte, 2660 Dombås, tel: 61.24.29.16; huts, camping possible, small shop.]*

Pass information board about animal life on Dovre fjell: *musk ox, wild reindeer, wolverine, mountain fox as well as golden eagles and the ubiquitous (and very vociferous) cuckoo. The musk oxen were reintroduced from Greenland in the 1950s; you are unlikely to see them, but keep an eye out in case you do (it is recommended to give them a very wide birth).*

Zigzag down to cross two FBs and after that you enter a nature reserve *(Dovrefjell has the largest concentration of such places in Norway)*. Pass 300–400m above a collection of 15–20 huts *(this is* **Furuhaugli***: turn L to sleep there)*.

Pass information board about **Haukstardmyrin** *(another marsh) and palsa bogs and cross river by FB.*

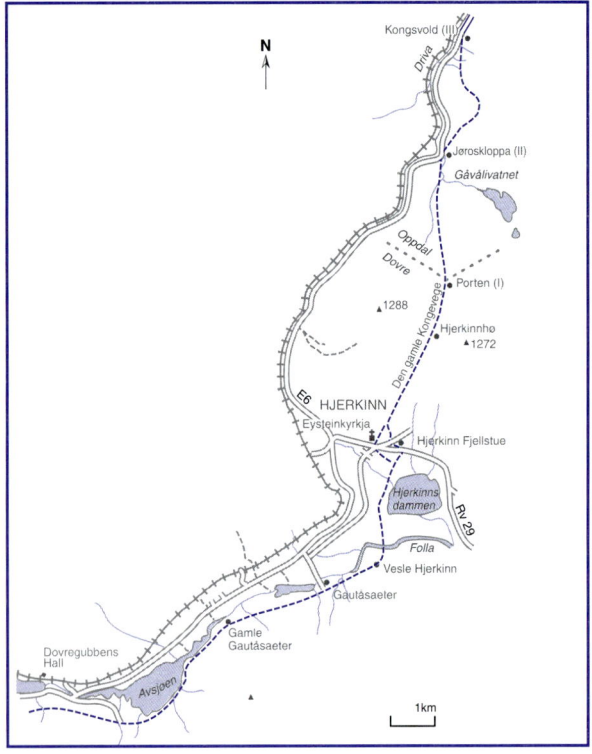

After another stream track veers L again and follows line of electric poles towards a lake (**Avsjøen**). Pass information board about plant life on Dovrefjell.

Reach old farm and join wide track. When track bends sharp L turn R under electric poles to cross stream and veer L to path leading down towards lake. *(To L, 800m away on the E6, is Dovregubbens Hall (accommodation, art gallery.) [Dovregubbens Hall, Vålåsjø, 2660 Dombås, tel: 61.24.29.17.]*

Pass waymark 'Bågåstelle', *indicating a site 30m to L, and an information board explaining what these were – hunters' hides used for shooting reindeer that passed by on the old migratory routes between summer and winter grazing grounds that criss-crossed the Dovrefjell. Pit traps or 'falls' were also used (hence the origin of the word – nowadays only with its figurative meaning – 'pitfall').*

Reach farm track, turn R over concrete bridge and KSO towards buildings ahead. 200m later turn L, cross FB and pass waymarks 'Gravhauger' *(information board about burial sites to R, indicating three graves 6m in diameter and 1m high).*

Continue along RH side of lake *(planks, duckboards in very boggy sections)*. Pass houses *(FB links them to E6 via minor road)*. Pass information board about Stone Age settlements in the area.

Pass waymark 'Gml Gautåseter' *(Hjerkinn Eystein church is visible ahead L here)*. Keep losing height. Cross river (FB).

Pass **Haugesetter Turisthytter and campsite**, *open all year, café. [Hagesetter Turisthytte, 2660 Dombås, tel: 61.24.29.60, E.]* Reach (walker's) signposts (at **Gautåsaeterin**), take 'Hjerkinn Fellstua' option and cross bridge over river ahead.

The FP is well waymarked (mini-waymark) and describes a large quarter circle over to Hjerkinn Fjellstue and church.

Pass waymark 'Dyregrav' *(i.e. animal grave; Villreingrav = wild reindeer pits). Trap pits were in use until 1700. The reindeer fell in but couldn't get out, so they had to stay there till the hunters arrived to kill them (and therefore the meat lasted longer). Pits were made of rock, with gravel ridges, often with walls leading reindeer straight into them. Traps were often built in rows and at crossing points of winter/summer migratory routes (in the summer they went to places nearer the coast for calving). Once you've seen one or two of these pits (as with burial mounds) you can easily spot others.*

1km later reach another signpost. KSO(L) ahead (**Hjerkinn Fjellstue**; *RH turn is Slettum)*. Reach

19km Vesle Hjerkinn 935m (428/215)

'Little Hjerkinn', where the base of a large rectangular house is a replica of the building that was situated here, along with five

other houses, between 950 AD and 1350. Located near the oldest route across Dovre mountains (the Gautstigen) it was a large house with broad benches – suitable for housing travellers – and there is evidence that pilgrims stayed here too.

Information board provides details about artefacts from the Viking Age and about reindeer trapping; there were over 500 pits registered between Dombås and Kongsvold (10 near here) and they were already in use by 600 BC.

Vesle Hjerkinn: replica of base of medieval saelehus (Eivind Luthen)

When you reach a small lake the path goes to its R and then turns hard R uphill, but if the waymark is standing in the water (!) go uphill ahead and you will pick up the next one shortly afterwards. Pass 'Ice and water carved the landscape' information board.

Cross bridge over the river **Folla**. *There are several* kalvbruer *('bridge roads') in this section: roads raised up above the bog, built of logs, like a causeway.*

Pass picnic area, reach minor road, turn R along it for 300m then fork R onto gravel track, trees to either side, and KSO. Pass 'Routes across the mountains' information board.

Hjerkinn (Eystein) church is visible to L and the Fjellstue ahead. Here you have a choice of routes: when you reach a gravel track coming from lake on your R, just before some gates, you can:

a) KSO through gates, veering R, to Rv 29 at Hjerkinn Fjellstue;

b) turn L 'til Eysteinkyrka' (i.e. on road), FP short-cutting bends.

   Alternatively you can go to the church from the Fjellstue by going through the campsite.

Kalvbru (log causeway) on Dovrefjell near Vesle Hjerkinn   (author)

Hjerkinn to Nidaros

3km Hjerkinn 950m (431/212)

Accommodation in Fjellstue, campsite, meals. [Hjerkinn Fjellstue, 2661 Hjerkinn, tel: 61.24.29.27.]

Eystein church was built in 1969, designed by the architect Magnus Poulsson and named not for a saint but after King Eystein Magnusson, who had a saelehus (hospice) built on Dovrefjell for pilgrims and other travellers, though it is uncertain whether it was at Vesle Hjerkinn or on the site where the Fjellstue now stands. The original church was built near to where the Fjellstue now stands, 1050–1300, and its bell is said to have rung out to guide pilgrims in bad weather. A 'pilgrim passport' dating from 1439 has been found (a document carried to ensure safe conduct). Nice place for a rest. The church is open every day from 10.00 to 17.00 from July 1st to end August, with services every Sunday during that period; when it is closed you can ask for the key from the Fjellstue.

Eysteinkyrja is a pilgrim church today, and every year, during the weekend before St. Olav's day (i.e. giving the walker time to continue on to Nidaros for the Olsokmesse on July 29th), there are 'Pilegrimsdager på Dovrefjell' ('Pilgrim Days') in Dovre and Hjerkinn, with walks, church services, concerts, lectures, theatre, exhibitions, etc., all with pilgrimage as their theme. The dates for the year 2002 are 26th–28th July, followed by 25th–27th in 2003, 23rd–25th in 2004 and 22nd–24th in 2005, etc. There are also plans underway to build a pilgrim centre (including sleeping accommodation) in Hjerkinn to be the focus of pilgrim tradition in both Norway and the rest of Scandinavia. Pilgrims interested in these events can contact the priest in Dovre (in English) on tel: 612.42.100 or consult the Internet site at www.dovrenett/pilegrimsdager (English translation in preparation).

To continue: there is no need to backtrack, as the path continues behind church (i.e. at altar end), through the woods and then L up earth road to pick up PL by waymarks. Otherwise – turn R (facing church) over stile to campsite.

The *pilegrimsleden* continues (from the Fjellstue) through campsite, passing to L of reception building. *(Notice board informs you that 'Gamle Kongveien over Hjerkinnhø startet her'.) The 'Royal Road' was a bridleway at first, but then in the 1700s it was made suitable for horse-drawn traffic.*

Go through gate and continue up hill on clear grassy track. Splendid views all round on a clear day. Path becomes gravel track and less steep. KSO for 4km to

4km Hjerkinnhø 1200m (435/208)

Literally 'Hjerkinn hill'. Waymark stone informs you that there are now 208km left to Nidaros. Stony area with a lot of cairns. Splendid views all round on a clear day.

KSO ahead, gently downhill for 2km, till you reach a stone cairn and waymark 'Porten', marking the boundary between Dovre and Oppdal *kommuner. Originally there was a big gateway here (hence the spot's name), informing the traveller that he/she was leaving Oppland and entering Trøndelag. (To L of lake ahead is Jøroskloppa, the place where you touch the E6.)*

The waymark is also no. I. In Oppdal the 'proper' PL waymarks bear only numbers I–XXVII, but there are no place or subject names on them. These waymarks will be indicated in the text (and on the maps) so that you can identify where you are.

KSO down into valley (sort of large bowl) for 3km to E6 at

5.5km Jøroskloppa (Waymark II) (440.5/202.5)

Continue across parking area, cross river by road bridge and fork R up FP (Waymark II) and signpost 'Pilegrimsleden' in blue and 'T Kongsvold' *(Olav logo waymarks in slate slabs – something like tombstones – here too)*. Small FP, but obvious and well waymarked over shoulder of hill ahead.

After 2km of open moorland the paths divide. Fork L *(the RH option continues the DNT waymarked path)* into scrubby woods, veering L and uphill before levelling out onto open ground again. Lose height gradually and after 1km veer R to cross river (by fording it). However, if this is a raging torrent, for example after the snow has melted in spring, you will find, if you go exploring upstream (i.e. to your R) some 100–150m higher up, that 'your' river is, in fact, the fusion of two smaller ones which you can therefore cross separately by stepping stones (even if you are only moderately agile). A small FP on the other side then brings you back to the place where you should have crossed in the first place.

KSO downhill on other side alongside river at first and then veering R downhill towards the E6, passing Waymark III and going through a gate to turn L and then R through buildings at

4.5km Kongsvold (445/198)

Accommodation (on the pricey side), meals, Kro (i.e. café) opens mid-June. [Kongsvold Fjeldstue, Dovrefjell, 7340 Oppdal, tel: 72.42.09.11.] Mountain botanical garden. Railway station, bus services along E6 to Oppdal.

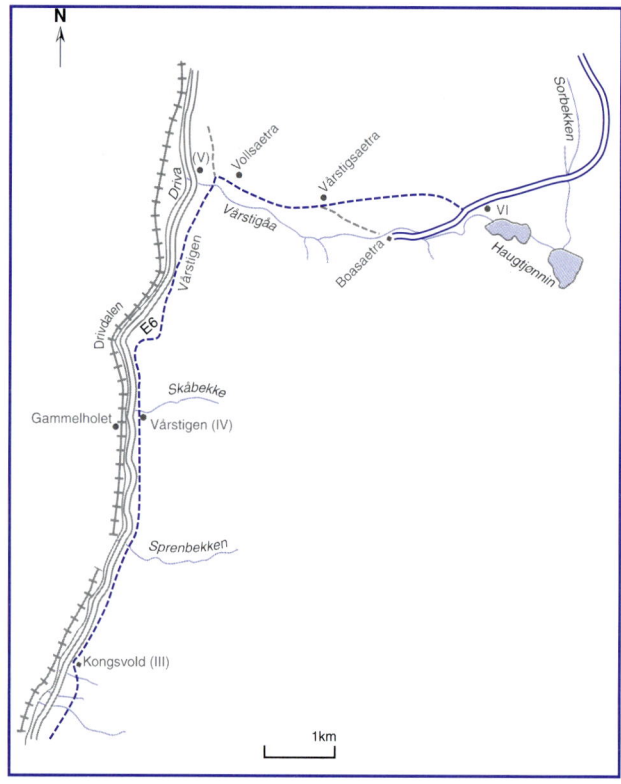

At end of buildings continue on FP alongside fence // to E6. Path then veers R uphill and through a fence with a trilingual notice *informing you about the musk oxen which have been reintroduced in this area, a notice you should not only read but also heed: you are unlikely to actually meet one of them as they normally keep well away from people, but if you do keep at least 200m away from it.*

Path continues through scrubby woods and then up and downhill for 3.5km to avoid the E6 – well waymarked but exhausting with its constant climbs and descents, as well as the terrain being slow-going to walk on. It goes under the cliffs of the **Knutshø** and you have to cross **Sprengbekken** half-way along. *Nice views. (The only alternative, though, is the hard shoulder of the E6.)*

You are now in **Drivedalen**, with the river **Driva** beside the road in the valley to L below. Return to the E6 again 3.5km later opposite **Gamleholet** *(the site of the original Kongsvoll Fjellstue)*, at the beginning of the

3.5km Vårstigen (448.5/194.5)

Waymark IV. 'Vårstigen' means 'spring path', i.e. one taken in the springtime when the valley paths were all full of water after the snow had melted. Picnic area on other side of E6 (via tunnel). Bilingual information board explains that the 'Old King's Road starts here. Wonderful view of the Driva valley. Mentioned as early as 1182 as Pilegrimsleden'. It then goes on to tell you that 'Frederick IV passed in 1704 with a two-wheeled carriage, and Kristian in 1733 with a four-wheeled carriage', something hard to imagine when looking up at the track!

Continue ahead up grassy lane // to the road. Cross bridge over **Skåkbekken** and pass information board about the 6230m long Vårstigen 'spring' route. KSO, climbing steadily for 1km, veering R at first information board and KSO at second *(indicating the site of* Tingsvaet, *the parliament place, 1000m)*, veering L downhill. Pass board with information about Vårstig pyrite mines *(remains of barracks for 18 labourers to R). This area is a paradise of wild flowers in mid-June.*

Pass ruins of **Driva Fjellstua**, *first built here in 1780s as a* saeter *(summer farm)*. After this the Vårstigen begins to climb steadily again until you leave it, 1km later, after crossing the

3.5km Bridge over Vårstigåa (Waymark V) (452/191)

At this point you leave the Vårstigen (it forks L downhill here) and fork R (Waymark V) up a FP through woods, steeply uphill to start with. (Nice in the evening sunlight if you know you aren't pushed for time.)

300m later turn R to join wider FP coming up from below L. Continue to climb, emerging above the tree-line, with the **Vårstigåa** now over to your R. Continue ahead, climbing more gradually, veering L and then R (river still to R), now a stony track.

Pass below **Vårstigsaetra** (a summer farm, on your L) and head for a small green house ahead, veering L. *(Track has become a FP by now, but the number of waymarks has increased, so you should have no difficulty finding the way across the boggy moorland.)*

Pass below green house (it is on your L) and KSO, veering slightly L, still gently uphill *(modern farm buildings away over to R)*. Watch out carefully for waymarks as path not always very clear in the boggy sections. *(Shortly you will see two lakes ahead, slightly to the R; Waymark VI is located to the north of these.)*

When you reach a ridge in front of you veer R (track has become more defined again). Join a farm road coming from back R, cross bridge over the **Vårstigåa** again and 400m later pass Waymark VI at

4km Haugtjønnin (456/187)

The lakes are now below you to R.

Continue ahead uphill all the time, the road continuing to climb for another 2.5km after the bridge, veering L, until it begins to level out (at 1250m). After this it descends very gradually *(you are now in Drotningdalen)* until you reach a junction just below the farm at **Ryin** *(though you can't, in fact, see it)*, with a road coming from above R and there there is a barrier across the road (that you are on): Waymark VII is here. KSO here and zigzag downhill, more steeply, and 1.5km later you will come to the *refuginen* at

8.5km Rypusan 1100m (464.5/178.5)

Cluster of houses by the river, with a pilgrim shelter, unattended, in the building on your R (picture of pilgrim with stick, hat and satchel on outside). [Simple CF, own food and sleeping bag needed.] Waymark VIII. You are now in Vinstradalen.

KSO downhill on **Saeterveg**, crossing and recrossing river **Vinstra** from

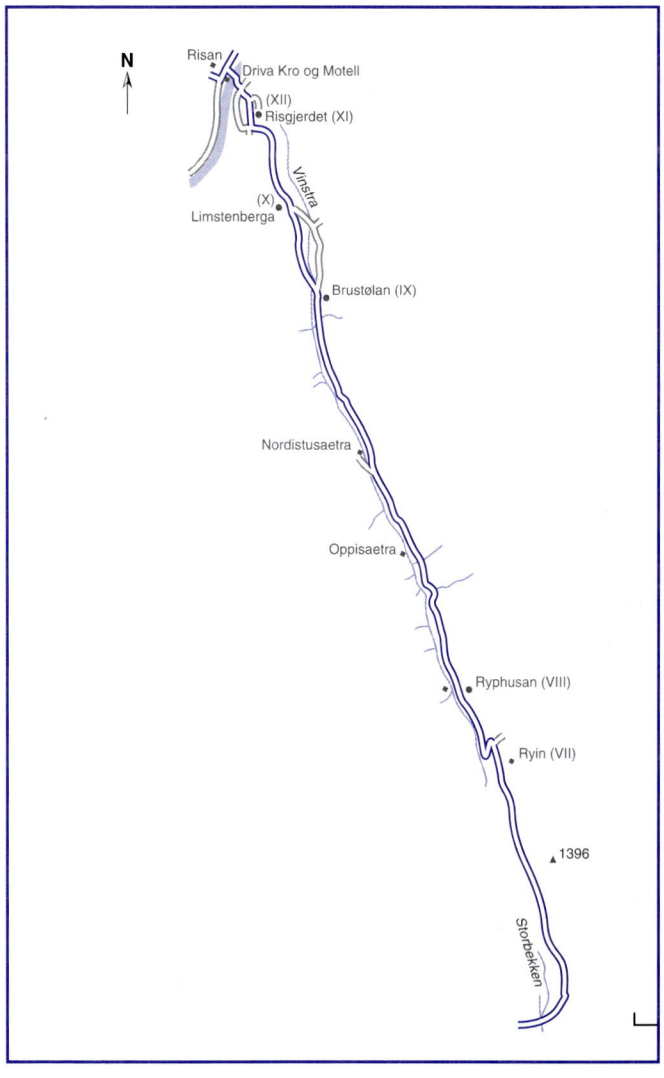

time to time. After 2km pass **Vannkilde** *(spring with drinking water and seat)*.

KSO. Pass three bridges over the river (the first one is at **Nordsaetra**, all three of them on the L). Pass turning to R and 8.5km after Ryphusan (Waymark IX) fork L off road onto grassy track at

8.5km Brustølen 900m (473/170)

This is an old, overgrown vehicle road leading downhill to the river Vinstra. Cross bridge and KSO(R) on other side, climbing at first then levelling out high above the river below.

Pass Waymark X (**Limstenberga**, *site of former limestone quarry*) and gradually descend *(view of Oppdal in distance as you do so)*. Reach a T-junction with a *grusvei* and turn L *(i.e. this is the same road as you were on before you crossed the river as it has now changed sides too)*. KSO for 1.5km and just before a sharp bend to L fork R off road onto grassy track downhill. Go through three gates and when you reach a fourth turn R *(Waymark XI, Iron Age burial mound here)* through a small gate on the R into a field. Go along its LH edge, through second small gate and turn L and then R in between buildings in the farm at **Risgrende** (L), towards a large flagpole. Continue down farm road, veering L *(waymarks may be missing from here, also Waymark XII)*. Turn R at staggered junction of farm roads, L at next junction, take next L turn and then turn R and L to cross railway line and meet the E6 by the

7km Driva Kro og Motell (480/163)

Café, accommodation (on L), meals, open every day.

Before you continue read the next section of the text as the next 5km of the waymarked route is extremely fiddly and an alternative is suggested.

The waymarked route indicates that you should turn R for 800m (passing supermarket on L), and just after bridge over a river turn R up a minor road beside campsite. *[Smedgården Camping.]* Turn second L (Fv 516) and pass farm. Road becomes a grassy track and at fork fork R towards field *(Waymark XIII appears to be missing)*, veering R towards railway line and then L alongside fence. Go through gate, continue ahead, go through second gate and two more fields. Turn R up farm track then L alongside very solid stone wall (on R) into woods, continuing along line of electric pylons.

When the track to the L of the wall becomes blocked you pass to its

R, cross a stream and continue along side of field, and half-way along pass beck to LH side again.

Continue through woods, watching out carefully for waymarks, and when you are about level with a farm (**Grisingran gård**) above you to R watch out carefully for marks. Go through small gate, continue alongside woods and pass Waymark XIV.

Continue along RH edge of field, go through gate, pass to RH side of fence and veer round LH edge of field and half-way up the end side, before forking L down bank (very overgrown in 1999) to pick up a wider track leading you to a small gravel road (coming from Grisingran).

The waymarks then indicate that you should turn R in order to be able to cross a small river, but the route is so fiddly and badly waymarked that it is suggested you turn left here to the E6, turn R along it for 800m, after which the cycle track begins, and the PL joins you again from the R at **Krossvegen**.

(Alternatively, however, you can turn left at the **Driva Kro** and 300m later turn R by farm at **Risen** onto a minor road. Cross bridge over river **Driva** and then turn R along a more minor road which you follow, more or less in a straight line, to the Rv 16 just before Oppdal church.

KSO, ignoring turns, for 3km until you reach a T-junction with a bigger road. Turn R to recross the **Driva** and then continue as described from *** below.)

5km Krossvegen (Waymark XV) (485/158)

Turn L down a minor road which then becomes a *grusvei*. After 1km (just before bridge to your L over the river **Driva**) turn R onto a slightly bigger road.*** 300m later turn L onto *grusvei* and KSO for 2km, passing Waymark XVI *(just after a Miljøstasjon – recycling depot)* and then cross the river **Olma**.

1km after the recycling plant cross a more main road and continue on other side (signposted 'Ridesenter' – riding school). Cross river **Skjørdøla** and reach Waymark XVII *(pointing to grave mounds on the other side of a stile to R)*: this is **Vang**, Norway's largest burial ground from heathen times. Over 750 burial mounds have been recorded here and excavations in 1990 revealed, among other things, bronze plates from Ireland, evidence of Viking raids to the west. The burial ground (over the stile) is a park with a marked path through the mounds that takes about half an hour to walk.

Continue the long, exhausting slog uphill, pass Waymark XVIII and reach the Rv 16. Cross it, go uphill again on other side and 400m later reach

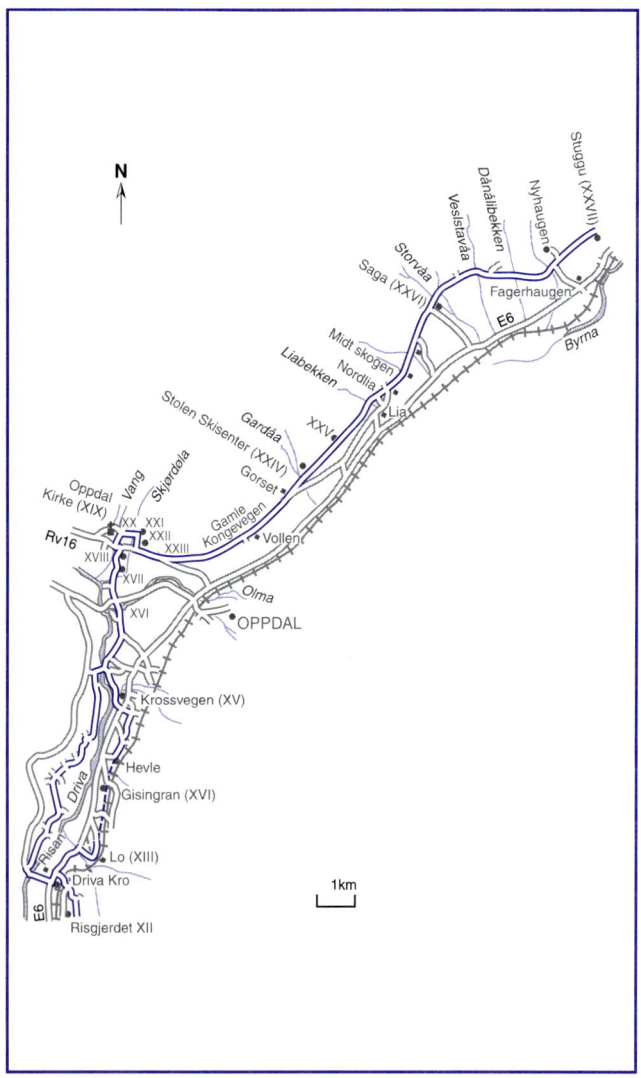

5km Oppdal kirke (490/153)

Waymark XIX. Marker stone informs you that there are now 153km left to Nidaros. The present church was built in 1651, replacing a medieval stave church dedicated to the English martyr St. Jetmund. The red (listed) building opposite, Raulåna, dates from 1675 and was used as accommodation for both civil and ecclesiatical dignitaries as well as royalty, who were housed in the state room on the first floor. It has been restored on several occasions, most recently in 1993.

After leaving church cross road and continue opposite on farm road, crossing bridge over the river **Skjørdøla** and turn R (Waymark XXI) and back down to the Rv 70. Turn L and 500m later turn L (Waymark XXIII) onto the **Gamle Kongeveg**; this is the Fv 501. KSO.

[To go into **Oppdal sentrum** (for shops, railway, etc.) turn R down **Aunevegen** and KSO. *(Hut accommodation at Vekve Hyttetun, Aunevegen 10, 7340 Oppdal, tel: 72.42.12.62, CF.)* However, to return to the route you do not need to backtrack but can fork R after the beginning of **Aunevegen** onto **Bjerkeveien** and then turn R along **Gamle Kongvegen** opposite the entrance to the **Gondolbane** *(cable railway)* and **Toppen Restaurant**.]

By the time you reach Oppdal your kph should have increased considerably, as not only will you be fit after all the ups and downs of the Gudbrandsdal but the walking is also much easier in this part, in a wide flat valley where the surface is better and there are less changes of direction.

Otherwise, to continue, KSO along **Gamle Kongvegen**. Pass the **Youth Hostel** *(on L).* [Oppdal Vandrerhjem Oppdalstunet, Sletvold Park Apartments, Gamle Kongevei, 7340 Oppdal, tel: 72.42.23.11, EE, simple CF.] 2km later turn L at a junction (Waymark XXIV) up a gravelled road to

5km Stolen Skisenter (495/148)

Veer R uphill, passing below ski-station buildings. At end, where the long-distance ski runs start (signposted) at junction KSO(R) ahead (Waymark XXV) on farm road. [Halsetløka Oppdal Camping, 7340 Oppdal, tel: 72.42.13.61.] An information board about the Gamle Kongveg tells us that the Old Royal Road from Dovrefjell through Drivdalen continued further from here through the Trøndelag to Trondheim and was used by several royal travellers, including Kristian V in 1685, Fredrik IV in 1704 and Kristian VI in 1733.

KSO, ignoring turns (road becomes a grassy track). This is a nice section, quiet, gently undulating for 2.8km till you join a farm road coming from back L (at **Nordli**) then another and KSO as local road, likewise ignoring turnings to L and R. 300m later join another road again and KSO(L) ahead, track becoming surfaced. KSO ahead for 3.5km. Then, near some houses and Waymark XXVI, cross the

7km Stor-Stavåa (502/141)

There was formerly a chapel on this spot.

KSO crossing **Vest-Stavåa** and **Dånålibekken**, through undulating terrain with no particular distinguishing features and old, straggly woods to either side. Pass signpost to Grytdalen and KSO.

Pass **Gamle Stuggu** *(old black and brown house on RH side of road)* and nearly 1km later pass the last numbered waymark, XXVII, at **Stuggu** on RH side of road, in front of tumbledown wooden house (after modern farm) which has obviously seen better days; *this was the site of a medieval hospice for pilgrims and other travellers.*

KSO ahead. Reach a junction preceded by a crossing sign and 350m later cross the river

10km Gisna (512/131)

This is the boundary between Oppdal and Rennebu komunuer; waymark in middle of bridge to indicate this.

KSO ahead, passing several farms. *[Langklopp, after 3km, has accommodation; Langklopp Fjellgård, 7393 Rennebu, tel: 72.42.54.62, EE, CF, camping possible; meals available if ordered in advance.]* KSO past signpost to 'Gisnadalen' (L). Cross **Merrabekken** and then the bridge over the river

6km Hevra (518/125)

600m later, just before the road you are on joins another at **Sundset**, fork L uphill and pass behind a house called **Veistad**. Cross stream and field, fence opposite by very large rocks (stile missing) and then you will pick up a small FP just inside woods to L of fields. At end of first field pass to other side of fence and veer R round edge of second field, down towards road, then turn L at bottom through wood. Cross farm road, KSO past yellow house on cart track ahead which becomes a clear forest road (old Kongeveien).

KSO, ignoring turnings *(another nice quiet section)*. When you reach a large field 2km later you can either turn R and return to road here or pass to L of house beyond and return 200m later. This is **Kastet**

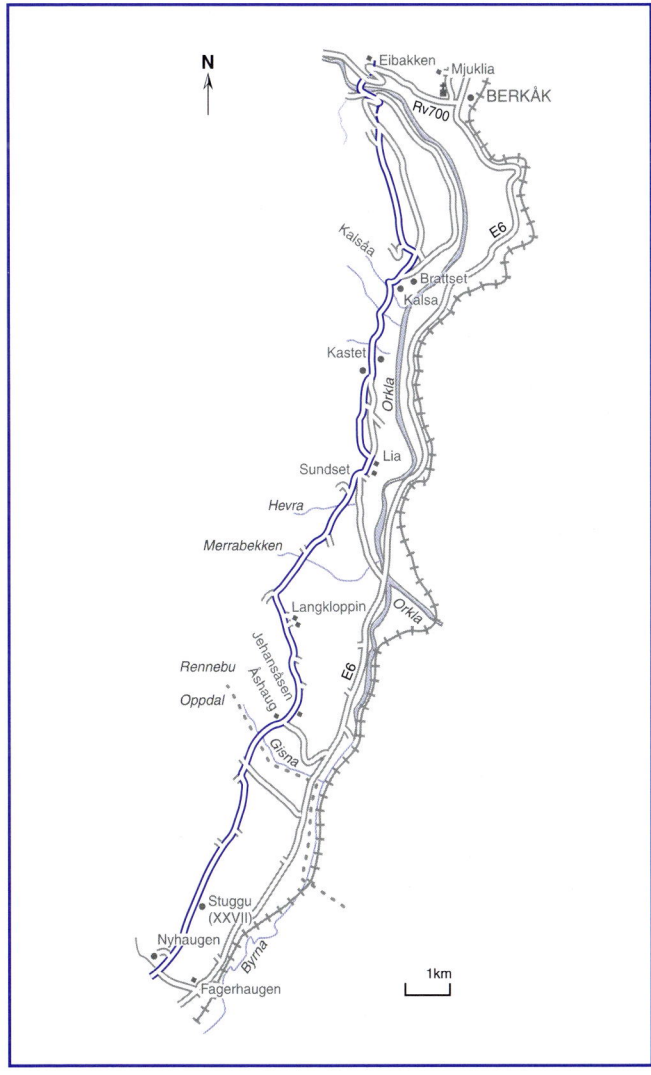

where, tradition has it, the giants living in the Våttåfjellet mountain above the route to the left were so irritated by the noise made by bleating goats on the farm below that they threw stones down on them ('kaste' = to cast). Continue on Fv 502 (Km 5) for 1km to

6km Brattset (524/119)

Fork L off road, veering R uphill on cart track behind farm, and continue along FP by fence, join **Nonhaugveien** coming from back L and KSO on forest road. Go through gate and KSO(L) ahead on track coming from back R. Go through another gate and KSO, level, quiet. Pass name boards (e.g. Kamban*), indicating the sites of crofts in centuries gone by.*

5km Gammelgraeva (529/114)

When you reach a local road at a T-junction (marked 'Gammelgraeva') continue ahead, down FP *(the remains of the old royal road)* which descends fairly steeply, in more or less a straight line all the time, becoming a *hulvei* after a while, // to stream (R). This short-cuts some of the bends in the surfaced road which you recross 500m later and then again by bridge 50m after that, this time to continue on other side on grassy track.

When you reach a fence blocking your path turn R alongside it, cross stream and follow fence down to road below. Turn L over cattlegrid (Fv 502) and continue to the *Skjepphaugbrua* (bridge) over the river

1.5km Orkla (530.5/112.5)

Remains of the short-lived St. Olavs Jernverk (iron works, 1852–65) and its buildings to LH side of road.

[If you want to go into **Bergåk** (2km off route, e.g. to sleep) you will have to turn R here, along the Rv 700. If you stay in **Mjuklia** *(accommodation)* you can rejoin the PL without having to retrace your steps, via a waymarked *tursti*, returning to it near the **Olavskleiva**. *[Mjuklia Ungdomssenter, 7391 Berkåk, tel: 72.42.82.30.]*

Otherwise – continue to junction with Rv 700 *(you are on Fv 502, Km 13.5; Løkken is signposted to L (44km), Bergåk to R).*

From here the waymarked route turns R for 250m, then turns L up a steep bank to short-cut bends in the road (Rv 700) and then takes you high up above it to the L (i.e. NW), crossing the **Breia** and the **Slippa** and passing an **Olavskleiva** and then returning you back down to the road again after 2.5km at **Kjønmoen**; it joins it by a bus stop at the

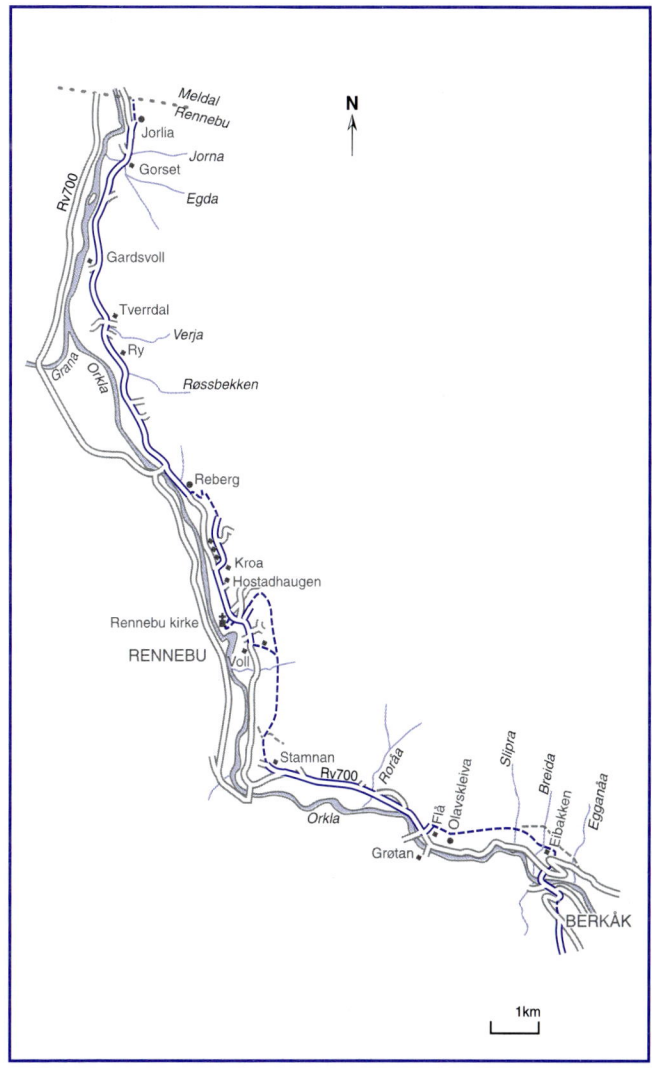

junctions of the 700 and 'Nerskogen' and 'Gunnes' roads. Turn R along 700, pass **Hoegsmoen Bedehus** *(a religious meeting-house)* and stay on road.

At present, however, this section is very inadequately waymarked, particularly at the start where the paths are not obvious, and it is suggested you turn L along the Rv 700 here, by the river, until you reach Stamnan. *(If you want to visit the Olavskleiva, however – and rejoin the route when you get there – you can do so via a small (marked) FP which leaves the road to the R just past road KM 12.5, after layby.)*

6.5km Stamnan (537/106)

The stuggu (log house) on your R is a replica of the original Jutulstugu ('Giant's house') from the 11th century, now used partly as a community centre. Inside there are benches around the walls, and the long tray-like board is half of the original 'table' – i.e. a sort of long, communal 'tray' propped up on the knees of all those sitting on the bench and used for eating (though presumably this arrangement would have been difficult if the diners were of very different heights...). The other half of the original is in the museum in Trondheim. The stuggu is often kept locked, but ask at white house with red roof opposite for key. Bank, supermarket.

100m after hut turn R up minor road, veering L uphill, then R and L to continue on forest road. KSO(L) at fork and then turn L through gate onto grassy lane uphill. At junction, when it levels out, turn R uphill, veering L to join forest track coming from back R. KSO(L) ahead and KSO(L) again at junction when track levels out.

KSO, go through gate, veer L in field to go through another and reach place marked 'Porkhuset'. *(Rennebu church visible below.)*

Here you can either:

a) turn L at stile to return to road and KSO along it to church;

b) (not well-waymarked later but possible if you are attentive) KSO on small but clear FP, still waymarked with the blue paint of a local walk. Ford the **Skørka** and KSO, veering L, descending continuously. Path disappears later, however, beneath trees. Keep as close to fence as possible and at a sort of 'storage box' cross fence to its R as best you can, after which you will pick up a clear stony track that veers L, following fence and leading to a gate at a T-junction with a farm road 250m later. KSO to the Rv 700 (this is

*Detail over farm
door (Rennebu)
(author)*

Voll). Pass supermarket with post office and veer L past **Korshaugen** *(a large burial mound)* and **Rennebu Bygdemuseum** *(of local history, on L)*. Cross bridge over river **Orkla** and turn L to

5km Rennebu kirke (542/101)

The original stave church, erected about 1250, was replaced by a new church in 1669, one of only three in Norway with a Y-shaped ground plan. 12th-century crucifix inside, with altarpiece and pulpit from 1672. Marker stone informs you that there are now 101km left to Nidaros.

Backtrack from church and turn L on Rv 700. 800m later turn R up farm road, veering L past farms (// to 700, on your R).

When you reach a second farm, a large one with the owner's name over the door and a large pond in a depression to the R, veer R alongside fence, go through gate and continue on green lane.

KSO(L) at fork, after which it becomes a narrow FP alongside fence all the time. Pass two small buildings (L) and KSO ahead, uphill, after which you join a clear forest track coming from R. KSO(L) ahead. This leads to a junction with a farm road at Reberg. Turn R *(waymark with 'kulturminne')*, pass between buildings and ahead L through field, going down grassy track in opposite LH corner, leading to Rv 700.

Turn R and fork R immediately onto a minor road (Fv 501). After 3km pass **Ry**, a farm (249m). Cross river and KSO. Pass another waymark with 'kulturminne'.

After 3km a minor road joins from back L. *This section is a gravelled road, but there is almost no traffic and very nice views out over the valley all the time.* 2km later pass **Sollhaugen**.

After 7km on Fv 501 cross the **Egda**, pass through farmyard at **Gorset**, cross the **Jorna** and fork R uphill by dilapidated hut, go through gate just below farm, up towards

12km Jorlia (554/89)

A listed farm, dating from the 10th century (note decorations on buildings).

Either a) pass to R (behind) buildings or b) pass through farmyard and continue ahead on other side through gates onto grassy track. Continue ahead, more or less level, *on what is a paradise of wild flowers in early June, another nice section, in which you cross the border from Rennebu into Meldal* kommune.

1km later reach an *utsiktspunkt* (to L), *with splendid views both back to where you have come from and forward to Meldal and where you are going next.*

Continue ahead on FP to descend through woods, veering L, and then R when you leave them, to continue on clear grassy track downhill (some waymarks) to rejoin local road by bridge over stream. You are now in **Orkladalen** *(valley).*

Turn R (Km 9.5) and KSO, right beside the river Orkla for 1km to start with, before it veers off to the L. Road is more or less flat, with farms to either side.

Pass turning to **Å**, go up hill. At **Fikke** *(road KM 6.5)* KSO(L) ahead at fork and 100m later fork L down minor road, veering L, into wide, flat valley. Turn R after first farm (marked 'Riksgrenda' at turning) and KSO for 1.7km; *this is the old road used for transporting ore from Kvikne in Østerdal.*

Grave mounds to L (in trees) after last of the three Rikstad farms.

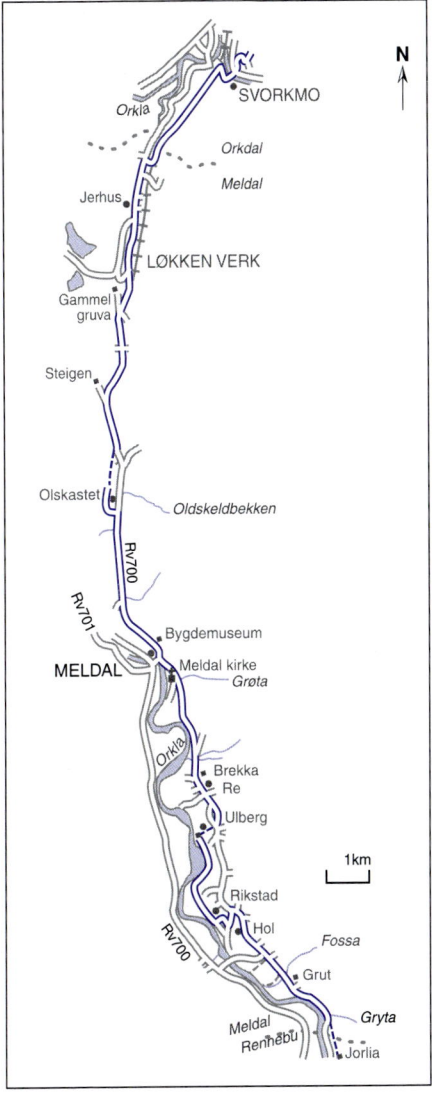

N

Orkla

SVORKMO

Orkdal

Meldal

Jerhus

LØKKEN VERK

Gammel
gruva

Steigen

Olskastet

Oldskeldbekken

Rv700

Rv701

Bygdemuseum

MELDAL

Meldal kirke

Grøta

Orkla

Brekka
Re

Ulberg

1km

Rikstad

Hol

Fossa

Rv700

Grut

Gryta

Meldal
Rennebu

Jorlia

KSO. Pass waymark with 'forminne'. The route veers L to continue along the banks of the river **Orkla** for a while *(one of Norway's finest salmon rivers)*, forks R towards a farm but then turns R across a field and uphill on forest road. Do not go on as far as the Fv 501 but turn L onto FP through woods, veering gradually L past the croft at **Ulberg** *(restored and maintained by the Meldal Historical Society)* and continuing on forest road to return to the Fv 501. Cross over, fork L into woods, fork L, join one track coming from back R then another and return to the Fv 501 800m later. *(The purpose of all this is to keep you off the road for a while.)* Turn R and KSO for 3.5km on road to

Croft at Ulberg, before Meldal (author)

10km Meldal (564/79)

Population 598. Pass church, built 1892 to replace earlier one (note figures outside front door and also enormously long barn in the prestegård).

Reach Rv 700 and turn R uphill *(shops, PO, bank, supermarket to L)*, passing café at bend.

500m later turn hard R to the **Meldal Bygdemuseum**, an open-air museum with a large collection of interesting buildings, then turn L through museum grounds and go out the other side on gravel road. KSO(L) at fork, turn hard R up minor road through residential area then L and then turn R 500m later and immediately L. Turn R at fork and KSO(R) at next, uphill, on gravel road. At bend KSO ahead on forest track, KSO(R) at fork, KSO(L) at next.

Cross river (FB) and KSO(L) on other side and then turn L onto grassy track. Veer L to return almost to road then turn R on grassy track beside it and continue on small FP through trees before returning to the Rv 700 by isolated house.

Cross over and turn R behind it onto grassy track, turning and then R after a while to continue higher up. At junction KSO(L) ahead on wide forest track for 1km to

Replica of travellers shelter at Olskastet, between Meldal and Løkken Verk (author)

3.5km Olskastet (567.5/75.5)

Little hut on L, a shelter for walkers, is a reproduction of a saelehus that stood here in former times to shelter pilgrims and other travellers. To see the Olavskilde (St. Olav spring) turn R (near to road) where it is boxed in, in a little wooden 'cupboard'. Water very cold but good to drink.

To continue: turn L through gates *(waymarked 'Olkortet', to L)* up gravel lane and veer R. At end continue ahead on grassy track through trees, veering R to gate. Continue ahead in straight line (// to road), pick up cart track and continue on it, turning R at junction alongside small river to return to Rv 700.

Turn L *(cycle track starts 500m later)* and KSO for 6km to **Løkken Verk**. *2km before you reach it (shop on L) you can see the old mine head and workings on the hill ahead of you; iron ore was discovered here in the 17th century and the mine was in continuous operation from 1654 to 1987. It is known, because of the scale of the mine, as the 'Cathedral of Toil and Work', and its largest space, the Fagerli Hall, is nowadays used for concerts. Guided tours available.*

7.5km Løkken Verk (575/68)

Population 1471. Orkla Industrimuseum (mining history), Gammelgruva (mine). The Thamshavn railway, Norway's first electric train, was built in 1908 to transport ore from the Løkken Verk mines and operated until 1963. It has now been restored as a museum train, running between here and Fannrem. Tourist office, shops, bank (+CD), PO, supermarket, café, campsite (huts – relatively expensive). [Løkken Camping, 7332 Løkken Verk, tel: 72.49.66.43, EE.]

Bus service Oppdal/Bergåk/Meldal/Løkken/Svorkmo is fairly frequent, including Sat and Sun, as it is on the Oppdal–Trondheim run, though its does not pass through places in between such as Rennebu.

KSO for 2.5km, on cycle track and then on road. Turn R up minor road *(opposite picnic area)* over river and railway line (the Thamshavn line) and veer round to L uphill. Shortly afterwards you leave Meldal *kommune* and enter Orkdal.

KSO for 2km then, when road bends sharp R, KSO(L) ahead towards houses and then down stony lane, descending steeply to a road. Turn R, then L, to cross bridge over the **Svorka**. On the other side is

6km Malmplassen ved Svorkmo (581/62)

The route does not go into Svorkmo itself, which is just a collection of houses with a supermarket. (If you do want to go there, however, e.g. to the campsite, turn left on road, go under railway and cross road bridge over the Orkla.) [Rønningen Camping, 7330 Svorkmo, tel: 72.48.41.14.]

Malmplassen was the site of iron ore (malm in Norwegian) smelting works from 1655 to 1845; the old smelting chimney is still there, by bridge.

Turn L on other side of bridge up the Fv 471. 2km later pass **Gården Gumdal**, *a former guest house dating from the 17th century and one of the best in the area (until the original house burnt down), indicating that this road was well used in former times.*

KSO for 3.5km (from Malmplassen) and just before road KM 12 turn R *(signposted 'Skytebane' – shooting range)* onto gravel road, veering L, passing a sportsground with floodlights.

'Lumpy' landscape changes here. After 1.5km turn L onto a grassy track that veers R uphill into woods and at barn fork L onto similar but more level track, passing under HT cables. It becomes a FP but quite well waymarked, roughly in a straight line all the time, over uneven heathland where trees were cleared some years ago.

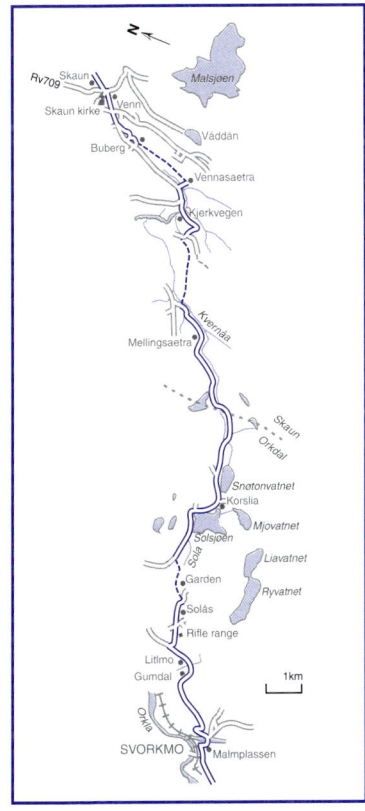

From the point where you leave the road (**) to the boundary with *Skaun* kommune the actual marker posts are not nearly frequent enough, but there are a lot of red ribbon markers tied to trees, obviously for a group walk, which guide you reliably through an area with indistinct footpaths and no obvious distinguishing features. Once you enter *Skaun* the ribbon markers stop but the posts increase considerably in quantity and frequency.

When you re-enter woods fork L downhill. After 1.5km (from road) reach BV and turn R. Pass large lake on R (**Solsjøen**) and turn R alongside it at junction (marked 'Privat vei') to

9km Korslia (590/53)

KSL(L) uphill here *(on a bomvei –* **Snøtenveg***)* and 1km later, at **Snøten** *(a group of houses)*, fork L onto a farm track, KSO ahead at junction (more houses) and fork R on FP to enter woods.

From here until the farm at Mellingsetra there is a stretch of 4.5km of semi-shaded woods and open, boggy heathland plateau, with no distinguishing features or views, across the Skona-Kjølen, a heath. The paths are not all that clear, but the route takes you in roughly a straight line all the time. You will, however, have to be extremely attentive to the waymarks, whether posts or ribbons, walking from one to the next all the time. The instructions may seem complicated but should be clear 'on the ground'.

On the way you pass waymarks indicating the boundary between Meldal and Skaun kommuner, 'Klopp' and 'Kvilstein' (the latter is a large 'resting' stone with graffiti on it –including some from 1905). When you finally begin to go downhill the ground becomes firmer, picking up a farm track just below a house (up to your L) at

6km Mellingsetra (596/47)

Continue to road (turning circle) 300m below, continue along it (river joins you // on R) and 100m after going through a gate turn R to cross the **Kvennåa** via stepping stones. Turn L onto forest track coming from R and KSO, ignoring turns.

Track becomes a (clear) FP for a while through open woodland, mainly descending before opening out to become a wider track again. When you meet another track coming from back R veer left, away from it, onto a grassy track.

KSO, descending gradually. *(Landscape opens out.)* Pass another 'Kvilstein' waymark. Turn R at T-junction 1km later then L through gate in fence (at junction with sheep pens L), back into the woods.

Continue on forest track, which reaches a quarry 150m later. Track coming from back R is waymarked 'Kjerkvegen' *(local road is now visible ahead)*. Fork R off it immediately down small FP through newly planted trees, leading to a minor road. Turn L. Cross two rivers, go through a gate and turn R into a wider road.

200m later turn R and fork L immediately up farm road, veering L past 'Vennasaetra' waymark and continuing ahead along edge of field when track stops, passing onto other (LH) side of hedge half-way along, to continue on forest track ahead, then uphill, continuing as a bridlepath (// to the Fv 754 away to L all the time) with high cliffs like a wall above you to R.

Pass third 'Kvilstein' waymark by two very large block-like rocks, on on either side of path.

KSO(R) at large farm (**Buberg**), passing between some buildings and to R of other and continue on farm road to FV 754. Turn R along it for 1km to

9km Skaun kirke (605/38)

First church at Skaun was a stone one built at Husaby (500m further along the PL). This one dates from 1150. Inside – oak altar frontal (communion table picture) from about 1250, one of only two in Norway depicting the Madonna, and the only

one in use in the church it belongs to. Baroque pulpit (1665).
Marker stone tells you there are now only 38km left to Nidaros.

Supermarket with PO, bank.

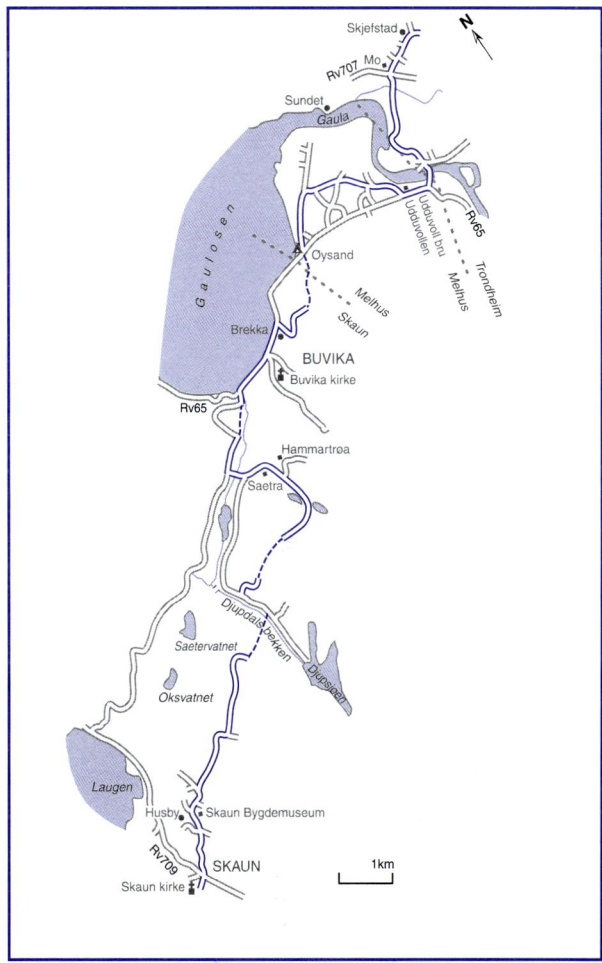

Cross road and continue uphill on other side signposted 'Eggutsalg'. Pass waymark 'Gildskålhaugen' (pointing to R).

300m later there is a short detour to **Husaby**, *with the ruins of original 12th-century Skaun church and a monument to Einer Tambarskelve who owned the land, one of Trøndelag's most well-known figures in medieval history. This is also the place where Sigrid Undset set her* Mistress of Husaby, *the second volume in her* Kristin Lavrandsdatter *trilogy. Seats – a nice place for a rest on a sunny day, with good views.*

Retrace you steps to junction and KSO(L) uphill at bend to **Skaun Bygdemuseum** *(details re. visits on information board at Husaby)*. Pass museum (R), KSO(R) at fork *(nice view back to where you have come from)* and KSO on road with woods to either side.

1.5km after museum turn L down forest track, then 150m later turn R onto another. KSO through semi-shaded woodland. Pass waymark 'Kolmille' (indicating to L) and a second one 50m later. KSO, ignoring turns to L and R.

Pass 'Husbysetrene' waymark. 500m later reach minor road and turn L. When it ends in a vehicle turning area KSO ahead on forest track. When you reach a junction fork L *('Gammel Setra' waymark)*.

200–300m later fork R (well waymarked) on small FP. Pass another 'kolmille' waymark. Fork slightly L in clearing 50m later and continue downhill, passing 'Fangstrop' waymark *(indicating the site of a former trap)* and descend steeply to the river **Djupa** 400m later.

6km Djupaelva (611/32)

Cross river via stepping stones and veer R and then L uphill to small gravel road and turn L.

300m later turn R up farm road past waymark 'Djupdalsvollen' *(picnic area here)* and continue ahead into woods. Pass waymark 'Postogården' (pointing R) and KSO ahead.

When you get to the top and the track flattens out you get your first view of Trondheim straight ahead *(the biggish place to R is Melhus)*.

Path descends, but when it starts to rise again watch out carefully for waymarks and turn hard L downhill on clear FP through woods, go uphill again, and then follow a long descent, crossing stream (with bridge), passing waymark 'Bakktroa' and reach a road at a bend.

Turn L (Fv 801) and follow road as it winds its way downhill, continuing on cycle track 1km *(Buvika church visible ahead R)*. At second bend (500m later, i.e. after starting on cycle track) cross road and go down FP, behind crash barrier on RH side, leading to a river.

(This manoeuvre is to short-cut bends in Fv 801.) Fork L on other side and continue on small FP veering round side of hill (waymark says 'Kvennhusbakken'). *This path is obviously well walked, but the vegetation to either side is often waist-high in the springtime.*

Descend fairly steeply (slippery if wet) with river now on your L, pass to L of electricity sub-station and turn L onto a gravelled road.

KSO to Fv 801 again – you have merely 'short-cut' a couple of its bends – cross over to cycle track and at bottom turn R to cross FB over river and continue alongside the lake on the E39's cycle track *(supermarket and PO to R).*

KSO, crossing bridge over the river into the 'centre' of

6km Buvika (617/26)

Population 820. Bank (CD), another supermarket.

The object of this next detour is to take you off the main road and down the historic path, but if you are in a hurry, tired or in bad weather you can, of course, merely continue along the (flat) main road.

Turn R (away from the fjord) up a minor road (next to the second supermarket) just before the E39 bends L. Follow road round to L under some enormous cliffs, passing 'Kjerkhaugen' waymark (pointing R). Turn R uphill with residential area, the **Brekkaberga**, veer L at top (picnic area on L) and turn R immediately (no street names) then fork L down a FP downhill (opposite house no. 6). This is the **Gamle Kongevei**, leading you back down to the E39 again, on the border between Skaun and Melhus *kommuner*, opposite

2km Øysand Camping (619/24)

Café. Campsite has huts and small flats and accommodates pilgrims in them if they have room (i.e. the other people who rent these normally stay more than just one night) – phone first, though if you have your own tent this is not necessary. [Øysand Camping, 7084 Melhus, tel: 72.87.24.15, EE.]

Cross over and continue ahead between petrol station and campsite, veering L to campsite office. Turn R there and 300m later turn R again on dead straight road towards farm ahead.

The original route continued ahead here to cross the river Gausa by boat to Sundet on the other side, but since there is no longer a ferry service you have to do a detour east to cross via the road bridge.

KSO past several farms, ignoring turnings to L or R, for 2.5km until you reach the E39. (The next to last farm you pass, on your R, is **Klomstad**.) Turn L along its cycle track and 1km later cross the **Udduvollbrua** (a bridge) over the river

4km Gaula (623/20)

This is the border between Melhus and Trondheim kommuner, with only 20km left to Nidaros.

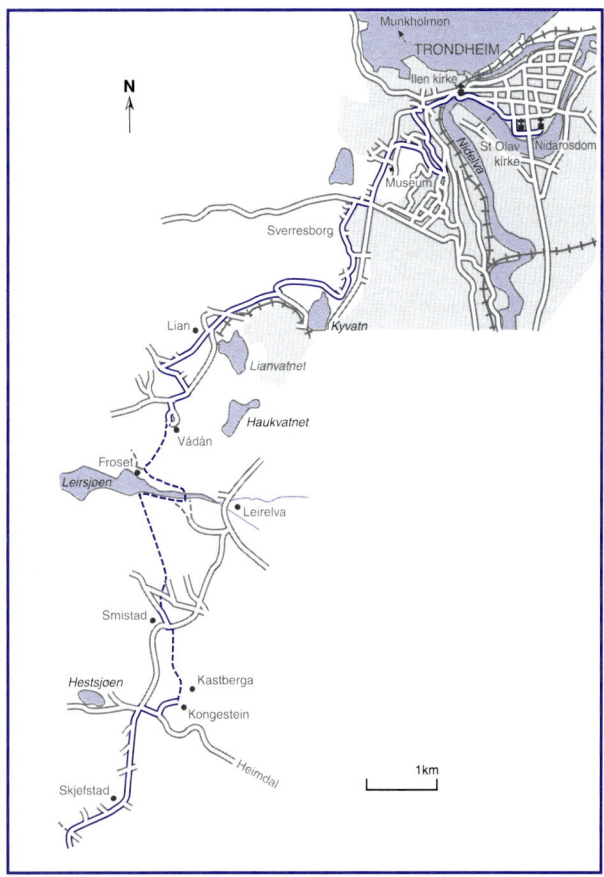

Turn hard L on other side then 300m later fork R on farm road along line of trees. Continue ahead, veering R, for 2km until you reach the Rv 707 at **Mo**. *(This is where pilgrims using the ferry crossing would have joined you from the L.)*

Cross over and fork R very steeply uphill (14%) on other side. KSO uphill for 2km, passing **Skjefstad**, till you reach the road (**Ringvålvegen**).

Turn R and 250m later turn L up minor road signposted 'Sivilforsvaret' ('Civil Defence'), veering R to parking lot. Turn hard L up forest track (marked 'Kastberga' at turn), passing 'Kongsteinen' waymark a little further on *(tradition has it that three kings are buried underneath)*. KSO uphill, ignoring turns, until you reach a view point *where one of the marble-type waymarks indicates 14km left to Nidaros.* This is

6km Kastberga 244m (629/14)

Continue ahead, forking L, and KSO, ignoring turns, until you reach a road 1km later.

Cross over, continue ahead on FP then turn L 100m later, veering R round side of hill up towards farm above you to rejoin road (thus short-cutting a bend). Turn L, go between buildings and KSO(R) ahead, uphill, on small gravel road.

When this forks R 500m later KSO(L) ahead on forest track in more or less a straight line, descending continuously, for 2km. *Boggy sections have log 'stair carpets' to walk on.* Reach a small gravel track, turn R and KSO for 800m, veering L, to the base of a big ski-jump and take third L turn onto a forest track back into the woods. Pass base of another (shorter) ski-jump (the **Høgåsen hoppbakke**) and KSO to a river (the **Leirelva**). Do not cross by FB ahead but turn L and cross by wooden vehicle bridge.

3km Leirelva (632/11)

Take RH of two roads opposite (uphill). 1km later, just before a farm, turn R onto a similar type of road (waymarked 'Froset'), cross stream and KSO ahead at junction on other side up track into woods, veering L. Turn R at junction with riding school opposite, L at T-junction shortly afterwards and almost immediately R onto a *turveg/rideveg* (this is **Vådan**).

Turn L 100m later *(this area has a lot of burial mounds)* and continue to road, via gate, 800m later. Turn R and R again onto wide minor road. 400m later turn L up **Skråstien**, veering R and then L, and

300m later turn R over FB onto FP into the woods. Pass information board about *Solem Søndre nedre* and veer L uphill *(view of Trondheim from top)*.

Continue ahead along ridge *(large lake below to R)* until you reach a road by a restaurant at

3km Lian (635/8)

The owner of the Gammeldagshuset in Trondheim (see page 201) has plans for a pilgrim hostel here (ring to check if ready by the time this book is published). If so you could sleep here and walk the remaining 8km the following morning unhurried; if it was a Sunday, you could then arrive at the cathedral in time for the main 11.00 service. The other option, if it is already late in the day, is to take the tram (see below *).

Continue ahead on road to bend then KSO(L) ahead on old minor road, joining a bigger one coming from back L (**Lianvegen**), and go downhill to a residential area and picnic area by tram stop (*). *(Line no. 11 goes to St. Olavs gate in central Trondheim; to return the next morning this stop is called 'Herlofsonløypa' – frequent service, even on Sundays.)*

Fork L down wide FP beside house called 'Granmo', which becomes a lane with woods to either side. KSO, gently downhill, for 2km, passing large lake *(Kyvatnet)* on R, until you reach a road in another residential area (**Antonie Løchens vei**). Turn L to a junction and then turn R, downhill, on **Dalhaugveien**. Turn L at the end and then R into the **Lagmann Linboes vei**, veering R and continuing until you reach a T-junction (**Fjellseterveien**). Turn R to junction with the **Sverreborg allé** and turn L. This is

4km Byåsen/Sverreborg (639/4)

Shops, bank (CD), PO, café.

Pass the grounds of the **Trøndelag Folksmuseum** *(worth a visit, view of fjord ahead)*, veering R at junction onto the **Fridthof Nansens vei**. Continue along here, veering R all the time, and just after house no. 39 reach waymark with *utsikt* (viewpoint). *This is near the* Feginsbrekka, *the 'mountjoy' from which pilgrims have their first proper view of Nidaros cathedral and all the city churches, akin to similar places on reaching Rome and Jerusalem and the Monte del Gozo just outside Santiago de Compostela.*

Fork L down FP here, zigzagging down to the **Sverdrupsvei** *(the island visible in the fjord ahead is Munkholmen, the first Benedictine* *monastery built in Scandinavia, 1000 AD; the church 'in front' of it is Ilen kirke).* KSO(L), veering L, and then turn R down **Dyrborgveien**, veering L. Turn R at end, cross a residential street, go down FP (**Steinerget**) and cross the **Byåseveien** via the underpass *(gangtunnel).* Turn L and then R on other side on the cycle track of the **Ilevollen** to

3km Ilen kirke (642/1)

Pass to R of church (this is the **Erling Skakkesgata**) past museum *('Slaveriet' Kriminalasylum, in use 1833–1961 and as an ordinary prison until 1971)* and an all-brick house and fork R along **Elvegata**. Continue at end onto the **Bispegata** and turn R along **Sverresgate** *(note more all-brick houses).*

Continue down FP to river at end, veering L. Go under the road bridge over the **Nidelva** and reach the **Olavskilde**, *a fountain on your L. One of the theories about the exact burial place of St. Olav is that his grave was here, beside the spring; the other, according to the saga, is that the high altar in the Nidarosdom lies over the exact spot on the river bank where the saint was buried, as the Olav Well (Olavsbrønnen) is actually inside the cathedral itself. You are now in the Hadriansplass, named after Pope Hadrian IV who established the Archbishopric of Nidaros in 1152–53.*

From the park in front of you the pilgrim path from the east joins you from Skalstugan in Sweden. Turn L up the steps, pass alongside long building on R, part of the **Vitenskapmuseet**, and reach the west front of the

1km Nidarosdom (643/0)

The first building on this site was a wooden chapel, put up over King Olav's grave immediately after he was made a saint on August 3rd 1031. Then in 1070 a church was built on the site, Kristkirke (Christchurch) – not dedicated to St. Olav, as is often thought – with the main altar with the saint's shrine positioned over the place where the grave had been. This was soon too small to cope with the numbers of pilgrims and others visiting his burial place, however, and from 1150 Archbishop Øystein set about enlarging and expanding the building, in Gothic style, and the work was eventually completed around 1300. It is also thought that the master builder responsible for much of the work on Lincoln cathedral also worked at Nidaros.

The cathedral has suffered extensive fire damage on five occasions and has been rebuilt again each time. When the

large-scale restoration work of 1869 began it was patterned on many of the places the well-educated and well-travelled Archbishop Øystein had visited on his extensive travels, so that the cathedral we see today is very much a European cathedral. Nidarosdom is also the Norwegian equivalent of Westminster Abbey, where the coronations of all its kings and queens take place.

Nidaros cathedral (Eivind Luthen)

The cathedral is open daily (entrance fee), with services on Sundays at 11.00 and 18.00. Guided tours available (including in English). On the outside of the building note, in particular, the Olav portal, with the saint (crowned with a wreath every year on July 29th) in the centre of the tympanum, flanked on either side by simple, ordinary pilgrims come to visit his shrine; St. Olav himself has both feet very firmly trampling underfoot the head of a full-figure representation of his former heathen persona, in armour and helmet. Note too, amongst the saints on the west façade, the one of St. James the pilgrim, with hat, staff and cockle shell, and the sculpture of St. Birgitta of Vadstena (a pilgrim destination in Sweden) on the south-west front tower, the 14th-century saint who not only made the journey on foot to Nidaros but also to Rome and Santiago de Compostela as well. The sculptures on the façade also include portrayals of ordinary pilgrims, people carrying out their daily routine tasks: bricklayer, farmer, shoemaker and so on.

Inside the great arched nave is in Gothic style, with the stained-glass rose window in the west made by Gabriel Kjelland in 1930. On the first floor (you may need to ask to be shown these if you take a guided tour) are two small chapels. The one to your L (with your back to the west entrance) is the Mariakapell, now used as a pilgrim chapel; the one on the right, no longer in use, is the Olavkapell. To appreciate the cathedral to the full it is worth buying a guide book.

TRONDHEIM

Large town with all facilities and plenty of things to see – it is worth spending a couple of days here if you can, and the town is an easy one to visit on foot. Railway station (daytime and overnight trains to Oslo, with or without sleeper), buses (daytime and overnight) to Oslo and Bergen. Tourist Office in Torget, in city centre.

Accommodation (1) Gammeldagshuset, Hvedingsveita 8, 7013 Trondheim, tel: 73.51.55.68, EE. B&B plus simple accommodation for pilgrims, 2 minutes walk from cathedral (off Prinsens gate), in listed building from 1837, now used as a museum of living history for educational purposes. (2) Youth Hostel: Trondheim Vandrerjem Rosenborg, Weidemannsvei 41, 7043 Trondheim, tel: 73.53.04.90, EE. (3) Trondheimn Inter-Rail Center, Studentersamfundet, Elgsetergata 1, 7030 Trondheim, 73.89.95.00, EE, sleeping bag needed, open end June to mid-August. For other accommodation (in all price brackets) ask at Tourist Office. (No campsite in Trondheim itself.)

Places of interest

There are several museums and other places worth visiting (ask at Tourist Office for more details), but of particular interest to pilgrims, apart from the cathedral, is the **Vitensapsmuseet** (Natural History and Archaeology), with the history of the area up to the Middle Ages and the development of church art from the 13th to the 18th century (look out for the altar panel painting from a church with the tiny depiction of *a pilgrim being refused hospitality in the corner). Other museums include the **Trøndelag Folkmuseum** (which you will have passed at Sverreborg on your way into town) and the extensive collection of musical instruments (in working order) at the **Ringve Museum** (which also has a botanical garden). Important buildings include the **Kristiansten festning** (fort), built when the town was being reconstructed after the fire in 1681, and **Erkebispegården** (Archbishop's Palace), the oldest secular building in Scandinavia (from the second half of the 12th century) and the Archbishop of Nidaros' residence until the Reformation.*

*Pilgrims interested in churches can visit **Lade kirke** (from 1180, near the Ringve Museum – you can also go there on foot along the Jarlstien (a footpath), built on the site of a pagan place of worship, and **Vår Frue kirke** (Church of our Lady, Kongens gate 5) was originally a 13th-century church dedicated to the Virgin Mary. The remains of the 12th-century **Olavkirke** are to be found in the courtyard of the Trondheim Public Library (Peter Egges plass, open when the library is), while the ruins of the 12th-century **Gregoriuskirke** are in the cellar of a large savings bank and can be viewed during the bank's opening hours (Sparebank 1 Midt-Norge, Kongens gate 4, at the Søndre gate entrance). The **Hospital Church** (Kongens gate) was built in 1705, the first octagonal timber church in both Norway and Sweden, while the original **Trondhjems Hospital** (Hospitalsløkkan 2–4), now an old people's home, was founded in 1277 as a hospice for lepers, pilgrims and the poor.*

St. Olav Catholic church *(Schirmers gate 1, near the river) dates from 1872 and has masses on Sundays at 09.00 and 11.00 and Vespers daily at 18.00, followed by mass at 18.30.*

*If you have time two other destinations outside Trondheim are worth visiting. **Munkholmen** (Monks Island) was the first Benedictine monastery in Scandinavia, built on an island in the Trondheimfjord at the beginning of the 12th century and converted into a prison fort in 1658. Hourly ferry from Ravnkloa. Further away (i.e. a day trip by bus) is **Stiklestad**, the site of the battle where King Olav was killed. Originally there was just a church (dating from 1180) there to mark the spot, but today it has become almost a pilgrimage centre in its own right; there is a folk museum, a Resistance museum and the Nasjonale Kultursenter (arts centre) has exhibitions and an open-air theatre where the events of July 1030 are re-enacted annually on the anniversary of the saint's death.*

A useful source of both practical and historical/cultural information is the booklet *On the Pilgrim Way to Trondheim* (see Bibliography in Appendix B), available from bookshops in the town or from the Tourist Office. This includes the last part of the eastern pilgrim route from Skalstugan, passing some of the sights along the coast on the city outskirts.

Finally, and as indicated in the Introduction, if you are returning to Oslo before going home, try to do so during the daytime so that you can 're-walk' in reverse the pilgrim journey in your mind.

APPENDIX A
Route from the Swedish Border

SKALSTUGAN TO NIDAROS (TRONDHEIM) 193KM

Skalstugan
7km Swedish-Norwegian border
14km Ådalsvollen
5km Sul
9km Salen
4km Brekkan
13km Årstad
3km Vuku kirke
6km Gjernstadhøgda
4km Stiklestad
4km Verdal
15km Munkeby kloster
4km Kolberg
13km Gården Troset
3km Movatnet
7km Sørdal–Levanger border
3km Tyldvatnet
9km Råa
4km Hofstad
11km Vaernes kirke
5km Lånke kirke
1km Hellkrysset
8km Høybydalenbrua
9km Homlaelva
3km Nygaardsvolden
4km Bakken
9km Bostad
4km Saksvikkorsen
8km Lade kirke
4km Nidaros

APPENDIX B
Suggestions for Further Reading

General

Donald Atwood and C.R.John, *Penguin dictionary of saints*, 3rd ed., Harmondsworth: Penguin, 1995.

Simon Coleman and John Elsner, *Pilgrimage past and present in the worlds religions*, London: British Museum Press, 1995.

J.G.Davies, *Pilgrimage yesterday and today: why? where? how?* London: SCM Press, 1988.

> Studies the nature of pilgrimages and motives behind them from patristic times to the Middles Ages, Protestant condemnation of pilgrimages and the 19th-century revival of pilgrimages amongst Protestants, ending with a review of the devotional aspects of modern pilgrmages.

Nancy Louise Frey, *Pilgrim stories*, Berkley & Los Angeles: University of California Press, 1998.

> This refers specifically to the experiences of modern pilgrims along the road to Santiago de Compostela, before, during and after after making their pilgrimage, but the questions raised confront any modern pilgrim on a route where the journey itself, rather than the destination, is the real issue at stake.

Martin Robinson, *Sacred places, pilgrim paths: an anthology of pilgrimage*, London: Fount 1997.

> An anthology reflecting the experiences of pilgrims through the ages, dealing with places of pilgrimage, preparation for the journey, the journey itself, the inner journey, worship on the way and on arrival and the questions raised once the pilgrimage is over.

Brian Spencer, *Pilgrim souvenirs and secular badges*, Salisbury and South Wiltshire Museum medieval Catalogue, Part 2, Salisbury: Salisbury and South Wiltshire Museum, 1990.

Illustrated catalogue of the museum's extensive collection of pilgrim badges, the largest in Britain.

Contesting the sacred: the anthropology of Christian pilgrimage, ed. John Eade and Michael J. Sallnow, London: Routledge, 1991.

Contributors examine particular Christian shrines (in France, Italy, Israel, Sri Lanka and Peru), analysing the dynamics of religious expression and belief but also the political and economic processes at local and global levels, emphasising that pilgrimage is primarily an arena for competing religious and secular discourses.

The way of a pilgrim, trans. R.M.French, London: Triangle, 1995.

First published in English in 1930 this book was written by an unknown Russian pilgrim in the 19th century, telling the story of his wanderings from one holy place to another in Russia and Siberia in search of the way of prayer.

Norway

Arne Bakken, *Pilgrimages past and present: a journey toNidaros*, trans. Margaret Ellson Davies, Trondheim: Restoration Workshop of Nidaros Cathedral Booklet No. 10, 1994.

Discusses pilgrimage in general, both today and in the Middle Ages, as well as Saint Olav in the context of the pilgrim tradition.

Mari Kollandrud, *Pilgrimsleden til Nidaros: en guide til vandringen*, Oslo: Gyldendal, 1997.

Guide to the pilgrim route in Norwegian, providing a route description and useful historical material, but less practical help on services and facilities along the way.

Morton Krogstad and Erik Schia, *Guide to Gamlebyen: medieval Oslo*, Oslo: Directorate for Cultural Heritage, Oslo City Museum and City Conservation Office, 1982.

Describes (in English) the buildings and history of Medieval Oslo.

Lars Roar Langslet, *Olav den Hellige*, Oslo: Gyldendal Norsk Forlag, 1995.

History of the life and activities of King and later Saint Olav, with discussion of his representation in art and architecture.

Eivind Luthen, *På Pilegrimsferd*, Oslo: Pilegrimskontoret, 1995

> Describes (in Norwegian) the history, background, pilgrim routes and practicalities of pilgrimage in the past, with a summary in English.

Snorri Sturluson, *Heimskringla (The stories of the kings of Norway*, 4 vols., trans. William Morris and Eiríkr Magnússon, London: Bernard Quaritch, 1893, 1894, 1895 and 1905.

> Volume 2 of this collection of the old Icelandic Sagas, 'The story of Olaf the Holy, the son of Harald', tells the story of the saint's life, travels, return to Norway and his death at the Battle of Stiklestad.

> For a modern English translation, the only version of the complete sagas, plus 49 connected tales, is the five-volume *Complete sagas of Icelanders*, ed. Vridar Hreinsson, Leifur Eiríksson Publishing: Iceland, 1997. Penguin Books publish a selection of ten Sagas with seven shorter tales (*Sagas of Icelanders*, London: Allen Lane, The Penguin Press, 2000) but these do not include the life of St. Olav.

Sigrid Undset, *Kristin Lavransdatter trilogy*: 'Bridal Wreath', 'Mistress of Husaby' and 'The Cross', London: Abacus 1995.

> One of Norway's most famous novels by Nobel prize-winning author. The saga of Kristin, her husband and seven sons is set in the first half of the 14th century in areas which the pilgrim road passes through. Gives an insight into the harsh life at the time the pilgrimage was still at its height, into the customs and beliefs of the period and the old superstitions that persisted alongside the newer Christian teachings.

On the Pilgrim Way to Trondheim, ed. Stein Thue, Trondheim: Tapir Publishers, 1998.

> Collection of short articles (in English) on different aspects of the St. Olav pilgrimage, with bibliography of pilgrim literature (in Norwegian).

USEFUL ADDRESSES

Pilgrim Office:

Pilegrimskontoret
Kirkegaten 34A,
0190 Oslo.   Tel: 22.33.03.11

Bookshops:

St. Olav Bokhandel
Akersveien 14
0177 Oslo   Tel: 22.20.72.48

Olaf Norlis Bokhandel
Universitets gaten 20-24
0162 Oslo

Tanum
Karl Johann gaten 37-41
0107 Oslo

APPENDIX C – Maps

The Statens Kartverk 1:50 000 maps in the Topografisk Hovedkartserie are given in route order, south to north. The figures given in brackets are those you will need when ordering or looking for them in a bookshop. Those marked with an asterisk* only cover a short (or tiny**) stretch of the route. For Oslo and its suburbs, however, Cappelan's Stor-Oslo 60 map is preferable to 1914 (1027) Oslo (both routes) and 1814 (873) Asker (western option).

Eastern (Historic) Route

* 1915 (1033) Nannestad

(1031) Ullensaker

(1029) Eidsvoll

1916 (1039) Tangen

* (1037) Løten

(1043) Hamar

* 1816 (889) Gjøvik

1817 (899) Lillehammer

* (897) Goppollen

Western (Cultural) Route

1815 (885) Hønefoss

* (883) Oppkuven

(881) Gran

* 1816 (891) Eina

1916 (1041) Østre Toten

** (1043) Hamar

1816 (889) Gjøvik

1817 (899) Lillehammer

* 1817 (897) Goppollen

Route after Skåe i Øyer

* * 1817 (897) Goppollen
* (903) Fåvang
* 1818 (909) Ringebu
* 1718 (755) Vinstra
* * (757) Skåbu
* (759) Otta
* 1519 (503) Hjerkinn
* (505) Snøhetta
* ** (499) Einunna
* 1520 (511) Oppdal
* (509) Innset
* (507) Rennebu
* 1521 (517) Holonda
* * (519) Løkken
* (515) Orkanger
* (651) Trondheim

APPENDIX D – Glossary

The vocabulary given below deals with geography, toponomy and practical matters such as food and accommodation.

Two points will be helpful:

a) The Norwegian alphabet has three extra letters (all vowels) which are not found in the English one: **ae**, **ø** and **å**. These are placed after 'Z' in dictionary entries and after the other vowels within letter groups. For example, *rød* (red) follows *rytter* (rider, horseman), not *robåt* (rowing boat).

   NB: sometimes you will see 'å' printed as 'aa'.

b) Unlike English Norwegian distinguishes between the genders of nouns, with correspondingly different words for 'a' (en, ei and et) which are placed *before* the noun, as well as for 'the', the same items added to the *end* of the words they refer to. Thus *skog* is the word for 'wood' and *skogen* '**the** wood'; *veg* is 'way' or 'road' and *vegen* '**the** road'; *elv* is 'river' and *elva* '**the** river'; *land* is 'land' or 'country' and *landet* '**the** land/country'. This should help with toponymy.

   You will also see variant forms – e.g. gat**e**/gat**a**, as the masculine and feminine forms are often combined into a common gender.

almuevegen	public road (for use by all: *almue* = common people)
bakke	hill, earth
barna lekker	(seen on street signs): 'children playing'
bautastein	stone monument
bedehus	(religious) meeting-house (lit. 'prayer house'), (non-conmformist) chapel
beite	pasture, grazing
bekken	beck, brook, stream
bomvei	gated road, toll bar
bru/bro/bu	bridge
by	town
bygdevei	lit. 'built' (as opposed to unmade up) local road
daglivarer	(i.e. 'daily wares') = groceries

dom	cathedral
domkirke	cathedral church
driftvei	drove road, temporary or works road
elv	river
Feginsbrekka	mountjoy (fegen = glad, happy, brekka = steep hill)
fjellstue	mountain hostel
folkmuseet	'folk museum', i.e. one concerned with ethnography and local history and customs
forminne	archaeological site, old tombstones, historical remains
foss	waterfall
fredet	listed (e.g. buildings)
frokost	breakfast
furu	pine tree
fylke	county
fylkesvei	main (local) road
gamle	old
gangbru	footbridge
gangtunnel	underpass
gangvei	pedestrianised street
gate	street
gatekjøkken	snack bar
gjestegiveri	guesthouse
gravlund/gravplass	graveyard, cemetery (i.e. not attached to a church)
grend	group of farms, neighbourhood
grendehus	communal hall
gutua	cow passage, cow path
gågate	pedestrianised street
gård	building, yard. courtyard; a *gård* is also a farm or a collection of buildings around a large farm, forming a unit of population
gårdtun	farmyard
haug	heap, mound, pile
hof	sacred place (where offerings were given)
hoff	court, royal house
hulvei	'hollow' (i.e. sunken) road
husmannsplass	cotter's (i.e. tenant) farm or smallholding
hø	hill, mountain

kiosk	news stand
kirke	church
kirkegård	churchyard, cemetery
kirkentjener	verger
kirketuft	site of (former) church
kloster	monastery, convent
kolkropp/kolgrop	depression in the ground where charcoal was burnt
kommune	district (subdivision of a *fylke*)
kongsgård	king's or royal farm
kors(et)	cross, crossroads
kro	inn, café,
krypinn	little shed, poky place
kultursti	(local) waymarked footpath
leden	path, course (originally used for shipping)
lund	grove
løypa	trail, track
menighethus	parish hall
merkestølpe	waymark
minibank	cash dispenser, 'hole-in-the-wall' machine
mo	heath, moor, (military) encampment
myrin	bog, mire
nedre	lower, nether (in place names)
nistepakke	packed lunch
nord	north
ny	new
Norrønt	old Viking times
odde	headland, point
omvisning	guided tour
pensjonat	boarding house, B&B
pilegrim	pilgrim
plass	square, place, space
prest	priest
prestegård	presbytery, manse (lit. 'priest's farm')
rak	straight, direct
riksvei	main (national) road
rodestein	stone border marker

røyse	heap of stones, mound
rådehus	townhall
selvhushold	self-catering
seng	bed
sengtøy	bedding
servering	meals (served)
seter/saeter	summer farm
sjø	lake (cf. 'sea')
skog	wood (forest)
stabbur	storehouse (raised up on pillars)
sti	track, path
stor	big, large
stue/stuggu	cottage, hut; room, living-room
sykehjem	hospital
saelehus	overnight shelter originally provided by religious or other charitable bodies (saele = charity)
sør	south
telt	tent
ting	parliament, assembly
tjern	tarn, small lake
tre kirke	wooden (lit: 'tree') church
tun	yard
tursti	walking route (often waymarked)
utsiktspunkt	viewpoint, panorama
vann	water; lake (small)
vatn	lake (small)
veg/vei	street (i.e. 'way')
veitslehall (archaic)	room or hall for entertainment (veitsle = feast)
vesle	small
vest	west
vik	inlet, cove
voll	meadow; bank, dike; rampart
våpenhus (lit. 'weapon house')	entrance hall (in a church) where weapons were left before entering
øst	east
øvre	upper (in place names)
å	stream

APPENDIX E
Index of Principal Place Names

NOTES

NOTES

LISTING OF CICERONE GUIDES

NORTHERN ENGLAND LONG DISTANCE TRAILS

THE DALES WAY

THE ISLE OF MAN COASTAL PATH

THE PENNINE WAY

THE ALTERNATIVE COAST TO COAST

NORTHERN COAST-TO-COAST WALK

THE RELATIVE HILLS OF BRITAIN

MOUNTAINS ENGLAND & WALES VOL 1 WALES. VOL 2 ENGLAND.

CYCLING

BORDER COUNTRY BIKE ROUTES

THE CHESHIRE CYCLE WAY

THE CUMBRIA CYCLE WAY

THE DANUBE CYCLE WAY

LANDS END TO JOHN O'GROATS CYCLE GUIDE

ON THE RUFFSTUFF -
84 Bike Rides in Nth Engl'd

RURAL RIDES No.1 WEST SURREY

RURAL RIDES No.1 EAST SURREY

SOUTH LAKELAND CYCLE RIDES

THE WAY OF ST JAMES
Le Puy to Santiago - Cyclist's

LAKE DISTRICT AND MORECAMBE BAY

CONISTON COPPER MINES

CUMBRIA WAY & ALLERDALE RAMBLE

THE CHRONICLES OF MILNTHORPE

THE EDEN WAY

FROM FELL AND FIELD

KENDAL - A SOCIAL HISTORY

A LAKE DISTRICT ANGLER''S GUIDE

LAKELAND TOWNS

LAKELAND VILLAGES

LAKELAND PANORAMAS

THE LOST RESORT?

SCRAMBLES IN THE LAKE DISTRICT

MORE SCRAMBLES IN THE LAKE DISTRICT

SHORT WALKS IN LAKELAND

Book 1: SOUTH

Book 2: NORTH

Book 3: WEST

ROCKY RAMBLER'S WILD WALKS

RAIN OR SHINE

ROADS AND TRACKS OF THE LAKE DISTRICT

THE TARNS OF LAKELAND Vol 1: West

THE TARNS OF LAKELAND Vol 2: East

WALKING ROUND THE LAKES

WALKS SILVERDALE/ARNSIDE

WINTER CLIMBS IN LAKE DISTRICT

NORTH-WEST ENGLAND

WALKING IN CHESHIRE

FAMILY WALKS IN FOREST OF BOWLAND

WALKING IN THE FOREST OF BOWLAND

LANCASTER CANAL WALKS

WALKER'S GUIDE TO LANCASTER CANAL

CANAL WALKS VOL 1: NORTH

NORTH-WEST ENGLAND

WALKS FROM THE LEEDS-LIVERPOOL CANAL

THE RIBBLE WAY

WALKS IN RIBBLE COUNTRY

WALKING IN LANCASHIRE

WALKS ON THE WEST PENNINE MOORS

WALKS IN LANCASHIRE WITCH COUNTRY

HADRIAN'S WALL
Vol 1 : The Wall Walk

Vol 2 : Wall Country Walks

WALKS FROM THE LEEDS-LIVERPOOL CANAL

NORTH YORKS MOORS

THE REIVER'S WAY

THE TEESDALE WAY

WALKING IN COUNTY DURHAM

WALKING IN THE NORTH PENNINES

WALKING IN NORTHUMBERLAND

WALKING IN THE WOLDS

WALKS IN THE NORTH YORK MOORS Books 1 and 2

WALKS IN THE YORKSHIRE DALES Books 1,2 and 3

WALKS IN DALES COUNTRY

WATERFALL WALKS - TEESDALE & HIGH PENNINES

THE YORKSHIRE DALES

YORKSHIRE DALES ANGLER'S GUIDE

THE PEAK DISTRICT

STAR FAMILY WALKS PEAK DISTRICT/Sth YORKS

HIGH PEAK WALKS

WEEKEND WALKS IN THE PEAK DISTRICT

WHITE PEAK WALKS
Vol.1 Northern Dales

Vol.2 Southern Dales

WHITE PEAK WAY

WALKING IN PEAKLAND

WALKING IN SHERWOOD FORES

WALKING IN STAFFORDSHIRE

THE VIKING WAY

WALES AND WELSH BORDERS

ANGLESEY COAST WALKS

ASCENT OF SNOWDON

THE BRECON BEACONS

CLWYD ROCK

HEREFORD & THE WYE VALLEY

HILLWALKING IN SNOWDONIA

HILLWALKING IN WALES Vol.1

HILLWALKING IN WALES Vol.2

LLEYN PENINSULA COASTAL PATH

WALKING OFFA'S DYKE PATH

THE PEMBROKESHIRE COASTAL PATH

THE RIDGES OF SNOWDONIA

SARN HELEN

SCRAMBLES IN SNOWDONIA

SEVERN WALKS

THE SHROPSHIRE HILLS

THE SHROPSHIRE WAY

SPIRIT PATHS OF WALES

WALKING DOWN THE WYE

A WELSH COAST TO COAST WALK

WELSH WINTER CLIMBS

LISTING OF CICERONE GUIDES

LISTING OF CICERONE GUIDES

COSTA BLANCA ROCK

COSTA BLANCA WALKS VOL 1

COSTA BLANCA WALKS VOL 2

WALKING IN MALLORCA

ROCK CLIMBS IN MAJORCA, IBIZA & TENERIFE

WALKING IN MADEIRA

THE MOUNTAINS OF CENTRAL SPAIN

THE SPANISH PYRENEES GR11 2nd Ed.

WALKING IN THE SIERRA NEVADA

WALKS & CLIMBS IN THE PICOS DE EUROPA

VIA DE LA PLATA

SWITZERLAND

ALPINE PASS ROUTE, SWITZERLAND

THE BERNESE ALPS A Walking Guide

CENTRAL SWITZERLAND

THE JURA: HIGH ROUTE & SKI TRAVERSES

WALKING IN TICINO, SWITZERLAND

THE VALAIS, SWITZERLAND. A Walking Guide

GERMANY, AUSTRIA AND EASTERN EUROPE

MOUNTAIN WALKING IN AUSTRIA

WALKING IN THE BAVARIAN ALPS

WALKING IN THE BLACK FOREST

THE DANUBE CYCLE WAY

GERMANY'S ROMANTIC ROAD

WALKING IN THE HARZ MOUNTAINS

KING LUDWIG WAY

KLETTERSTEIG Northern Limestone Alps

WALKING THE RIVER RHINE TRAIL

THE MOUNTAINS OF ROMANIA

WALKING IN THE SALZKAMMERGUT

HUT-TO-HUT IN THE STUBAI ALPS

THE HIGH TATRAS

SCANDANAVIA

WALKING IN NORWAY

ST OLAV'S WAY

ITALY AND SLOVENIA

ALTA VIA - HIGH LEVEL WALKS DOLOMITES

CENTRAL APENNINES OF ITALY

WALKING CENTRAL ITALIAN ALPS

WALKING IN THE DOLOMITES

SHORTER WALKS IN THE DOLOMITES

WALKING ITALY'S GRAN PARADISO

LONG DISTANCE WALKS IN ITALY'S GRAN PARADISO

ITALIAN ROCK

WALKS IN THE JULIAN ALPS

WALKING IN SICILY

WALKING IN TUSCANY

VIA FERRATA SCRAMBLES IN THE DOLOMITES

OTHER MEDITERRANEAN COUNTRIES

THE ATLAS MOUNTAINS

WALKING IN CYPRUS

CRETE - THE WHITE MOUNTAINS

THE MOUNTAINS OF GREECE

JORDAN - Walks, Treks, Caves etc.

THE MOUNTAINS OF TURKEY

TREKS & CLIMBS WADI RUM JORDAN

CLIMBS & TREKS IN THE ALA DAG

WALKING IN PALESTINE

HIMALAYA

ADVENTURE TREKS IN NEPAL

ANNAPURNA - A TREKKER'S GUIDE

EVEREST - A TREKKERS' GUIDE

GARHWAL & KUMAON - A Trekker's Guide

KANGCHENJUNGA - A Trekker's Guide

LANGTANG, GOSAINKUND & HELAMBU Trekkers Guide

MANASLU - A trekker's guide

OTHER COUNTRIES

MOUNTAIN WALKING IN AFRICA - KENYA

OZ ROCK – AUSTRALIAN CRAGS

WALKING IN BRITISH COLUMBIA

TREKKING IN THE CAUCAUSUS

GRAND CANYON & AMERICAN SOUTH WEST

ROCK CLIMBS IN HONG KONG

ADVENTURE TREKS WEST NORTH AMERICA

CLASSIC TRAMPS IN NEW ZEALAND

TECHNIQUES AND EDUCATION

SNOW & ICE TECHNIQUES

ROPE TECHNIQUES

THE BOOK OF THE BIVVY

THE HILLWALKER'S MANUAL

THE TREKKER'S HANDBOOK

THE ADVENTURE ALTERNATIVE

BEYOND ADVENTURE

FAR HORIZONS - ADVENTURE TRAVEL FOR ALL

MOUNTAIN WEATHER

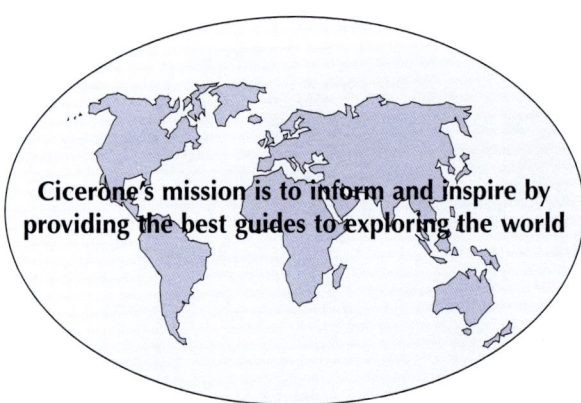

Cicerone's mission is to inform and inspire by providing the best guides to exploring the world

Since its foundation over 30 years ago, Cicerone has specialised in publishing guidebooks and has built a reputation for quality and reliability. It now publishes nearly 300 guides to the major destinations for outdoor enthusiasts, including Europe, UK and the rest of the world.

Written by leading and committed specialists, Cicerone guides are recognised as the most authoritative. They are full of information, maps and illustrations so that the user can plan and complete a successful and safe trip or expedition – be it a long face climb, a walk over Lakeland fells, an alpine traverse, a Himalayan trek or a ramble in the countryside.

With a thorough introduction to assist planning, clear diagrams, maps and colour photographs to illustrate the terrain and route, and accurate and detailed text, Cicerone guides are designed for ease of use and access to the information.

If the facts on the ground change, or there is any aspect of a guide that you think we can improve, we are always delighted to hear from you.

Cicerone Press, 2 Police Square, Milnthorpe, Cumbria LA7 7PY

Tel 01539 562 069   Fax 01539 563 417
email info@cicerone.co.uk   web: www.cicerone.co.uk

CICERONE